EBBETS TO VEECK TO BUSCH

Ebbets to Veeck to Busch

Eight Owners Who Shaped Baseball

by Burton A. Boxerman
and Benita W. Boxerman

McFarland & Company, Inc., Publishers
Jefferson, North Carolina, and London

Library of Congress Cataloguing-in-Publication Data

Boxerman, Burton Alan, 1933–
    Ebbets to Veeck to Busch : eight owners who shaped baseball /
by Burton A. Boxerman and Benita W. Boxerman.
        p.   cm.
    Includes bibliographical references and index.

    ISBN 0-7864-1562-2 (softcover : 50# alkaline paper) 

    1. Baseball team owners—United States—Biography.
I. Boxerman, Benita W.   II. Title.
GV865.A1B644   2003
338.7'61796357'0922—dc21   2003009937

British Library cataloguing data are available

*Front cover, top to bottom: left—Charles H. Ebbets, Barney Dreyfuss,
Clark Griffith, Bill Veeck; right—August Busch, Jr., Helene Britton,
Walter O'Malley, Charles Finley. Background ©2003 Comstock*

Manufactured in the United States of America

McFarland & Company, Inc., Publishers
    Box 611, Jefferson, North Carolina 28640
        www.mcfarlandpub.com

With love to

Cynthia and Sanford
Arlene and Leonard
Hannah and Robert
Benjamin and Matthew

Acknowledgments

In writing this book, we are very grateful for the help and support of many people:

Steve Gietschier, Senior Managing Editor, News Research, and Jim Meier, Senior Editor, News Research, *The Sporting News,* generously provided their archives and their expertise, and were always willing to answer our many questions. Their baseball knowledge is surpassed only by their patience and they made our research both possible and pleasurable.

Bill Marx and other members of *The Sporting News* staff of expert writers, as well as Steve and Jim, helped us greatly in compiling and then trimming the list of owners to be included.

Tim Wiles, Director of Research, Baseball Hall of Fame, also contributed ideas and knowledge that helped us build the list of owners.

Ken Holtzman, former major league star pitcher, graciously shared his experiences and provided unique insights on the character and contributions of owners he knew personally.

Librarians at the Missouri Historical Society, the St. Louis Public Library, the St. Louis County Library, the Detroit Public Library, and the libraries of Washington University in St. Louis, St. Louis University, and the University of Missouri — St. Louis were resourceful in helping us locate material needed in our research.

Liz Jones, at the Society for American Baseball Research (SABR) Lending Library, supplied us with microfiche of hard-to-acquire periodicals.

Candy Vogt, a friend and Certified Professional Secretary, converted an unintelligible resource into a useful format for our periodical research.

Elizabeth O'Farrell, trivia maven, one of the best writers we know, and a friend of long standing, read each chapter and provided invaluable editing advice and support.

Dr. Walter Ehrlich, historian, teacher, author, and friend provided answers relating to proper forms of footnotes and bibliography.

Our many friends, associates, and family always seemed genuinely interested in the writing and contents of this book, and patiently allowed us to bore them with tales of our progress and problems.

Finally, we wish to thank the countless individuals we trapped and barraged with the question, "Which baseball owners do you think did the most to shape the game of baseball?" Surprisingly, they were eager to volunteer their answers.

All the information aided us in our research; however, we take full responsibility for any errors.

Burton A. Boxerman
Benita W. Boxerman
St. Louis, Missouri
June 2003

Table of Contents

Preface

Baseball historians, sportswriters, and fans have written prolifically about various aspects of baseball. They have compiled histories of the game from many different points of view, written books about minority groups in baseball, and profiled numerous players, managers, and even umpires. Surprisingly, very little has been written about the men and women who invested their time and, frequently, their fortunes, in baseball — the team owners. What has been written tends to focus, for the most part, on the financial aspects of ownership. And yet there have been a number of owners whose participation in baseball has had a lasting effect on the game. This book is about eight of them.

In writing this book, our first challenge was to select which owners to include. We disregarded time frame, and geographic and team identity, and focused instead on two requirements: these owners had to be hands-on individuals who firmly ran their clubs, and their contributions had to have shaped the national pastime on or off the field — or both. Keeping those requirements in mind, we then brainstormed, solicited suggestions from knowledgeable friends and acquaintances, and prevailed upon experts at the Baseball Hall of Game and *The Sporting News* to send us their candidates to consider. In the end, we had a list of approximately 20 possibilities.

Our next step was to research briefly each of these owners. After much deliberation and discussion, we pared the list to 10 names. Next we conducted extensive research on the ten, using primary and secondary resources in numerous libraries, microfilm of the *New York Times* and other newspapers, the files of the Society for American Baseball Research (SABR) and the Missouri Historical Society, and the archives of *The Sporting News* and the Baseball Hall of Fame. Based on the additional research and the size limitations of the book, we eliminated two of the proposed subjects, leaving the seven men and one woman profiled.

We don't attempt to rank these eight owners in any order of importance, but rather present them chronologically. Furthermore, we don't claim that these owners are the eight greatest in the history of major league baseball, nor are they the only hands-on owners who contributed to the game in some significant way.

Baseball purists can — and will — argue that there are other owners with these same characteristics. Our goal is not to prevent anyone from asking why we didn't include Charlie Comiskey, or Phil Wrigley, or George Steinbrenner, or any number of other owners. Our goal is prove convincingly that the eight we did choose met our criteria so well that no one after reading the book can legitimately argue that they didn't deserve to be there.

Ongoing debates of who should or should not be part of any baseball list are among the many things that make baseball such a wonderful sport. We hope you enjoy our book. Please read and then we would enjoy discussing the merits of owners who shaped baseball.

1

Charles H. Ebbets
The Visionary

Eighteen eighty-three marked the beginning of the baseball career of Charles Hercules Ebbets and the founding of the Brooklyn Dodgers. Ebbets and the Dodgers were to be inextricably linked for the next 42 years.

The man who established the Brooklyn Dodgers, however, was George Taylor, city editor of the *New York Herald* and a dedicated baseball fan. Taylor suggested to three friends, Charles H. Byrne, Joseph Doyle, and Ferdinand A. Abell, that they form a baseball team to play in the Interstate League, an offshoot of the American Association, a rival of the National League.[1]

Abell put up most of the money, but Byrne became president of the club.[2] Byrne, who was in the real estate business, found a site for the team's ballpark on a parcel of land between Fourth and Fifth Avenues that extended from Third to Fifth Streets. He called it Washington Park, for it was thought to have been George Washington's Continental Army headquarters when he fought the Battle of Long Island.[3]

The team was dubbed the Trolley Dodgers, because Brooklyn fans were forced to dodge a maze of trolley-car lines to get to the park.[4] The name was eventually shortened to just Dodgers. [5]

Eighteen ninety was a momentous year for the Brooklyn Dodgers, as they entered the National League and won the pennant their first year. They also drew more fans than the Brooklyn Wonders, the newly organized Brotherhood or Players' League entry in Brooklyn. Indeed, the Wonders fared so badly that Brooklyn financier George Chauncey, the team's owner, folded them at the end of the 1890 season, bringing down the entire league. Chauncey, an ardent baseball fan, quickly joined forces with the Dodgers, who made him a stockholder, and accepted his conditions for merging the two teams.[6] Under his terms, the original Dodger owners would retain control, Charles Byrne would continue as president, and the Dodgers would leave Washington Park and make their home at Brotherhood Park in East New York, where Chauncey had vast real estate holdings.[7] Chauncey's final condition was to prove the most significant for baseball: his new partners were to retain the services of Charles H. Ebbets.

Charlie Ebbets was born in Manhattan on October 29, 1859, and educated in the New York public schools. He had married in 1877, and was the father of four children. Ebbets had trained as a draftsman and also worked as a printer, but he found neither trade satisfying.[8] In 1883 his brother got him a job with the Dodgers performing a variety of duties such as keeping the books, printing line ups and selling tickets.[9] No task was too difficult or too demeaning for Ebbets. He hawked scorecards through the stands and took care of little drudgeries in the business office that other employees refused.[10]

Chauncey was the first to recognize Ebbets' gift for baseball. Early in 1890 he offered to sell Ebbets part of his own stock because he liked the sociable young man, and also because he felt that by owning stock, Ebbets would have an incentive to work even harder.[11] When one of the Dodgers owners, Joseph Doyle, died in 1896, Ebbets replaced Doyle as secretary of the club.[12]

The merger of the Dodgers and the Wonders and the move to East New York was not a success. Attendance dropped and the team began to slip in the standings. In 1897, Bill Barnie, who had managed the Baltimore club of the American Association, was chosen as manager. He fared only slightly better than his predecessors, and the Dodgers finished in sixth place.[13]

The following year, 1898, club president and chief stockholder Charles Byrne died. Of the three original owners of the Dodgers, only Abell survived; and, although he was now the largest stockholder, he took very little interest in club operations. Acting on a suggestion from Chauncey, Abell backed Ebbets in his successful bid for president of the club.[14]

Charlie Ebbets' first decision as Dodger president was to move the team back to Brooklyn, where he wanted to build a new ballpark. He personally selected a site near the most populous part of the city, diagonally across from the location of two earlier ballparks; it would also be called Washington Park.[15] Chauncey enthusiastically supported the move, since the land under the East New York site had increased so much in value that it was worth much more to him as building lots.[16]

To pay for the new Washington Park, Ebbets persuaded two trolley companies that stood to gain from the additional business to put up more than $15,000. Using his skills as a draftsman, he drew up the architectural plans himself. The roofed grandstand was pleasantly gabled and he set aside two rooms over the main entrance for his office. He also designed something new — ramps to direct fans into the stands and move them halfway up so they wouldn't block the view of those sitting in front. Ebbets was convinced that the location and novelty of his new ballpark would increase attendance and even improve his team's play.[17]

He was only partially right. There *was* an overflow crowd of 14,000 at the opening game in 1898, but his Dodgers lost 6–4. Ebbets then made the first of what he thought were useful suggestions to manager Billy Barnie on how to improve the team. Barnie, however, continued to manage his own way and Ebbets soon replaced him with outfielder Mike Griffin. After losing three games in four days, Griffin decided to return to the outfield and Ebbets hired the only man he felt he could trust — himself. Sporting the top hat that all

CHARLES H. EBBETS — Brooklyn Dodgers 1898 to 1925 — Charles Ebbets designed and built one of the first steel baseball stadiums, led the effort to permit New York teams to play ball on Sundays, and envisioned a bright future for the game (*Sporting News*).

major league owners wore and a dark handlebar mustache, the boyish-looking Ebbets sat on the players' bench and directed his athletes on the field. The Dodgers finished the season tenth in the 12-team league, winning only 38 of 110 games under Ebbets' leadership. Ebbets never again attempted to manage his team in person, although he was not averse to second-guessing his managers on occasion.[18]

Throughout the late 1880s and 1890s, teams struggled for operating capital in the face of competition from rival leagues and declining attendance. In an effort to get good players cheaply, the stronger clubs in the 12-team National League would buy into the weaker ones and appropriate the better players. This cross-ownership of major league baseball clubs, known as Syndicate Ball, resulted in a mini-farm system that kept the poor clubs stuck at the bottom of the standings.[19]

The Brooklyn Dodgers and the Baltimore Orioles of the late 1890s were classic examples of Syndicate Ball. In 1898, the Dodgers' poor play and the impending war with Spain contributed to a 40-percent drop in attendance from the previous year. Ebbets decided that it was time to make a major move. Before the 1899 season opened, Ebbets and Baltimore owner Harry B. Von der Horst agreed to create an interdependent relationship between the two franchises.[20]

Baltimore had won pennants in 1894, 1895, and 1896, but finished in second place behind Boston the following two seasons. By 1898, Von der Horst, like Ebbets, was losing money. Von der Horst had always eyed the New York area as a potentially more lucrative market than Baltimore, and, through the agreement with Ebbets, he was able to buy into the New York market while he continued running the Baltimore team. Van der Horst sent many of his best players to Brooklyn and, in return, obtained stock in the Dodgers. For his part, Ebbets was allowed to purchase stock in the Orioles. Ned Hanlon, president and manager of the Orioles, became the Dodgers' new manager but remained president of the Baltimore club. He also received stock in both teams. Of course, this was a conflict of interest; but, according to baseball's code of conduct, the transactions between the two teams were perfectly legal, and, by the end of the 1890s, quite common.[21]

When all the shuffling of stock was completed, Chauncey and the Byrne estate had been bought out and two factions—Abell and Ebbets from Brooklyn and Von der Horst and Hanlon from Baltimore—each owned half of both clubs. While Abell and von der Horst held most of the stock, Ebbets and Hanlon kept operating control.[22]

Von der Horst was elated—he had finally penetrated the New York market. Ebbets was no less pleased. He received a top-notch manager in Hanlon, as well as a number of outstanding players—first baseman, Dan McGann, shortstop Hughie Jennings, outfielders "Wee" Willie Keeler and Joe Kelley, and pitchers Doc McJames and Jim Hughes—in fact, many of the players responsible for the Orioles' finishing in first or second place from 1894 to 1898.[23]

The *Brooklyn Eagle* hailed the new syndicate as a "progressive policy" in baseball management. The *Eagle* also dubbed the Brooklyn team the Superbas, a name derived from a popular vaudeville troupe at that time. However, most fans in Brooklyn preferred the Dodger name.[24]

When Hanlon retained his title as president of the Baltimore Orioles, many Brooklyn fans questioned his loyalty to the Superbas, but Hanlon erased those doubts by leading his team to consecutive pennants in 1899 and 1900. The 1900 Dodger team was helped when the National League eliminated its teams in Baltimore, Cleveland, Louisville, and Washington, reducing the league from twelve clubs to eight. This streamlining allowed Oriole ace pitcher Joe (Iron Man) McGinnity, to leave his collapsed franchise and join the Dodgers where he won 29 games for his new team.[25]

Ebbets, delighted by the back-to-back pennants, gave bonuses to his champion players. Members of the 1899 team each received $160, but in 1900, when the Dodgers lost money, Ebbets presented them cufflinks.[26]

Nineteen hundred marked both the end of the National League's brief monopoly on professional baseball and Brooklyn's dominance in that league. In October 1899, the Western League, founded by Cincinnati newspaperman, Byron Bancroft Johnson, changed its name to the American League and began efforts to legitimize itself as a second major league.[27]

Ebbets bitterly opposed the formation of a rival league because it was competition on two levels. First, the American League was building its rosters by raiding the National League for players. Ebbets had to compete to keep his own players and it was soon apparent that he didn't have the funds. No team suffered more in this bidding war than Charlie Ebbets' Superbas. Ebbets lost his entire outfield of Wee Willie Keeler, Fielder Jones and Joe Kelley. Second baseman Tom Daly went to the Chicago White Sox, while pitcher Wild Bill Donovan and catcher Jim McGuire went to the Detroit Tigers. The loss of such key players was reflected in the National League standings. After winning pennants in 1899 and 1900, the Superbas ended in third place in 1901 and second in 1902.[28] The second level of American League competition came in the form of an American League team in New York City, where the struggle for fan support, already difficult against the New York Giants, increased.

As the American League became more and more established, Ebbets was the only magnate to express a willingness to fight them to the end. "I will never listen to a proposition looking for peace with the American League. I consider that a thief has robbed us in the night. A ball club has no other assets than its players and the American League has taken these from us," Ebbets angrily told *The Sporting News*.[29] *The Sporting News* replied, "While Mr. Ebbets is undoubtedly sincere in all he says, he is not adopting a policy beneficial to the game. There is room for two big leagues in this country."[30]

Although American League teams began playing in 1901, it was not until 1903 that the so-called "Junior Circuit" was officially recognized. At a meeting in Cincinnati on January 10, 1903, to ratify an agreement between the leagues, only New York and Brooklyn strongly opposed the peace settlement. Ebbets was still outraged over the loss of his players and both he and New York Giant owner, John Brush, were bitter over the establishment of the American League Highlanders (later called the Yankees) in New York. When it appeared that the vote for ratification would go against him, Ebbets, and eventually Brush, surrendered. The final peace agreement between the American and National Leagues was endorsed unanimously.[31]

According to this agreement, organized baseball was to consist of two leagues, the National and the American. National League teams were to remain in Boston, Philadelphia, Brooklyn, Pittsburgh, Cincinnati, St. Louis, New York, and Chicago. The American League was firmly established with teams in Boston, Chicago, Cleveland, Detroit, New York, Philadelphia, St. Louis, and Washington.[32]

Official peace did nothing to help the Dodgers. The team fell into the second division, finishing fifth in 1903 and sixth in 1904. In 1905, they experienced the most humiliating season in Brooklyn baseball history, ending in the cellar with 105 losses, 56½ games behind the World Champion New York Giants. The fact that their archrivals, the Giants, had emerged as baseball's newest power, while the Superbas finished in last place, was particularly galling.[33]

The roots of Dodger-Giants rivalry, considered by many the most passionate in baseball, stretched back to pre–National League contests between the Brooklyn Atlantics and the New York Knickerbockers. No one knows exactly why such bitter feelings existed between the two clubs, but their close proximity and the "class distinction" perception of "blue-collar" Brooklyn against "white-collar" Manhattan likely contributed. In 1898, Brooklyn, because of economic and political reasons, was forced to become part of New York City, increasing the rivalry between the two ball clubs.[34]

This rivalry was intensified even more during the first years of the 20th century as Ebbets' Dodgers continued their downward slide, while manager John McGraw's Giants grew stronger. Because his team had won back-to-back pennants in 1904 and 1905, McGraw, never a likeable character, had become even more contentious and defiant. He would swagger into town, fighting with the umpires and taking extreme pleasure in taunting the Dodgers and their fans. Brooklyn fans grew to hate the Giants and, in their rage and frustration over the Superba's inability to beat them, they turned on Ebbets, a conspicuous figure in the grandstand at all games and an open target for the fans' anger. On a number of occasions McGraw would publicly insult Ebbets, who finally decided to bring McGraw's actions before Harry Pulliam, the National League president. Although Pulliam had had a number of brushes with McGraw about bullying rival managers and owners, he felt powerless to take action against him. This animosity between Ebbets and McGraw continued as long as both were active in baseball.[35]

The feud between the National League and the upstart American League, combined with the poor showing of the Dodgers, had major repercussions in the team's front office. In 1902, Ferdinand Abell sold his interest in the team to Charles Ebbets. Von der Horst, who was ill, also lost his enthusiasm for baseball and decided to pull out of the sport and sell his stock.[36] Hanlon, despite his success in bringing two pennants to the Dodgers in four years, was unhappy in Brooklyn. He told his friends that his goal was to move the Dodgers to Baltimore. Although he was not especially fond of Charles Ebbets, Hanlon tried to persuade Ebbets to go along with him, but he encountered a strong refusal. "I still have faith in Brooklyn," exclaimed Ebbets. Hanlon scoffed at Ebbets, "You can keep it. If I get that stock, we're moving."[37]

Fortunately for Ebbets, Van der Horst disliked Hanlon and told Ebbets that he preferred to sell his stock to him. Losing his beloved Dodgers was unthinkable to Ebbets and he was determined to raise the money needed to buy the stock. A Brooklyn furniture dealer, Henry W. Medicus, came to the rescue of Ebbets and Brooklyn baseball fans by loaning him the $30,000 Van der Horst was asking. To the chagrin of Hanlon, Ebbets and Van der Horst completed the deal and Ebbets became the majority owner of the Brooklyn Dodgers.[38]

Ebbets demonstrated that he was boss by getting himself re-elected as president, and by electing Medicus as treasurer and his son, Charles H. Ebbets, Jr., an easygoing young man, as secretary of the club. Ebbets' next priority was money. Before Ebbets was majority stockholder in the team, he had made less than his manager, Hanlon. Now Ebbets was able to raise his own salary as club president from $4,000 to $10,000 and at the same time cut manager Ned Hanlon's salary from $11,500 to $7,500.[39]

Surprisingly, Hanlon continued as Dodger manager for three more years despite a mediocre team to manage and a less-than-friendly relationship with Ebbets. When the Dodgers ended the 1905 season deep in last place, Ebbets finally fired Hanlon.[40]

Hanlon may have stayed with Brooklyn even after losing out to Ebbets in the Van der Horst deal because he still had hopes of getting the team. As a Dodger stockholder, Hanlon challenged Ebbets' control of the club in the courts. The Baltimore stock Ebbets had acquired in 1899 when Brooklyn and Baltimore had consolidated their clubs, became the center of litigation. Hanlon and heirs of the late Von der Horst sued Ebbets for $30,000, the price paid by the National League for the Baltimore club, which Ebbets had spent during the heat of the American League player battles. Although Dodger stockholders were nervous about the suit, Ebbets was confident he would win.

In the midst of the trial, the New York Giants, realizing that the Dodgers were sorely in need of money, offered Ebbets $30,000 for the two players many considered the nucleus of the Dodger team — Tim Jordan and Harry Lumley. Ebbets' attorneys urged him to dispose of the players and acquire enough money to pay off the damage suit if he lost.

Ebbets mulled over his lawyers' advice for 24 hours and then refused the Giants, once again demonstrating his great devotion to Brooklyn. He later stated: "I took a gambler's chance and turned the offer down…. To my way of thinking, it was my duty to Brooklyn fans to keep these players in spite of the fact that we needed money worse than we did players at that time. It wouldn't have been fair to our patrons to sell those players."[41]

After the court ruled in favor of Ebbets, Hanlon sold his shares of stock in the Dodgers and left to manage the Cincinnati team. Ebbets replaced Hanlon with a succession of managers, none of whom could inspire the team to play better. Patsy Donovan, former Pirate and Cardinal outfielder, managed the Dodgers from 1906 to 1908. Harry Lumley, who lasted only one year, succeeded Donovan. From 1910 until 1913, Bill Dahlen, a 19-year veteran shortstop in the National League, managed the Dodgers. The Dodgers would have their poor teams during the 1920s and 1930s, but the years between 1903 and 1914 were the most appalling in team history. The Dodgers ended in the second division during that entire span of time.[42]

The poor showing of the Dodgers during this period brought Ebbets' financial situation, never robust, to new lows. Attendance continued to dwindle at Washington Park and though Charlie tried to curb his operating costs, they mounted even while receipts dwindled.[43]

Desperate to attract more fans to the game, Ebbets tried a number of inventive promotions. As early as 1899, he offered a Ladies' Day, admitting female fans to the ballpark at a reduced rate. Other leagues had used this scheme previously, but Ebbets was the first in the National League to have a Ladies' Day. Unfortunately, male fans bitterly complained that the women chattered throughout the entire game and allowed their children to run around the grandstand. Ebbets quickly did away with it.[44]

Ebbets regularly advertised his team on Brooklyn's elaborate trolley car system. He also distributed lithographs of the players to prominent sporting goods stores throughout the borough.[45] He handed out free passes to local politicians and members of the press who might publicize the club.[46] Another attendance gimmick was to designate a special day to honor an individual player. The idea was so successful that Ebbets came close to overdoing it with a whole series of player days, plus a day for his manager and another for the league president. One newspaper referred to Ebbets' ideas as "bargain counter fads."[47]

Not all of Ebbets' innovations were promotional. Baseball historians have also credited Ebbets with a number of new ideas which changed the game, including one which literally created order from chaos. It was the custom before games for both teams to take hitting practice at the same time, often batting in front of the stands where spectators could easily be hurt. In 1906 Ebbets suggested and the league adopted a rule which allowed each team separate times for batting and fielding practices, very much as it is done today.[48]

Another Charlie Ebbets innovation actually eliminated one of the game's most colorful features, but was a boon to visiting teams. Visiting players used to don their uniforms in their hotel and then horse-drawn carriages paraded them through the streets to the ballpark and back. This custom subjected the players to jeers and worse, as fans often lined the streets to hurl objects at them. In 1906 Ebbets persuaded the National League to require that all parks install dressing rooms equipped with lockers and hot and cold running water for both home and visiting players. Ebbets led the way, spending $5,000 to provide such facilities, not only for the visiting team but also for the umpires at his newly constructed Washington Park. In addition, he installed a private telephone so the umpires could call the police if needed.[49]

A third Ebbets innovation also continues to this day virtually unchanged from when Ebbets created it. When the Brooklyn club was organized in 1883, patrons who purchased tickets were given a stiff ticket, 2½ by 4 inches in size, which they turned in when they entered the park. If a game was rained out or couldn't be completed, separate rain checks were handed to the spectators as they left, practically encouraging dishonesty among the patrons. In 1911 the league adopted Ebbets' design of a single ticket that would be separated when the fan entered the ballpark. The detached part of the ticket was handed back as the rain check.[50]

Charlie Ebbets is credited with two additional contributions to major league baseball. In 1892, the National League recognized his mathematical skills and had him devise an annual schedule for all the teams in the League at that time. First he calculated the total miles all the teams would travel during a season and deduced that each club would need to average 15,528 miles of travel.[51] Based on these figures, Ebbets reasoned that each team should play 154 games during the regular season. Except in 1918 when World War I forced baseball to shorten its season, Ebbets' schedule of 154 games was the standard format from 1904 until 1961, when expansion required a longer schedule.[52]

A second and far more important contribution Ebbets made dealt with the player draft. Prior to 1913, all major league clubs put requests for the minor league players they wanted in the form of drafts, which would be selected in random drawings. The lucky clubs won the players and often the weaker clubs had to be content with whatever they got. Ebbets proposed that the last team in each league should get first and second choice of any player in the minor leagues. Then the next-to-last club could draft third and fourth and so on up to the league leaders. "In this way," said Ebbets, "the weak clubs get first pick of the material…. If I finish last, I don't have to take a chance on [the player I want] being grabbed by one of the strong pennant contenders."[53] The *Sporting News* heartily endorsed Ebbets' plan, commenting, "The general adoption of the drafting plan of President Ebbets presents an opportunity to eliminate greed in baseball and help the weaker clubs. It is hoped that the Ebbets plan will soon be in general use."[54] Needless to say, not only baseball but also the perpetually second-division Brooklyn Dodgers, benefited from the plan.

Ebbets also influenced the rules governing the World Series. In 1924, at the last owners' meeting he would attend, he persuaded the other owners to agree to play the World Series on a 2-3-2 basis, an arrangement that not only is still the pattern today, but that also has been adapted for league playoffs.[55]

Despite these great ideas and his active role as a leading magnate of the National League, Ebbets had yet to achieve his major goal of a winning team. In 1908 Ebbets met someone who would help. Larry Sutton was also a printer by trade, but even more, he was a devoted baseball fan who had hoped to be a major league player. When he realized he would never play baseball on any level, he decided to become an umpire. For the next three summers he worked minor league games, returning each winter to his print shop in New York.

In December, Sutton attended the National League winter meeting in New York at the old Waldorf Hotel, standing around in the lobby, just listening to the owners talk baseball. Charles Ebbets talked with him for a while and quickly realized that Sutton was a perceptive judge of baseball talent. On a hunch, Ebbets hired him as a scout for his Dodgers.[56] Sutton was to become one of the best-known figures in baseball and, except from 1916 to 1919, he remained a Brooklyn scout until ill health forced his retirement from the game.[57]

Sutton's first discovery was a left-handed hitting outfielder from Missouri, Zach Wheat. Sutton was impressed by Wheat's ability to hit line drives all over the ballpark. Wheat was to spend 18 seasons with the Dodgers, and was considered one of the finest left-handed hitters of his era. He collected 2,884 hits with a lifetime batting average of .317 and, in 1959, he was elected to the Hall of Fame.[58]

The following season, Sutton found Ebbets a first baseman. Jake Daubert, a future National League batting champion, was to play for Ebbets from 1910 until 1918. He won the National League batting title in both 1913 and 1914.[59] That same year Sutton also sent the Dodgers Otto Miller, a wily catcher with an uncanny rapport with his pitchers and the ability to call an excellent game. Miller remained with Brooklyn for 13 years and became the team's coach after his retirement.[60] The acquisition of Wheat, Daubert, and Miller gave the Dodgers the core of a team that would eventually bring a pennant to Brooklyn.[61]

At the same time that Charles Ebbets was trying to improve his team on the field, he was also involved in another major activity that demonstrated his vision for the game of baseball — the construction of a new steel-reinforced concrete ballpark. In 1912 he argued in *Leslie's Weekly* that Brooklyn fans deserved a safe and comfortable park and that he wanted to build for the future. "I want a structure," Ebbets wrote, "that will fill all demands upon it for the next thirty years. I believe that baseball will continue [to be] America's most popular sport for centuries to come and will improve both in play, character and attendance for many years yet."[62]

Ebbets had actually begun working on a new ballpark in 1908. Ten-year-old Washington Park had several major problems. Located near a can factory, a coal yard, and the Gowanus Canal, the park was often filled with smoke and unpleasant odors. Its wooden stands were not only a fire hazard, but also inadequate for the crowds that turned out as the popularity of baseball kept increasing during the first decade of the 20th century. Ebbets often pointed to the April 12, 1912, opening day game in Washington Park, when crowd overflow resulted in spectators lining the field lines and standing in the outfield, not only blocking the view of seated fans, but even interfering with play. Washington Park's only advantage was its easy access due to the number of nearby trolley lines.[63]

For the new park Ebbets chose what seemed an unlikely spot — an area of Brooklyn at the southeast corner of Prospect Park, between the Bedford and Flatbush sections. It was commonly referred to as Pigtown because of the gaping pit right in the middle where local farmers used to feed their pigs. Occupied by squatters and grazing goats, to most people, Pigtown was simply a four-and-a-half acre slum.[64]

Ebbets, however, could see beyond the site's squalid appearance. He believed that Brooklyn's growth, the proximity of Pigtown to Prospect Park, and the fact that Bedford and Flatbush were becoming upscale residential areas, would eventually result in a boom in land values. He proved to be quite a prophet.[65]

When Ebbets checked to see who owned the land, he discovered that there were forty claims of ownership, either by deed or squatters rights. Ebbets promptly formed the Pylon Construction Company, a front which disguised his true purpose, and bought the first parcel in Pigtown in 1908. Unfortunately for Ebbets, midway through the three years it took him to secure the other parcels, word leaked out about his plans, and many of the owners hiked their prices sharply. By the end of 1911, Ebbets had all of the ground except one parcel. When detectives finally located the missing landholder in New Jersey, he had forgotten that he even owned the plot. Unaware of Ebbets' purpose and amused that anyone would want land in Pigtown, he asked only $500. Ebbets had the entire plot of land he needed.[66]

The cost for constructing the stadium soon became higher than Ebbets' original estimate and his personal funds were depleted. Since none of the other baseball magnates had answered Ebbets' call for financing, he welcomed the offer of backing from two Brooklyn contractors, Steve and Ed McKeever. Neither brother had been involved in baseball except as fans, but they had known Ebbets for more than 30 years and were certain that the new ballpark would be a success. In return for their support, Ebbets gave the McKeevers half interest in the Dodgers.[67]

Groundbreaking ceremonies took place on March 14, 1912. Ebbets, wearing a black bowler and an elegant overcoat, pushed a shovel into the ground to begin the excavation. "What are you going to call the park?" a reporter asked Ebbets. "I hadn't even thought about it," he replied. The writer persisted, "Why don't you call it Ebbets Field?" Ebbets nodded and replied, "All right. That's what we'll call it then."[68]

The completed stadium seated 25,000 people and, with supplemental benches, could accommodate another 10,000. Made of concrete and steel, it was considered a palatial structure by 1913 standards with a tile-inlaid entrance rotunda of Italian marble adorned by chandeliers made of crossed baseball bats, an architectural distinction throughout its lifetime. Reporter Abe Yager of the *Brooklyn Eagle*, who covered the Dodgers games, wrote that in theory the rotunda might have been the last word in baseball entrances, but it wasn't very practical. "The crowd piled into that enclosure like a leaderless suffragette army and ran in all directions for tickets."[69] Eventually, Ebbets created two new entrances to divert some of the rotunda traffic.

Double-decked stands extended from the right field corner on Bedford Avenue around the infield to just past third base on the Cedar Place side. There, they met a section of concrete bleachers that stretched to the left field wall on Montgomery Street. It was anything but a regularly shaped park. The nine-foot high outfield walls were completely out of balance — the left field foul pole was 419 feet from home plate, while the distance down the right field line was a scant 301 feet. Fans sitting behind home plate could hardly see center field 477 feet away. In later years the dimension of the playing field would be trimmed to the point that it would be known as a "bandbox."[70]

Ebbets Field opened on schedule on a cold and dreary April 5, 1913, when the Dodgers met the New York Yankees in an exhibition game. The Dodgers won the game on an inside-the-park home run by a rookie outfielder named Casey Stengel.[71] The first National League game at Ebbets Field was played four days later when Philadelphia defeated the Dodgers 1–0.[72]

As Ebbets had foreseen, the area around Ebbets Field developed rapidly. The park area's nine trolley lines eventually connected to thirty-two others and in time, the stadium was within three blocks of two subways. Fans could easily walk to ball games from buses which traveled Flatbush and Reid Avenues and Empire Boulevard. In later years, motorists could drive to the park on broad thoroughfares such as Ocean and Bedford Avenues. Moreover, Wall Street and Manhattan's City Hall were barely 20 minutes away, putting the ballpark within easy reach of some four million people.[73]

Some baseball historians consider Ebbets Field the foremost legacy of Charles Ebbets' nearly 30 years as owner of the Dodgers. It symbolized civic pride and community development centered on a sports franchise and became a model emulated throughout American sports history.[74]

Although Ebbets had his ballpark, he did not yet have a winning team to play in it. To make matters worse, he would soon face a serious problem from another team in Brooklyn. In 1913, a new league independent of organized baseball was formed in the Midwest. The Federal League had wealthy backers who saw all the new concrete and steel ballparks and wanted a part of what they perceived as baseball's golden age of money-making. Frustrated in their attempts to buy into the Major Leagues, these men put their money into the new league, which set up franchises in six big-league cities. The Federal League originally signed only players not under contract to a team in organized baseball, but by 1914, they began to raid the big league rosters, just as the American League had done a decade earlier. They also added franchises in the East, including a team in Brooklyn run by Robert Boyd Ward. Ward and his brother, George, owned the Brooklyn-based Ward's Bakery Company, bakers of popular TipTop Bread.[75]

Before the 1914 season, Ebbets had announced a deal with Cincinnati that was to bring well-known shortstop Joe Tinker to the Dodgers. Part of the double-play combination of Tinker to Evers to Chance, Tinker had been with the Cubs pennant-winning teams of 1906, '07 and '08, and was traded to Cincinnati in 1913.[76] Ebbets was to pay the Reds $25,000, with Tinker receiving $10,000 of that amount as a bonus. Tinker never arrived in Brooklyn. Unhappy with the $7,500 salary offered by Ebbets, he ignored the $10,000 bonus and signed a three-year contract as player-manager of the new Federal League Chicago team.[77]

The loss of Tinker was only the beginning. Ebbets heard rumors that other members of the Dodgers were considering defecting. Players like Casey Stengel, whose contract had expired, were bound to Brooklyn only by the lifetime option of the reserve clause, which the Federal League didn't recognize. Even Ebbets' star first baseman, Jake Daubert, who had signed a three-year contract, had been talking to the Federal League. Ebbets was extremely nervous. Here he was with a brand-new ballpark; he desperately needed fans to fill it and a team to attract them. With competition from the Brooklyn TipTops in mind, Ebbets began to court his own players, urging them to sign long-term deals by offering generous salaries. Most of his players signed either two- or three-year contracts. Casey Stengel liked the salary Ebbets offered but, looking to the future, signed for only one year. Ebbets argued, pleaded, and even threatened players who hesitated to sign a Dodgers contract or who were likely to jump to the Federal League. "Remember," he warned, "this league won't last long. And if you join it, when the crash comes, you will be out of a job, because nobody that goes to the Federal League ever can return to organized baseball."[78]

After Ebbets had signed his team to long-term contracts, he boasted, "I have assumed the burden of the biggest payroll I have ever been called upon to meet. The Federal League wanted my stars—well, so did I. That meant I had to outbid them, and I assure you those fellows certainly did boost their figures. But I met them. I didn't let one of my good players get away."[79] Throughout 1914, the Federal League continued going after players from the established teams. Stengel's one-year contract expired at the end of the 1914 season and Ebbets moved quickly to sign him to a longer one. He finally got Stengel to agree to two years at $6,000 a year, or roughly six times the amount he had made when he joined the Dodgers two years earlier.[80]

The rival Federal League existed for two years, straining the finances of virtually every team in all three leagues. When Robert Ward of the Tip-Tops died unexpectedly, the Federal League was ready for a peace conference, which took place in December 1915, in Cincinnati. Two Federal League owners were each allowed to buy an existing major league club and, contrary to what Ebbets had told his players, all Federal Leaguers were eligible to play anywhere in organized baseball. The Federal League — and the Brooklyn TipTops — ceased to exist.[81]

War with the Federal League had not prevented Ebbets from his main goal — a good Dodgers team. At the conclusion of the 1913 season, Charles Ebbets asked his manager, Bill Dahlen, to resign. In his four seasons as skipper of the Dodgers, Dahlen had a record of 251 victories and 355 losses; his teams had finished in sixth place twice and in seventh place twice.[82]

Wilbert Robinson, Ebbets announced, would be the new manager of the Brooklyn Dodgers. Some baseball historians think that Ebbets' selection of the jovial Robinson was as important to the team as the building of Ebbets Field.[83] Robinson had been a coach under John McGraw. After the two had a falling out during the 1913 World Series, Ebbets jumped at the chance to hire the extremely talented Robinson. At the same time, he could hurt his long-time enemies, John McGraw and the hated Giants.[84] Robinson was very popular with the Brooklyn fans and New York sports reporters. Noted sportswriter Damon Runyon dubbed the new manager, "Your Uncle Wilbert" although later he would be known as "Uncle Robbie."[85]

Under Wilbert Robinson in 1914, the Dodgers' second season in Ebbets Field, they improved to a fifth-place finish, and in 1915, they climbed out of the second division for the first time in a decade, coming in third.[86]

The Dodgers won their first pennant in sixteen years in 1916. Robinson was aided by the acquisition of four pitchers — Jack Coombs, a former Philadelphia hurler; spitballer Larry Cheney, from the Chicago Cubs; left-hander Rube Marquard, a former Giant; and Jeff Pfeffer, from the St. Louis Browns. They combined to win a total of 79 games for the Dodgers in 1916.[87]

Unfortunately, the Dodgers were no match for the Boston Red Sox that year, losing the World Series four games to one. The highlight of the series was Game Two, which featured one of the greatest pitching duels in postseason play, a fourteen-inning thriller in which Boston's Babe Ruth outlasted Brooklyn's Sherry Smith by the score of 2–1. The Dodgers scored their lone run in the first inning and then were held scoreless by Ruth the remainder of the game.[88]

Uncle Robbie's 1916 champion Brooklyn Dodgers were not built to last. For the next three years they finished seventh once and sixth twice.[89]

During those years, Ebbets certainly didn't use salary to motivate better performances. In effect, his dealings with some of his most popular and outstanding stars made it appear that he was putting the financial interests of his club ahead of winning. He had vowed that once the war with the Federal League was over, he would bring players' salaries back in line with "pre-war" pay. Despite his team's pennant-winning achievement in 1916, as soon as the season ended Ebbets began offering far lower salaries as each player's contract expired. He particularly focused on Casey Stengel, who had had a good season in 1916, but whose raucous, often disrespectful behavior irritated Ebbets. Very conscious of the "class distinction" between owner and player, Ebbets was deeply offended by Stengel's letter of response to Ebbets' attempt to cut his wages from $6,000 to $4,000. "Dear Charlie," Stengel began, and then went on to ask if Ebbets had confused him with an assistant club house attendant.[90]

The situation dragged on. Spring training for the 1917 season began, but Stengel still refused to sign a contract. Finally, Robinson brought Ebbets and Stengel together and Stengel accepted a $4,600 contract just two weeks before the season started. But Ebbets didn't forgive or forget Stengel's holding out so long or his attitude. Despite the strong support Stengel received from the press, Ebbets traded him to the Pittsburgh Pirates on January 18, 1918.[91]

Ebbets also had a long struggle with his star outfielder, Zach Wheat, ostensibly over a $500 salary increase. Ebbets offered Wheat, "the idol of Flatbush," the same $8,300 he had earned the previous year, even though Wheat had led the team in hitting with a .355 average. When Wheat insisted that he was worth more, Ebbets advised him to "show loyalty to the Brooklyn club.... Players are only money grabbers. They never show any loyalty to the club owners. All they think about is the dollar."[92]

Predictably, Ebbets was not intimidated by the threat of a union to protect players' interests. "I will not be black-jacked into meeting unreasonable demands by my players... If they go on strike ... I will fight them with every means at my command."[93]

It was becoming clear that Ebbets, dependent on baseball for his livelihood, was now putting more and more emphasis on the business aspects of the game. It wasn't his fault, he explained. "The fans want faster and more skillful playing which entails the employment of expert players at largely increased salaries. Better and safer stands and diamonds and the same conveniences that the fans are accustomed to in their homes have all helped to run up the cost of baseball."[94] And he added, "I am not in baseball for my health."[95]

Ebbets soon realized that Ebbets Field itself could be a productive source of revenue, even when the Dodgers were on the road. During their trips, he leased the ballpark for many purposes, including one that had an impact on the greater entertainment world. Ebbets worked out a deal with movie entrepreneur Marcus Loew, to show a six-reel film, *The Wrath of the Gods,* followed by a live show in front of the grandstand. More than 21,000 people paid their way into the park to see the movie and the show and Ebbets got half the proceeds. The showing was so successful that Loew began buying up theaters that were to bear his name for decades. Many people still credit Ebbets with playing a major role in the consolidation of the Loews movie theater chain.[96]

During most of his years as Dodger owner, Ebbets was considered tightfisted and stingy. He was always ready to cut salaries where he could, and if he had to increase an individual's pay, he did it grudgingly. Ebbets argued constantly with sporting goods suppliers over the price of bats, balls, and uniforms and, at times, he delayed or even avoided paying his bills. His pride kept him from admitting publicly that he simply did not have the money to spend. The rain check incident was a case in point. After a home game with the Phillies had been rained out, Ebbets scheduled two games the following day. Rather than accept the rain checks for a double header, he scheduled the first game in the morning and the second game later that afternoon and sold separate tickets for each. Those who knew Ebbets well, however, agreed that the Dodger owner was generous when he had the funds, giving freely to many Brooklyn charities.[97]

The fans were well aware of Ebbets' frugality. The Squire of Flatbush, as he was known in Brooklyn, could always be seen at the games sitting on an elevated bench behind the last row of the grandstand in back of home plate. For many years he had to endure the taunts of fans chiding him for his stinginess. He was not bashful about occasionally answering them back, reminding them that the Dodgers were his only source of income. "You call me cheap, but I am the only club owner in the major leagues who cannot afford his own automobile."[98]

The press showed even less mercy towards him, especially New York journalists. On one occasion, they ridiculed Ebbets because he would charge his players for their postgame soft drinks and beer.[99] A columnist for the New York *Herald* who covered the opening game of the 1922 season, asserted that "Ebbets was in a parade but dropped a dime just before the band signaled the start of the procession and the parade moved on while Ebbets was searching for it." When Ebbets protested such a caricature, the columnist came back the following day to declare, "I was in error when I wrote that Squire Ebbets held up the Opening Day parade by searching for a dime he had dropped. The president of the Brooklyn club has informed me that the amount involved was fifteen cents."[100]

An astute businessman, Ebbets recognized that Sunday baseball was a way to generate additional revenue for his team and had long advocated scheduling Sunday games in Brooklyn. His successful battle to force the repeal of the New York blue laws prohibiting Sunday ball was one of his major legacies to the game.

The history of Sunday ball began in 1876 when the National League ruled that no league games were to be played on Sunday. The league waived the edict in 1892 to stimulate fan interest and made Sunday baseball a local option with the approval of the visiting team.[101]

In 1889, the city of New York became a major battleground of Sunday baseball when opponents took the owner of a semi-pro park to court to protest a noisy Sunday game. It wasn't just baseball that was singled out. Blue law supporters, known as Sabbatarians, opposed virtually everything but church-going on Sunday, even printing newspapers and opening libraries and museums.[102]

During the late nineteenth and into the twentieth centuries, professional Sunday baseball was not played in New York's three largest cities, but was permitted by local consent in smaller cities such as Albany, Schenectady, Syracuse, and Utica. Playing professional ball in upstate New York was one thing; playing ball in New York City where the Sabbatarians were more vigilant, was another.

After the 1903 season, the New York Giants decided to test the waters by scheduling a Sunday benefit game against a semi-pro team at Olympic Field in Harlem. A crowd of 7,000 people bought 25-cent scorecards instead of the usual admission tickets, and no police action was taken during or after the game.[103]

The success of this event was not lost on Ebbets. Early in 1904 he defiantly proclaimed, "Other clubs are playing Sunday ball right under our noses and there is no reason why we should not do so."[104] On April 17, 1904, Ebbets announced that there would be no charge for a Sunday contest between the Dodgers and the Braves; the only requirement was that fans had to buy scorecards. These scorecards just happened to be color-coded and priced to correspond to seating prices in the boxes, grandstands and bleachers. The game attracted 12,000 spectators who bought the 25-, 50-, and 75-cent scorecards. Again, there was no police objection.[105]

The Dodgers scheduled another Sunday game the following week against the Philadelphia Phillies. This time, just as the game got underway, the police marched on the field and arrested Brooklyn starting pitcher Ed Poole, Brooklyn catcher Fred Jackson, Philadelphia leadoff batter Frank Roth, and three ticket sellers. The game was allowed to continue, but Poole, Jackson, and Roth were taken to court and tried before Justice William Gaynor, a long-time friend of Sunday baseball. Gaynor ruled that the "peaceful repose and religious liberty" of the community had not been disturbed and chastised the police for reviving an obsolete law.[106] Ebbets' victory was short-lived, however. Just a few weeks later, on June 18, 1904, Gaynor reversed his earlier decision and ruled that Sunday games where scorecards had been sold instead of tickets did indeed violate the blue laws.[107]

Gaynor's decision put an end to professional Sunday ball in Brooklyn for the 1904 season. New York Police Commissioner William Gibbs McAdoo issued instructions to his department that, "If a game of baseball is played either in the Borough of Brooklyn or the Borough of Queens on next Sunday and the game is a public exhibition ... for which an admission fee is charged, the police must arrest all the offenders." The words "all the offenders" rang in Ebbets' ears, since it obviously included even club officials.[108]

Ebbets was convinced that the state legislature had to overturn the blue law that prohibited Sunday ball in New York City. Ebbets had long been active in Brooklyn's Democratic politics and had strong support in Tammany Hall, whose immigrant constituency fervently opposed the blue laws.[109] The energetic Ebbets had been elected to the Brooklyn City Council and the Lower House in Albany and in 1904 ran for the New York State Senate. However, 1904, which saw Theodore Roosevelt heading the national ticket, was a banner year for Republicans. Despite a whirlwind campaign, Ebbets lost his senate race by fewer than 1,000 votes. *The Sporting News* noted that had Ebbets won his race, he would have certainly proposed a bill legalizing Sunday baseball.[110]

In 1906, Ebbets tried again to resume Sunday baseball at Washington Park by having spectators get in by placing money in a "donation" box, but new Police Commissioner, William Bingham, also ordered his men to halt Sunday games.[111]

Several bills were introduced in the New York General Assembly during 1907 to legalize amateur and semiprofessional Sunday baseball. Ebbets strongly backed these proposals and lobbied on their behalf. Debate on all bills dealing with Sunday baseball was fierce. The Sabbatarians claimed that the American Sabbath was necessary for the welfare of working-class people, while Al Smith and other proponents of Sunday reform argued that most people, especially those in New York City, wanted Sunday baseball. None of the reform bills introduced at the 1907 session passed; in fact, only one made its way out of committee.[112]

From 1907 until 1917, Ebbets fought a losing, rather lonely, battle for Sunday baseball. A number of factors helped turn the tide in his favor. The outbreak of World War I gave Ebbets another opportunity to skirt the blue laws. He held a band concert at Ebbets Field on July 1, 1917, to raise money for the Red Cross and war-related charity organizations. As an extra inducement, he announced the Dodgers and Phillies would play a baseball game immediately after the concert. Even though 1,500 marching sailors appeared on the field prior to the concert, the New York police arrested Ebbets and manager Robinson. They were both found guilty, but won a moral victory when their fines were suspended.[113]

Another factor favoring Ebbets' position was the changing attitude of other owners. Franchisees in the New York State and International Leagues, and even the other two New York major league owners, who had been hesitant to support Ebbets' position, began to join Ebbets in calling for legalized Sunday baseball.[114] In 1917 both the New York Yankees and the New York Giants played their first "illegal" Sunday games, the Yankees on June 17, and the Giants on August 19. The Yankees had no difficulty with the police and were able to donate $10,000 from ticket sales to a reserve regiment about to go overseas. The Giants were not so lucky. Both Giant manager John McGraw and Reds manager Christy Mathewson were arrested. The arrest received nationwide attention, because Mathewson was considered the idol of American youth. Magistrate Mathew X. McQuade, another long-time judicial friend of Sunday entertainment, quickly dismissed the charges, chided the Sabbatarians, and commended both managers for their services to the patriotic cause of war relief.[115]

Ebbets now changed his strategy. Instead of a repeal of the blue laws, he began working for home rule — the right of each city in New York State to decide for itself "if in its bailiwick Sunday games shall be permitted."[116] In 1917, a full year before the 1918 elections, he began his home rule campaign by interviewing candidates for local and state offices to learn their position on the issue, lining up many prominent politicians such as New York's Mayor John P Mitchell; Al Smith, the Democratic gubernatorial candidate who had led the fight for Sunday ball in the 1907 State Legislature; and John H. Cooey, Democratic leader in Brooklyn.[117] In turn Ebbets supported local candidates who were pro–Sunday baseball and helped to elect many of them.

With political support in place, Ebbets then shrewdly turned to a group that could influence public opinion in favor of Sunday ball — the clergy. "Statistics of cities where Sunday baseball is played," he told them, "prove that the Church has not been interfered with; that the morals of the community have been improved; that less intoxication prevails, and that many clergy and public officials who were first opposed to Sunday baseball now approve it."[118]

By the time the New York State Legislature convened in 1918, a broad-based, statewide, urban coalition had been formed favoring home rule. It included baseball club owners, motion picture entrepreneurs who wanted to show films on Sundays, the majority of New York State newspapers, organized labor, progressives, and veterans' and women's groups concerned with providing wholesome entertainment for the returning soldiers. The support of the women's groups was a vital development since they previously had opposed the measure.[119]

Al Smith was elected governor, and although Democrats were still a minority in the legislature, some of the newly elected Republican members, for both political and patriotic reasons , helped pass the legislation that Charles Ebbets had championed for more than 20 years.[120] Governor Smith promptly signed the measure and Sunday ball in New York City was now left up to that city.[121]

Despite continued protest by the Sabbatarians, the New York City Board of Aldermen quickly passed a bill permitting professional baseball to be played on Sundays. Brooklyn played its first legal Sunday game at Ebbets Field on May 4, 1919, defeating the Braves 6–2. That same day, the New York Giants also played their first Sunday game, losing to the Phillies 4–3, and the Yankees played theirs the next Sunday, a 12-inning 0–0 tie against the Washington Senators.[122]

The payoff to Ebbets' 20-year crusade was the beginning of financial success, due in large part to the huge crowds coming out to see Sunday ball. In 1920 they also came out to see a winning team.

Robinson won his second pennant for Ebbets in 1920 with a patchwork of castoffs. Ed Konetchy, a veteran of twelve National League seasons played first base; Pete Kilduff, discarded by the Giants and the Cubs, played second. Jimmy Johnston, who had played the outfield in 1916, shifted to third base; Zach Wheat played left and Hi Myers played in center as they had done in 1916. Tommy Griffith played right and Otto Miller again was the catcher. Robinson's greatest strength was his pitchers. Holdovers from the 1916 staff included Leon Cadore, Rube Marquard, Sherry Smith and Jeff Pfeffer. Additions included Clarence Mitchell, who had pitched for the Reds in 1916 and 1917, and Al Mamaux and Burleigh Grimes, who were sent to Brooklyn from the Pittsburgh Pirates in the trade for Casey Stengel. Grimes pitched for the Dodgers through 1926 and won 270 games over a 19-year career. In 1964, Grimes, the last pitcher to throw legal spitballs, was elected to the Hall of Fame. In 1920 he had an outstanding year, compiling a record of 23–11, and his percentage of .676 led the National League pitchers that year.[123]

Nineteen twenty was one of the years when organized baseball experimented with a best-of-nine World Series, but the Dodgers came up short again when the Cleveland Indians beat them, five games to two. Tris Speaker's Indians won two of three games played at Ebbets Field, and when the Series moved to Cleveland, they beat the Dodgers four straight. The real story of the 1920 World Series was the remarkable fifth game, one of the most extraordinary in the history of the World Series. Played in Cleveland's League Park on October 10, Cleveland won easily 8–1. Cleveland's Elmer Smith, facing Burleigh Grimes, hit the first World Series grandslam, and Cleveland hurler Jim Bagby followed up two innings later for the first home run by a pitcher in World Series play. The following inning Brooklyn had the bases loaded with nobody out. Relief pitcher Clarence Mitchell was allowed to bat for himself and hit a line drive that seemed headed for center field. Cleveland second baseman, Bill Wambsganss, speared the ball for the first out, and then tagged both the runner darting for third and the runner headed for second, completing a miraculous unassisted triple play.[124]

On September 27, 1920, the day the Dodgers clinched the pennant, the *Philadelphia North American* ran a front-page headline, "Gamblers Promised White Sox $10,000 to Lose." The following day, a grand jury in Chicago indicted eight White Sox players on charges of conspiring to throw the 1919 World Series in what became known as the infamous Black Sox Scandal.[125] The suspicion that gamblers had corrupted all ball clubs cast a shadow over the Dodgers, too. The *New York Evening Sun* cited rumors that the same clique of gamblers involved with the White Sox was trying to get the Dodgers to throw the 1920 World Series. Harry E. Lewis, an ambitious Brooklyn District Attorney, promptly announced that he would question all the Dodger players regarding another fix. Ebbets defended his players, telling Lewis, "The boys of the Brooklyn baseball team are as clean-cut and as honest fellows as can be found anywhere in the world of athletics." After the questioning, Lewis agreed, stating, "My investigation has not disclosed a single suspicion that there has been any attempt to fix the coming Series."[126] The announcement did much to reinstate the integrity of the Series.

Although there was nothing even resembling a major scandal connected with the 1920 World Series, two incidents did embarrass the Dodgers. During the Series, Dodger pitcher Rube Marquard was accused of scalping tickets in the hotel lobby. The police claimed that he was overheard trying to sell eight box seats— original cost $52.80 —for $350. Marquard claimed that he had only been joking with a fan. He was found guilty, but only fined $1 and court costs. The judge felt that the Dodger hurler "had been punished enough by being written up more than any presidential candidate."[127]

Ebbets did not let Marquard off so lightly. He normally allowed Robinson to handle discipline, but the Marquard incident upset him deeply. "I am through with him absolutely," Ebbets declared. "Marquard will never again put on a Brooklyn uniform."[128] Just before Christmas,

Ebbets got rid of Marquard just as he had Casey Stengel, who had also mortified him. The trade actually turned out very well for the Dodgers. Dutch Reuther, who came from Cincinnati in exchange for Marquard, won 21 games for Robinson in 1922 and finished his career as a member of the great 1927 Yankees.[129]

The second incident involved the Dodger owner himself. During Game One of the World Series, Ebbets had given half-pint bottles of rye to the sportswriters to help keep them warm in the nippy weather. Normally, this would have been a thoughtful gesture, but, in 1920, Prohibition was the law of the land. The newspapers became aware of the episode, which brought a horde of federal agents prowling through Ebbets' executive offices looking for more booze. Fortunately, Ebbets had been tipped off to the upcoming raid and hid the illegal liquor in an attic.[130]

During the following seasons, Ebbets' finances improved even more, as Sunday crowds kept increasing even though the team was again not playing well. The 1920 National League Champions fell to fifth place in 1921, then sixth the following two seasons. Although his team was mired in the second division again, Ebbets, for the first time in his life, could call himself a millionaire and even looked the part, having become heavy and full-faced over the years. He also was treating his players generously, making his Dodgers the highest-paid club in the league, and proving to his friends what Ebbets had been telling them all along, "When I had it, I was really a good guy."[131]

The Dodgers had won two consecutive pennants in presidential election years—1916 and 1920 — and it appeared that they would continue this pattern in 1924. In 1922, thanks to the advice of scout Larry Sutton, the Dodgers had acquired a towering, broad-shouldered right-handed pitcher, Dazzy Vance. In 1924, Vance had an outstanding year, leading the National League with 28 victories and 30 complete games. He ended his career in 1935 with a lifetime record of 197–140 and entered the Hall of Fame in 1955.[132] Many consider Vance the greatest pitcher in Brooklyn history.

Other outstanding players on the Dodger roster in 1924 included Andy High, a steady left-handed hitting infielder; Zach Taylor, a welcome addition to the catching staff; Jacques Fournier, a slugging first baseman who played that position in both leagues; Eddie Brown, who came from Indianapolis to play center field; and two former St. Louis Cardinals, third baseman Milton Stock, and veteran spitball pitcher, Bill Doak.[133]

Despite a 15-game winning streak in late August, the Dodgers were unable to hang on to a very tenuous hold on first place. On the final day of the season, the New York Giants clinched the pennant and the Dodgers ended the season in second place, 1½ games back.[134] It was to be Ebbets' final season.

As early as 1920, Ebbets had talked about retiring from the game he had loved for so many years. "I have been in the game for 38 years," he said that year, "and I think it's about time for me to quit. I am 61 years old now."[135] In 1923, he stated firmly that because of his ill health, "I will retire from baseball next year if I can sell the club for a satisfactory price."[136]

Although Charles Ebbets had been suffering from heart trouble for several years, he refused to curtail his activities. His partners, the McKeever brothers, offered to relieve him of some of the club's executive duties, but Ebbets stubbornly refused, claiming he was strong enough for the annual meetings and the usual contract battles with his players. During the winter following the 1924 season, he made several tiring railroad trips to major league and even minor league meetings, delivering a number of speeches along the way. Ebbets then went to Clearwater, Florida, where he had his winter home and where his Dodgers conducted their spring training. When he arrived in Clearwater, he was near collapse, but was confident that the warm Florida weather would improve his health.

He had once joked to a writer for the *New York Sun,* "When the end comes, I'd like to be out there in the grandstand watching the game and hearing the cheering of the fans—that would be a fitting place to die."[137] Ebbets returned north with the ballclub, but not to the grandstand nor even to Brooklyn. Ill again when he reached New York, he was taken to a suite he maintained in the Waldorf-Astoria. Shortly after 6 A.M. on Saturday, April 18, 1925, with his second wife, Grace, and his children at the bedside, Ebbets died of heart failure at the age of 65. At the time of his death he was the senior club official in the National League and had been with the Dodgers during his entire 42 years in baseball.[138]

The Dodgers and Giants were scheduled to play the day Ebbets died. The McKeever brothers and manager Robinson decided to go ahead with the game anyway. Said Robbie, "Charlie wouldn't want anybody to miss a Giant-Brooklyn series just because he died." Ed McKeever was chosen to act as president of the Dodgers until a formal election could be held."[139]

The Dodger players wore mourning bands on their sleeves and there was a moment of silence at home plate prior to the first pitch. Shortly after 5 P.M., while the game was still in progress, the hearse carrying the body of Charles Ebbets passed by the ballpark en route to the family's Flatbush home on Glenwood Road.[140]

Ebbets' death deeply shocked the entire baseball world. John Heydler, National League President, ordered that all National League games be postponed the following Tuesday, the day set for the funeral, and flags at the ballparks remained at half-staff for 30 days. Most of the club owners made the trip to New York to attend the funeral.[141]

More than 2,000 baseball dignitaries and just plain Brooklyn fans crowded into Trinity Church to attend the brief funeral services. Honorary pallbearers included Baseball Commissioner Kenesaw Mountain Landis, manager "Uncle Robbie" Robinson, and the sportswriters who covered the team. There was no eulogy, simply the chanting of a few brief hymns. Then Ebbets' body was buried in Greenwood Cemetery.[142]

Tragically, the death of Ebbets led to a second blow to the Dodger organization less than a week later. Ebbets' burial had taken place on a cold and rainy day and when the funeral cortege reached the family plot, they discovered that Ebbets' outsize casket wouldn't fit into the grave. For an hour and a half the mourners huddled in the rain while the opening was enlarged. Ed McKeever, the new team president, was already chilled and sniffling with a cold, and went home to bed. By the next morning, the cold had become pneumonia and within a week, he, too, died. Ebbets' heirs made Wilbert Robinson the new president because of his long association with Charlie.[143]

While there were no eulogies for Ebbets at his funeral, there was no lack of them afterwards. W. O. McGeehan, the sportswriter who wrote the story about the dropped dime, wrote a moving tribute to Ebbets: "Professional baseball will always owe much to the abiding faith of Charles H. Ebbets in the game, the kindly Squire who was misunderstood to the last."[144] The *Sporting News* praised him for "his intense loyalty to the league," adding that he was "a man who was for the game from the innermost fiber of his being."[145] The 1926 Reach Baseball Guide, marking the 56th anniversary of Ebbets' death in 1981, commented, "Ebbets was one of the comparatively few old time magnates whose interest in the affairs of the game never faltered. His counsel and efforts toward the improvement of the game were always wise and practical."[146] Forty years after Ebbets' death, Ford C. Frick, National League President from 1934 to 1951 and Baseball Commissioner from 1951 until 1965 honored Ebbets in his book, *Games, Asterisks, and People: Memoirs of a Lucky Fan,* praising his "everlasting enthusiasm for the game of baseball and his belief in baseball's future."[147]

Ebbets had played a major role in developing professional baseball, but above all, through his actions and his words, Ebbets had demonstrated his vision for the game. A phrase he spoke in 1909 truly was his guiding philosophy. The Pittsburgh Pirates had won the pennant and at the winter meetings that year, the other magnates gave a dinner for Pirate owner Barney Dreyfuss. Called upon to make a speech, Ebbets began by reviewing the history of baseball, and then looking into the crowd, he loudly proclaimed, "Baseball is in its infancy." The remark was met with amusement and outright laughter. "What did you say?" they responded, "She's been around since 1839." But Ebbets insisted and was to repeat many times throughout the years, "Baseball is in its infancy."[148]

In his book Frick noted that although the critics had fun with Ebbets' declaration, Ebbets was convinced he was right. "Unfortunately," wrote Frick, "Charles Ebbets didn't live to see his prophecy come true. But if, somewhere in the Great Beyond, there is a Valhalla for baseball war-horses, I'm sure Charlie Ebbets is there.... And if sometimes he should look down, chuckle to himself, and indulge in a Brooklynesque 'I told you so,' who can blame him? That last laugh, philosophers tell us, is always most enjoyable."[149]

2

Barney Dreyfuss
The Purist

When Charlie Ebbets died in 1925, Barney Dreyfuss became the senior club owner in major league baseball. Dreyfuss was affiliated with professional baseball for more than 40 years, 32 of them as owner of the Pittsburgh Pirates. During those 32 years, Dreyfuss developed Pirate teams that won six pennants and two World Championships, and finished in the first division all but six times. But his influence extended far beyond the Pirates.

Bernhardt (Barney) Dreyfuss was born February 23, 1865, in Freiberg, Germany, the son of Samuel Dreyfuss, an American of German-Jewish extraction and Fanny (Goldsmith) Dreyfuss. Samuel had become a United States citizen, but returned to Germany for business reasons. He never failed to tell his son how wonderful America was, and what economic advantages its residents enjoyed. In 1861, he advised 16-year-old Barney, a bank clerk with little chance of advancement in Germany, to sail for America.[1]

Barney arrived in the U.S. with barely enough money for train fare to Paducah, Kentucky, where his uncles, Isaac and Bernard Bernheim, owned a distillery. Because he had such a deep desire to see the great Niagara Falls that had been described in his schoolbooks, he scrimped on meals and slept sitting up on the trains so he could travel to Kentucky by way of Buffalo.[2]

Dreyfuss began working at the Bernheim Distillery, washing barrels nine hours a day. After work, he studied English until midnight and eventually mastered the language, although he was never able to lose his German accent.[3] His uncles soon recognized Barney's intelligence, and he was promoted to head bookkeeper and, in time, to credit manager. In 1890, Dreyfuss was given a working interest in the business.[4]

Dreyfus' doctor was largely responsible for launching Barney's baseball career. Because he was small and never robust, his physician advised him to spend more time outdoors. "Why don't you play baseball?" the doctor suggested. Dreyfuss knew little about the game, but he learned it watching youngsters playing on an empty lot. Before long, he became so interested in baseball that he organized a semiprofessional team in Paducah where he occasionally played second base.[5]

In 1888, his uncles moved the distillery to Louisville — an action that was to have two profound effects on Dreyfuss. First, in Louisville, he met his future wife on a Sunday excursion train to a band concert in Cincinnati. Barney Dreyfuss and Florence Wolf married on October 16, 1894, and had two children: Samuel, born November 9, 1896, and Eleanor, born April 30, 1898.[6]

The second major event happened in 1889, when Dreyfuss became part of a group of local distillers who purchased an interest in the Louisville Colonels baseball team. During their ten years in the American Association, from 1882 to 1891, the Colonels finished in first place only once.[7]

In 1892, the Colonels joined the National League as one of the clubs added when the league expanded to 12 teams.[8] Unfortunately, Louisville was no more successful in this league, either on the field or at the box office, consistently finishing near the bottom of the standings.

Despite the team's poor performance, by 1898 Dreyfuss was hooked on baseball. He sold his interest in the Bernheim Distillery and bought full control of the Louisville Colonels. In February 1899 he became team president, swapping titles with Harry Pulliam, who became club secretary.[9] In the deal, he acquired future Hall of Famer Fred Clarke. Clarke never hit below .300 at Louisville, reaching a high of .390 in 1897, when he also managed the team. 1897 also marked the debut of a young outfielder named Honus Wagner, who was to become one of the greatest players in the game.

Dreyfuss worried that when the National League expansion agreement expired in 1901, his Colonels would be dropped. To make sure he stayed in baseball, Dreyfuss began purchasing stock by proxy in Pittsburgh's ball club, one of the "old" teams likely to remain. The Pittsburgh team, first known as the Innocents, had joined the National League in 1887. They became the Pirates a few years later, when another team sued them for using "piratical" measures to sign a free agent. The ballclub kept the player and the name.[10]

When it became apparent that Dreyfuss was right and that the Colonels were to be eliminated from the National League, Dreyfuss approached William W. Kerr, principal owner of the Pittsburgh team, with an offer to buy the club. Kerr was not interested, but Dreyfuss persisted.

In late November 1899, the two men worked out an agreement. Dreyfuss would sell his interest in the Colonels and he and Pulliam would purchase half of the Pirates stock. Kerr would retain controlling interest in the team, but Dreyfuss would be the club president. Equally important, Dreyfuss would sell Kerr the best Louisville players for $25,000 and Kerr would send several of the more expendable Pirates to Louisville.

On December 7, 1899, one day after Dreyfuss announced his ownership in the Pittsburgh Pirates, one of the greatest trades in the history of major league baseball was completed. The Colonels sent to the Pirates not only outfielders Clarke and Wagner, but also pitchers Elton Cunningham, Rube Waddell, Deacon Phillippe, Pat Flaherty, and Walter Woods; catchers Charley Zimmer, Cliff Latimer and Tom Messitt; and infielders Mike Kelley, Claude

BARNEY DREYFUSS— Pittsburgh Pirates 1899 to 1932 — German-Jewish immigrant Barney Dreyfuss began the tradition of the World Series between the National and American leagues and was known both for his high personal integrity and his passion for the game (National Baseball Hall of Fame Library, Cooperstown, NY).

Ritchey, and Tommy Leach. Five players went from the Pirates to Louisville including future Hall of Fame pitcher, Jack Chesboro, who would actually return to Pittsburgh before the 1900 season opened.[11] In this trade, the Pirates had received four future Hall of Famers, a number of 20-game winners and batting champions and, in Leach, a home run leader.[12]

It was no accident that Dreyfuss had assembled such an array of talent during his tenure at Louisville. Baseball experts considered Dreyfuss the best judge of player talent in his time, better, in fact, than most baseball scouts. Dreyfuss was primarily his own scout when he ran both the Colonels and later the Pirates. He found players by regularly scanning baseball publications such as *The Sporting News, Sporting Life,* Spalding and Reach's *Guides,* and the sports pages of the daily newspapers.[13] Friends all over the country would also send him tips on prospects. He carried with him a little black book filled with the names of minor league players and the statistics for those players he considered talented enough to eventually play for the Pirates.[14]

Dreyfuss' dope book soon became a formal file kept in his office, which he meticulously updated. When he saw a prospective player or heard about one from a friend, Dreyfuss would write all the details on a file card — age, favorite positions, batting and fielding averages, etc. Whenever he needed to know something about a player in the minor leagues, all he had to do was find the card.[15]

Dreyfuss, of course, was not infallible and despite his astuteness, he occasionally made mistakes. Once, a tipster extolled a young semipro pitcher from Idaho and even offered to bring him to Pittsburgh for a tryout if Dreyfuss would pay for the trip. Dreyfuss felt the salesman was just a little too eager and he turned him down. Shortly afterwards, the prospect, future Hall of Fame pitcher Walter Johnson, signed with Washington.[16]

On March 9, 1900, the National League officially became an eight-team league again, buying out the franchises in Louisville, Cleveland, Washington and Baltimore. Louisville would be the only one of the four cities where major league baseball would not return.[17]

In 1900, Dreyfuss' first year as co-owner of the Pirates, the team ended in second place, six games behind the pennant-winning Brooklyn Dodgers. The club also had its first league-batting champion — Honus Wagner, who finished the season with a mark of .381. Moreover, in 1900, the team made money for the first time in decades.[18]

But problems were brewing in the front office. William Kerr was growing uncomfortable in what he considered a subordinate role to Dreyfuss and Pulliam. A minor incident caused a major rift and the eventual sale of the club to Dreyfuss. A fan at Exposition Park, home field of the Pirates, tore his coat while attending a game. When he complained to secretary Pulliam, Pulliam told the fan to have his coat repaired and bill the Pittsburgh ball club. Kerr overheard the conversation and shouted that any matter involving money ought to be referred to him. Pulliam immediately walked off the job until Dreyfuss interceded in his behalf.

The conflict reached its climax at the annual stockholders meeting in January 1901, when Kerr attempted to gain complete control of the club by lining up enough investors to elect a handpicked board and dump Dreyfuss and Pulliam. But Dreyfuss came to the meeting well prepared. The Pirates, incorporated in New Jersey, were not allowed to elect anyone as an officer or board member if he counted the ballots at the meeting where he was chosen. This law, Dreyfuss pointed out, disqualified Kerr from serving on the Pirates' board. Kerr was enraged, but to avoid a legal battle, he sold his interest for $70,000 cash to Dreyfuss and Pulliam, who were backed by a group of local businessmen. Dreyfuss now owned 50 percent of the stock outright, with the balance in friendly hands. He had become the dominant owner of the Pittsburgh Pirates at the age of 35, and would hold that post until his death in 1932.[19]

Although Dreyfuss controlled the team, he and Fred Clarke, who came to Pittsburgh with Dreyfuss and managed the Pirates from 1900 to 1915, soon clarified who controlled the players on the field. Once, after the Pirates had lost a ball game, Dreyfuss burst into the team locker room and demanded to know why the players had not played harder. Clarke completely agreed with Dreyfuss, but he ordered the owner out of the players' quarters, telling his boss, "As far as these players go, if there is criticism, they'll hear plenty from me, and me, alone." Dreyfuss knew Clarke was right and seldom appeared in the locker room again before or after a game.[20]

Dreyfuss quickly realized that owning a major league baseball team involved a number of intricate problems unrelated to the activity on the field. The first one he encountered as Pirate owner involved the very structure and governance of Major League Baseball. Cross-ownership of Major League clubs, known as Syndicate Ball, was widespread during the early years of baseball through the 1920s. Shares in weaker clubs would be bought by stronger teams, who would then acquire the better players. Dreyfuss had taken part in this practice with the "trade" he arranged between Louisville and Pittsburgh.[21]

New York Giants owner Andrew Freedman wanted to go even further. He proposed to three National League moguls, Cincinnati's John Brush, St. Louis' Frank Robison, and Boston's Art Soden, that the National League reorganize as a trust, pool its resources, and divide the profits of all the teams. The teams would no longer be individually owned; the trust would own them all.[22]

Freedman needed one more vote to ratify his plan. Jim Hart of the Chicago Cubs, Charles Ebbets of the Brooklyn Dodgers, and John Rogers of the Philadelphia Phillies, had fought him for years and would never go along with any of his schemes. This left Dreyfuss as the pivotal vote. Despite heavy pressure, Dreyfuss stood firm. "I am against [a Baseball Trust]," he argued, "because it would kill baseball."[23] He also knew that the Pirates had been the most profitable team in 1901 and yet Freedman and the Giants would have received the largest share of the redistributed monies.[24]

With four teams supporting the Trust and four teams opposed, the issued boiled down to the tie-breaking vote of the President of the National League. Naturally, the feuding magnates couldn't agree on who would hold this post. Led by Dreyfuss, the four owners opposed to the Trust backed Albert G. Spalding, a baseball pioneer and sporting goods entrepreneur. Freedman and his group supported incumbent president Nick Young.

After much acrimony, the eight owners compromised by establishing a three-person executive board to run league affairs. To be known as the National Commission, this board would consist of Arthur Soden of Boston, James Hart of Chicago, and John Brush of New York as chairman. When the American League became a Major League two years later, the makeup of the Commission changed to the American League President, the National League President, and a third member chosen by the two. Dreyfuss had been successful in thwarting Freedman's plan for a Baseball Trust and indirectly bringing about the governing body of baseball that lasted from 1902 until 1920.[25]

At the same time that Dreyfuss and the other National League owners were arguing about the proposed Trust, Cincinnati journalist, Ban Johnson, was forming a second Major League, signing top-quality players from existing National League teams to staff it. Originally, Dreyfuss supported Johnson's plan and even suggested cities for American League franchises. "This would be a good thing for baseball and would relieve the National League of the necessity of keeping up parks in Baltimore and Washington."[26]

Unlike other National League teams such as Ebbets' Dodgers, the Pirates emerged relatively unscathed from Johnson's initial player raids because Dreyfuss had moved quickly to sign his players before they could be lured away. By the end of September 1901, Dreyfuss announced that all of his players had been signed for the 1902 season.[27] He was able to accomplish this feat because of the loyalty his players felt for him. Many had signed blank contracts, trusting Dreyfuss to fill in the amount at a later date. Honus Wagner was offered larger salaries by American League teams, but authorized Dreyfuss to pay him what his boss felt he was worth. Pirate star, Tommy Leach, took pains to write Dreyfuss after the 1902 season to reassure him, "I will be with you and no one else next season. Do not pay any attention to the gossip you may hear to the effect that I am going to the American League."[28] The American League was able to woo only two of the Pirates star players. Pitchers Jesse Tannehill and 28-game winner Jack Chesboro went to the New York Highlanders (later the Yankees.) In 1904, Chesboro posted an amazing record of 41 wins and only 12 losses for the American League club.[29]

At one time, Ban Johnson had tried to talk Dreyfuss into moving to the American League, receiving a courteous but firm "no" from Barney. "This refusal," noted the *Sporting News,*" marked the end of the American

League's 'hands-off' policy toward Pittsburgh."[30] According to rumors, Johnson was now ready to place a rival club in Pittsburgh. Dreyfuss, however, outmaneuvered him again. For a reported total of $15,000, Barney leased all the suitable sites in and around Pittsburgh where a competing ballpark could be built.[31]

In mid–January, 1903, with Barney Dreyfuss among the chief negotiators, the National and American Leagues reached a compromise. The American League kept its club in New York and retained all of its players. In return, they agreed not to place a club in Pittsburgh. Both leagues promised to observe the reserve clause and honor each other's contracts. At the same baseball meeting, Dreyfuss nominated his friend and co-owner, Harry Pulliam, as President of the National League. "I can promise you that Harry Pulliam is the soul of honor, and if he is elected, I expect no favors and I shall ask no favors." Pulliam was unanimously elected the National League's fifth president. He was scrupulously fair in his dealings with Dreyfuss, but he did appoint him chairman of the schedule committee. Pulliam, together with American League President Ban Johnson, and Cincinnati owner Garry Herrmann, now comprised baseball's National Commission.[32]

Dreyfuss may have been busy with the Baseball Trust and the American League, but these battles certainly did not affect the performance of the Pittsburgh Pirates, who won consecutive pennants in 1901, 1902, and 1903. In 1901, the Pirates reached first place on June 16 and never looked back, finishing 7½ games ahead of the second place Phillies. Wagner was the key to the Pirate pennant-winning team, with a batting average of .353, and league-leading totals of 38 doubles and 49 stolen bases. His versatility in the field was outstanding — he played 64 games at shortstop, 51 in the outfield, and 24 at third base.[33]

In 1902, the Pirates, untouched by American League forays, swept to the pennant by winning 103 games and finishing 27½ games ahead of the second-place Dodgers. For the second consecutive year, the Pirates had the league's leading hitter, but this year Ginger Beaumont won with a .357 batting average. Wagner's batting average was only .329. Jack Chesboro, Jesse Tannehill and Deacon Phillippe were all 20-game winners for the Pirates, while Tommy Leach led the league with six home runs, all of them inside the park.[34]

In 1903, the Pirates were without two of their top pitchers, Chesboro and Tannehill, but three other pitchers— Sam Leever, Deacon Phillippe, and Ed Doheny —combined for 65 wins and the team set a major league record with six consecutive shutouts.[35]

For Dreyfuss, his first years as Pirate owner had been eventful and successful. He had the game's greatest team, had helped make his best friend

President of the National League, and had played a major role in writing the peace between the two leagues. Unlike many fellow National League magnates, Dreyfuss was more convinced than ever that a rivalry of two strong, well-conducted leagues was beneficial to baseball.

By August of 1903, there was little question that the Pittsburgh Pirates would win the National League pennant and the Boston Pilgrims the title in the American League. After the season, Dreyfuss had intended to take his team to Hawaii and Australia as a reward for their third straight championship. Sports writers and fans, however, began to call for a series of games between the two pennant winners. Post-season competition in the Majors was not new. In 1894 the Temple Cup, an early version of the World Series, was awarded to the winner of a playoff between the first- and second-place finishers of the old 12-team National League. This competition ended after four years because of rumors that the two teams divided the money equally regardless of which one won.[36]

Dreyfuss realized that a World Series would have a number of benefits. It would help restore the pride of the National League moguls (since Dreyfuss fully expected to win the series), legitimize the American League, and most importantly, revive fan interest in baseball.[37] Beyond the altruistic reasons, Dreyfuss also realized it could provide extra money for his players and perhaps a little extra profit for both clubs.[38]

Dreyfuss contacted Henry Killilea, president of the American League Pilgrims, about participating in a post-season championship series. "The time has come for the National League and American League to organize a World Series ... we would create great interest in baseball, in our leagues, and in our players. I also believe it would be a financial success."[39]

Killilea and Dreyfuss worked out a number of rules for the 1903 World Series. Although they decided on a best five-of-nine series for that year, two of the other provisions agreed to in 1903 are followed to this day. First, the series was to be played in the home parks of the two participants, rather than on a neutral field. Second, any player not on the team's roster prior to September 1 could not participate in the contest.[40] The text of the agreement was made public but not the plan for dividing the receipts. There is evidence, however, that the two owners agreed to split only the income from the basic admissions—75 percent to the winner and 25 percent to the loser. Each owner would retain any monies exceeding the basic admission charge from the sale of higher priced seats and each owner would determine what his own players received for participating in the series.[41]

It appeared that the Pirates had the superior team. That year, Honus Wagner had won another batting title with a .355 average. He was followed closely by player-manager Fred Clarke at .351 and 1902 batting champ

Ginger Beaumont at .341.[42] Star players also included slugging third baseman Tommy Leach and a pitching staff led by twenty-five game winners
Sam Leever and Deacon Phillippe. Dreyfuss did not think for one minute
that any team could beat his Pirates.

The Pilgrim team was composed mainly of players recruited from the
National League. The great Cy Young had come from St. Louis and Bill
Dineen from the Boston Braves. Other stars included third baseman and
manager Jimmy Collins, and outfielders Chick Stahl, Pat Dougherty, and
Buck Freeman, the 1899 National League home run champion.[43]

In a surprising upset, before overflow crowds in both cities, the Pilgrims won the 1903 Series, defeating the Pirates five games to three, and
becoming the first World Champions of modern baseball. The great Pirates
pitching staff had broken down. Sam Leever developed a lame arm and
pitched only one complete game. Ed Doheny, the Pirates eccentric southpaw, went berserk shortly before the series and was put in an insane asy-
lum. That left the Pirates with only one hurler, Deacon Phillippe. He made
a noble effort, pitching five complete games in a little less than two weeks,
and winning three of them, but Boston's Cy Young and Bill Dineen were
outstanding. In addition, batting champ Honus Wagner was held to a lowly
.214 average during the series. In his final 14 at-bats, he managed only one
hit — a single.[44]

Despite the loss, Dreyfuss showed his appreciation for the good showing his team had made by tossing his entire share of the club's receipts into
the players' pool — a magnanimous gesture that illustrates why the Pirates
were so loyal to him.[45] Dreyfuss said it was just his way of thanking his
players for three pennants and for sticking by him during the league war.
"The boys deserve it," he said. As a result, the Pirate players each collected
$1,316 for losing the World Series, while the winning Boston players were
each paid only $1,182.[46]

Not only was Dreyfuss loyal and generous to his players, he was a
good sport and a gracious loser. He told *The Sporting News,* "The Boston
club squarely won the world's championship series playing the cleanest
kind of baseball."[47] He was especially pleased to have initiated what he
hoped would be the beginning of many contests between the leagues. Dreyfuss was far ahead of his time in advocating inter-league play, both during and after the regular season. He wanted fans in all major league cities
to have the opportunity to see players in both leagues.[48]

If Barney Dreyfuss had any visions of a fourth consecutive pennant
for his Pirates in 1904, his hopes were dashed early in the season. A poor
start in April was impossible to overcome and the Bucs had to be content
to finish the season in fourth place.[49]

The New York Giants won the National League Pennant in 1904 chiefly because of great pitching from their new college star, Christy Mathewson, and from veteran Joe McGinnity. The Pilgrims captured the American League flag again.[50]

Baseball fans were ready for a 1904 World Series. After the 1903 Series, Boston manager Jimmy Collins told *Sporting Life*, "I should not be surprised to see postseason games each fall as long as there are two big leagues."[51] But Giant manager John McGraw, backed by his owner John Brush, refused to play the American League champions, stating, "There is nothing in the constitution or playing rules of the National League which requires its victorious club to … a contest with a victorious club in a minor league."[52] Baseball experts speculate that the reason McGraw and Brush refused to play stemmed from their dislike of American League president Ban Johnson. As a sportswriter in Cincinnati, Johnson had been quite critical of Brush, who was then owner of the Cincinnati team. McGraw and Johnson had disliked each other since the days when McGraw was the Baltimore manager in the American League and his constant heckling had upset Johnson. A third reason might have been that the Giants didn't want to be embarrassed by the "upstart" American League who had weakened the Senior Circuit by recruiting so many of its stars.[53]

Fans were so upset about not having a World Series that Brush relented — somewhat. He agreed to an annual World Series on two conditions: it would a best-of-seven event, as it is today, and the series would not begin until the following year, 1905.[54]

Barney Dreyfuss was also outraged. As chairman of the National League schedule committee, he accused Brush and McGraw of reneging on the agreement between the two leagues' joint schedule committee to hold a World Series. According to Dreyfuss, "The National League gave its word to the American League that postseason games would be played … and I will keep my word with them as far as the Pittsburgh club is concerned."[55] Dreyfuss and his fourth-place Pirates then challenged Cleveland, the American League's fourth-place club.[56]

Even though it was not a World Series in the truest sense, the postseason event brought together both leagues' batting champs of 1904, Pittsburgh's Honus Wagner, and Cleveland's Napoleon Lajoie. It was the third batting championship for each of them.[57] Neither team really won the series. Cleveland had two victories and the Pirates one, but the other two games ended as ties, even though one went 14 innings.[58]

Dreyfuss' position as chairman of the schedule committee required long hours, incredible computational abilities, and diplomatic finesse as he attempted to appease teams in both leagues. He favored a uniform schedule with both leagues playing the same number of games, and for many years he tangled with the American League who wanted to play 168 games while the National League adhered to the 154-game schedule Ebbets had developed many years before.[59] Dreyfuss also had to satisfy owners who wanted to begin the season later in April and finish later in October and he fought long and hard for a uniform closing date for both leagues. Within his own league, Dreyfuss had to be completely fair to the other seven teams, giving them an equal opportunity to play holiday games at home, and making sure that no team received preferential treatment. When a representative of *The Sporting News* visited the office of Barney Dreyfuss, he noted that Dreyfuss' desk was littered with calendars, almanacs, railroad guides, dry figures and dates which, the reporter said, would drive ordinary men to distraction.[60]

Dreyfuss held the post of schedule committee chairman from the time he was appointed by Harry Pulliam until he resigned in 1927. He was lauded for his expertise, his evenhandedness, and the integrity he exhibited as committee chairman.[61] According to some students of the game, his schedules were models of compactness not equaled since his death.[62]

Integrity was only one of the attributes which marked Dreyfuss' life. He was also recognized throughout his baseball career for his intellect and his financial acumen, assets he happily shared with his ballplayers. He would offer to establish bank accounts for his players, particularly those men with wives and families. Dreyfuss also volunteered to invest some of the pay for his higher-salaried players with the understanding that he would guarantee the principal if the investments lost money. Later in his career, Honus Wagner often allowed his paychecks to accrue. With Dreyfuss using his keen business sense to invest the funds, Wagner collected a substantially higher sum each fall.[63]

On the other hand, Dreyfuss could be rough on players who did not cooperate with him, especially holdouts. When Burleigh Grimes refused to accept a contract, Dreyfuss traded him to the Boston Braves, a team with much less talent than the Pirates. "[Grimes] is a hard worker during a ball game and he knows how to pitch. But I hold the interests of my ball club above everything else and when he refused to accept our terms, I decided to trade him and make the best bargain possible." He admitted that he could have sold Grimes to a number of teams, but he had a lifelong policy of never selling a player he could trade.[64]

Like most other owners of his day, Dreyfuss watched every penny that would increase his team's profits. He even complained about Ladies' Day and Knothole Gang promotions, citing figures showing that in a two-day series in St. Louis, boys and women admitted free comprised 40 percent

of the total attendance. When the owner of the Cardinals reminded Dreyfuss that the Knothole Gang was a charity program for poor children and
that his team had to complete with the Browns, one of the clubs that held
Ladies' Days, Dreyfuss was unmoved and unsympathetic.[65]

Dreyfuss was also a man of firm convictions who tenaciously clung
to them, even when they seemed petty. Dreyfuss once scouted a prospect
in Texas reputed to be a great batter, but he smoked cigarettes. Dreyfuss
refused to sign the young man who was to become one of baseball's leading hitters—Tris Speaker.[66] And even though Dreyfuss denied the story,
the rumor persisted.[67]

Dreyfuss was not a smoker, but since he had been in his family's distillery business, he was not opposed to an occasional drink. His players,
however, were distinctly told that, during the season, "….anyone desiring
to draw salary from the Pittsburgh Club will have to stay on the water
wagon."[68] Pittsburgh pitcher Howard Camnitz once discovered that Dreyfuss had deducted $1,200 from his paycheck because Camnitz had been
drinking. Camnitz admitted his guilt but told Dreyfuss it was only on the
advice of his physician. Dreyfus bluntly replied that he, not the physician,
was running the club.[69]

Dreyfuss firmly believed that integrity should be an integral part of
baseball. He favored laws which would make it illegal for anyone to sell
tickets higher than their face value.[70] He also strongly opposed gambling
anywhere near his ballpark and often complained that the Pittsburgh police
did not take the matter seriously enough.[71]

Dreyfuss was a stickler for what he considered fair play on the ball
field. For many years, he campaigned to abolish the spitball and all "doctored" pitches because he claimed they gave pitchers an unfair edge.[72] "The
spitball is unsanitary and not a natural delivery…. It is not the stock in
trade of first class twirlers but a last resort measure…. I believe baseball
would progress more rapidly without any of these freaks like the spitball
and the emery ball."[73] Major league baseball eventually agreed with Dreyfuss but compromised. Dreyfuss favored outlawing the spitball at once, but,
over his opposition, legislation was passed allowing spitball pitchers registered by their owners to continue using the pitch until the end of their
major league careers. Hal Carlson, who pitched for the Pirates from 1917
until 1923, threw the spitter, but Dreyfuss refused to put him on the register, even though it reduced the strength of the Pirate pitching staff.[74]

What most upset Barney Dreyfuss, however, was unseemly behavior
on the part of baseball fans, players, and managers. One of his first stands
as Pirate owner was to oppose the National League's return to using just
one umpire per game. Dreyfuss, who always wanted baseball to be civil

and sportsmanlike, felt that this move would only encourage the "rowdy-ism" which had plagued the game for many years.[75] During one 1901 Pirate home game, the umpire's calls so angered the Pirate fans, that two thousand of them chased the umpire off the grounds. He was saved from injury only because Fred Clarke and Honus Wagner protected him from the mob. Dreyfuss declared that he would not tolerate such behavior by the fans and that bad umpiring was no excuse. "Rowdyism destroys the game of baseball," he reiterated.[76] He also had to frequently remind his fiery manager, "Fred, I want a hustling, aggressive club, but I don't want rowdies and umpire fighters."[77]

No one did more to test Dreyfuss' concept of proper behavior in baseball than John McGraw, the New York Giant manager who had insulted Dodger owner, Charlie Ebbets. After the Giants won the National League pennant in 1904, they became bitter rivals of the Pirates and generally the most hated team in baseball. John McGraw was a bully—loud, crude, aggressive, and belligerent both on and off the field. Grantland Rice, noted sportswriter once said of McGraw, "His very walk across the field in a hostile town was a challenge to the multitude."[78] McGraw harassed umpires, opposing players, and managers and offered to fight everyone in the stands.

Obviously, McGraw also considered baseball owners fair game. On May 18, 1905, the Giants and Pirates met at the Polo Grounds. After badgering the Pirate pitcher, he and Pirate manager, Fred Clarke, nearly came to blows and McGraw was ejected from the game. Before the next day's game, McGraw greeted Dreyfuss derisively as the Pirate owner headed toward his box behind third base. He then continued to taunt Dreyfuss, shouting repeatedly, "Hey, Barney." At the top of his lungs, McGraw accused Dreyfuss of welching on gambling debts and receiving special favors from his friend, National League President Pulliam.

Dreyfuss lodged a formal protest with Pulliam, who referred the matter to the National League's four-man Board of Directors. Three of them could hardly be called neutral: John Brush, owner of the Giants and McGraw's boss; Arthur Soden, owner of the Boston National League team and also part-owner of the Giants; and Dreyfuss. The remaining member was Chicago Cub owner Jim Hart. Even before the board had ruled, McGraw called Pulliam and denounced him as a puppet of Dreyfuss. Pulliam promptly fined McGraw $150 and suspended him for 15 days.[79] McGraw was livid. "Why, there is no organization on the face of the earth, except the National League, that will convict an accused man without a hearing. We might as well be in Russia."[80]

The matter was settled in a most unsatisfactory way from Dreyfuss' point of view, indicating the influence of Giant owner, John T. Brush, and the liberties that baseball allowed John McGraw to take on the diamond. The National League Directors absolved McGraw of any guilt, but instead scolded Dreyfuss for "indulging in an open controversy with a ball player." At the same time, however, the league upheld Pulliam's suspension of McGraw, who was never out of uniform for one day.[81]

As for Dreyfuss, he was both embarrassed and angry. He resented the fact that his integrity could be questioned, for he considered himself a model of clean living, who never consorted with gamblers nor behaved badly in public. Although his feud with McGraw was handled strictly within the National League, the incident was one of the reasons that ultimately caused Dreyfuss to challenge the governing structure of Major League baseball.[82]

The Pirates' second-place finish in 1905, nine games behind McGraw's Giants, only added to Dreyfuss' unhappiness. Neither the Pirates nor the Giants won the pennant in 1906. The Chicago Cubs, led by its player-manager Frank Chance, compiled an unequalled record of 116 victories and 36 defeats, a winning percentage of .763, the major-league record for the twentieth century.[83] The Pirates ended in third place, 23½ games behind the league leader. Yet, there were a few bright spots for the Bucs that year. Pirate pitchers hurled two no-hitters and once again Honus Wagner led the league in hitting with an average of .339, his fourth batting title.[84] 1906 also was the year that Dreyfuss introduced another baseball innovation: a tarpaulin to cover the infield when it rained.[85]

The Cubs won the pennant again in 1907, with the Pirates finishing in second place and, much to the delight of Dreyfuss, McGraw's Giants finishing fourth.[86] Thirty-three-year-old Honus Wagner won his fifth batting title with a .350 average, and led the league with 38 doubles.[87]

In 1908 the Pirates, Giants and Cubs were neck and neck in the standings until the last game of the season when the Cubs won the pennant by one game. Honus Wagner was awe-inspiring in 1908. He won his sixth batting title with an average of .354. He also led the league with 201 hits, 39 doubles, 19 triples, 109 runs batted in, a slugging percentage of .542, and 53 stolen bases.[88]

After the 1908 season, Barney Dreyfuss began to look for another location for his ballpark. Exposition Park, where the Pirates had been playing, was so close to the Allegheny River that when the river reached flood tide, the outfield went under water. Dreyfus also felt the park was too close to Pittsburgh's red-light district, which discouraged women from attending Pirate home games. In addition, Dreyfuss feared that the wooden stands were a fire hazard. He had lost his stadium in Louisville to fire and was convinced that he needed to construct a fireproof park.[89] When the Baltimore and Ohio Railroad, owner of the land, hinted that it might want the grounds to expand its railroad yards, Dreyfuss made up his mind to construct a new ballpark.[90]

Dreyfuss discovered a seven-acre tract of land in Oakland-Schenley, a middle-class enclave midway between Pittsburgh's downtown and the east end, and three miles from the business district.[91] "When I found the land," said Dreyfuss, "there was nothing there but a livery stable and a hot house, with a few cows grazing over the countryside. A ravine ran through the property."[92] But it was close to trolley lines and far from the odorous mills. Dreyfuss planned to build stands that would hold the largest crowds anticipated over the next five years and designed the park so he could enlarge them if needed.[93] Critics immediately ridiculed the new location, claiming that "Dreyfuss' Folly" was too far away for the fans and much larger than it should be. Dreyfuss smiled and stood his ground.

He asked fans to suggest names for the new park, finally selecting Forbes Field as the name of his new steel-and-concrete structure. British General John Forbes, appropriately nicknamed "Old Ironsides," had been the leader of the forces which had captured the site where the British erected Fort Pitt, the forerunner of the city of Pittsburgh.[94]

Dreyfuss oversaw much of the ballpark's construction. In order to open the park on time, men worked double shifts, completing Forbes Field in just 122 days. On June 30, 1909, 30,338 fans packed the 25,000-seat park and thousands more stood behind a rope barrier to watch their Pirates lose to the Cubs 3–2. Dreyfuss was not happy with the results of the game but he liked the attendance figures. "A friend bet me a $150 suit we would never fill the park, and we filled it five times the first two weeks," he gloated.[95]

Forbes Field, constructed at a cost of $2 million, was a three-tiered stadium within the baselines and two tiered beyond the lines. Dressing rooms for the home and visiting clubs were underneath the stands and both had lockers, spacious baths, and clothes-drying apparatus. There was a lounge for Pirate employees, a custom-designed office for manager Fred Clarke, and well-appointed umpires' quarters.[96] For the fans, Forbes Field was equipped with electric lights, telephones and even maids in the ladies' rest rooms.[97] Ramps helped speed fans to and from their seats, and elevators were available for those able to afford luxury boxes on the third deck.[98]

The playing field was large, measuring 360 feet down the left-field line, 462 feet in dead center and 376 feet in right field, a reflection of Dreyfuss' aversion to cheap homeruns. He had vowed there would never be any in his park. Forbes Field was definitely not a hitter's paradise; yet, despite the seeming advantages for a pitcher, there was never a no-hitter pitched there during its entire history.[99]

Not only was Forbes Field beautiful, it was a revenue producer for Dreyfuss. He cut down sharply on the number of cheap bleacher seats and replaced them with grandstand seating. Patrons could purchase brass removable nameplates for a hundred dollars, even though the box holder was still compelled to pay the daily admission charge. When the Pirates were on the road, Dreyfuss, like fellow owner, Charlie Ebbets, made money by renting the park for horse shows, public gatherings, and other events.[100]

Dreyfuss could have brought in more revenue had he allowed advertising boards in his new ballpark, but he wanted to keep Forbes Field's pastoral setting free of commercials. He did allow ads for war stamps during World War I and war bonds during World War II. Many local firms offered Dreyfuss huge sums to advertise in the park, but he always turned them down. His son-in-law, William Benswanger, once estimated that advertising would have brought in more than $1 million in additional revenue.[101]

Baseball historians consider Forbes Field the beginning of a new era for ballparks. While Shibe Park in Philadelphia had opened earlier in 1909 and was the first of the major league concrete-and-steel parks, it was no rival in size or grandeur to Forbes Field. Shibe Park's grandstand sat 6,000 people, with seating for an additional 14,000 on concrete bleachers in both left and right fields. Forbes Field, on the other hand, contained far more higher-priced grandstand seats. Boasting of his new ballpark, Dreyfuss bragged, "Why, they told me the Giants don't have that large a park with all New York to draw from."[102]

Nineteen nine would have been the greatest year in Dreyfuss' baseball career had it not been for a personal tragedy. One month after Forbes Field opened, Harry Pulliam shot himself as the result of a nervous breakdown, provoked, many claim, by his run-ins with John McGraw and ongoing depression. Dreyfuss was heartbroken over the death of his good friend and paid tribute to him, "Pulliam was a true Kentucky thoroughbred; no finer man ever was born into this world. I am heartsick over what has happened."[103]

In spite of his private grief, Dreyfuss maintained his focus on his ballclub. The Cubs won 104 games in 1909, but the Pirates won 110 and their fourth pennant for Dreyfuss. Once again Wagner won the National League batting title, his fourth consecutive title and his seventh since becoming a Pirate.[104]

The American League champions in 1909 were the Detroit Tigers, who won their third consecutive pennant. The World Series featured the first series skirmish between the two batting champions, Wagner and Detroit's Ty Cobb. Wagner out-hit Cobb .311 to .231 in the Series and Pittsburgh pitcher Babe Adams became the first man to win three games in a seven-game Series. The two led the Pirates to victory over the Tigers, four games to three. The 1909 Series was the first to go the full seven games. Because of Dreyfuss' large new ballpark, it was also a huge financial success for both teams, drawing 145,807 fans paying $188,302.[105]

Although Dreyfuss predicted that the 1909 team would "stay up there for some time," he was soon proved wrong.[106] The 1910 Pirates finished in third place, 17 games behind the pennant-winning Chicago Cubs, causing Dreyfuss to remark, "Our 1910 team was my biggest disappointment in baseball. Never did I see a great team fold so quickly."[107] 1910 did see the Pirate debut of a young outfielder named Max Carey. Although he played in only two games in 1910, by the next year Carey would be a core player in the Pirate lineup en route to baseball's Hall of Fame.[108]

In 1911, the Pirates again finished in third place; and in 1912, the last great club of the Clarke-Wagner era, the Pirates finished second, only two games behind the New York Giants. In 1913, 40-year-old Fred Clarke ended his playing career and managed the Pirates from the bench. The Pirates finished in fourth that year but fell into the second division in both 1914 and 1915.[109] At the end of the season, manager Clarke told Dreyfuss that he was going to retire from baseball. He had been in the game for 21 years, but now he planned to raise mules on his Kansas ranch. "After handling ball players for many years, handling mules should be easy," exclaimed Clarke.[110]

From 1913 through 1916, Dreyfuss not only attempted to get his team back on track, but he and the other major league owners also began facing opposition from the rival Federal League. Following the 1913 season, the Federal League mounted an aggressive campaign to establish itself as a major league by building new ballparks and signing current big league players. In 1914, the Federal League established the Pittsburgh Rebels, and approached Honus Wagner with a multi-year deal worth $15,000 annually to manage them. Wagner was no more interested in this contract than he had been in the American League's lucrative offer years earlier, saying, "The Feds know there's no use talking to me."[111] Eventually, the Rebels signed former star Pirate pitcher, Deacon Phillippe, to manage their team.[112]

Thanks to Dreyfuss' shrewdness, the Rebels caused less trouble in Pittsburgh than Federal League teams did in other cities. Using the same strategy as when he was challenged by the American League, Dreyfuss actively began to sign his players. By the beginning of the 1914 season, only two Pirate players had jumped to the Federal League, catcher Mike Simon who signed with the Chicago ChiFeds and pitcher Claude Hendrix, who joined the St. Louis club.[113]

There was no love lost between Dreyfuss and the upstart Federal League. He argued that the Federal League had contributed to the poor showing of the 1914 Pirates, saying, "Our players talked, played, and ate Feds." Dreyfuss was especially irked that some of the Pirate players were using the Federal League to their advantage for what Dreyfuss termed "a holdup." Max Carey, a Pirate outfielder, who never missed a chance to coax a little more money from his employer, received a new two-year deal with a raise.[114]

Early in January 1915, the Federal League sued organized baseball in U.S. District Court in Chicago, claiming the Major Leagues violated the Sherman Antitrust Act, which prohibited monopolies operating in interstate commerce. The case was presided over by Judge Kenesaw Mountain Landis, an ardent baseball fan who refused to render a verdict. He hoped that the longer he delayed, the more likely the parties would reach some kind of agreement on their own. Landis' plan worked. A year later, the Federal League fell apart and the suit was dropped.[115]

In 1916, the wealthiest owner in the Federal League, oilman Harry Sinclair, threatened to move his New Jersey team to New York. Suddenly the National League, with two New York area teams to protect and a Federal League team already competing in Brooklyn, was willing to talk compromise. A secret meeting was held in Cincinnati between Dreyfuss, who had again accepted the role of negotiator, National League President John Tener, and three Federal League team owners. Dreyfuss was called on because his good relations with the American League gave him a unique standing with both major leagues. The settlement, finalized in December 1916, called for Federal League owners Phil Ball and Charles Weegham to buy the St. Louis Browns and the Chicago Cubs, respectively. Dreyfuss was instrumental in the plan to get Federal League players into the American and National Leagues, by allowing the teams to choose the players in inverse order to their 1915 standings.[116] Dreyfuss, however, stated that he would not purchase any of the former Federal Leaguers.[117]

Major League Baseball and the Federal League had settled their battle, but in 1917 there were still a number of problems. The Players' Fraternity, baseball's labor union, headed by David Fultz, threatened a strike which could possibly bring all play to a halt; and the United States had entered World War I. Dreyfuss had no control over events in Germany, but he had plenty to say about the union. "Our club has not made money for three years. We have been paying out to the players all we took in — and sometimes more. I believe that baseball might be benefited by a year's layoff. So far as I am concerned, I would be willing to shut up Forbes Field throughout 1917 ... before I will consent to give in to the demands which have been made by Fultz."[118]

To make matters worse, a series of disputes erupted among baseball's executives, which ultimately caused the downfall of the National Commission and nearly disrupted the entire structure of organized baseball.[119] At the center of these disputes was Barney Dreyfuss.

Ever since the National Commission had been established, Barney Dreyfuss had been skeptical of its organization and work. In the fall of 1909, Dreyfuss had called it a joke, claiming that its members did too much drinking and ran its affairs too loosely. "If I were to run my business in the manner of the National Commission," he stated, "I would consider myself a poor businessman indeed."[120] He was even critical of Ban Johnson, President of the American League. Dreyfuss had been the only National League owner really sympathetic to the American League during the early 20th century, but he had become so badly disenchanted with the work of the Commission, that Johnson, as its dominant figure, received some of Barney's ire.[121]

The major clash occurred in 1916, although its roots went back six years. George Sisler, a star high school pitcher, signed a contract in 1910 with the Akron club in the Ohio-Penn League. His father voided the contract, claiming that his son was a minor, and enrolled him at the University of Michigan.[122]

The Columbus Club of the American Association, which controlled Akron, sold Sisler's contract to the Pittsburgh Pirates for $5,000, with the National Commission approving the sale on September 1, 1912. Sisler consulted his college baseball coach, Branch Rickey, who was also a lawyer and former major league catcher. Rickey advised the young pitcher that the contract was not binding.[123]

By 1915, Dreyfuss had been holding the contract he had bought from Columbus for three years. Since the National Commission had approved his purchase, he wrote them asking for a clarification of Sisler's status. The Commission's attorney unequivocally nullified the Commission's earlier action, stating that Sisler's contract was invalid and that Pittsburgh had no legal claim to him. The Commission unanimously declared Sisler a free agent.[124]

Sisler then solicited offers from Pittsburgh and other major league teams. Dreyfuss proposed a salary of $700 a month for the balance of the 1915 season plus a bonus for a total of $5,200. In mid–June Sisler wired Dreyfuss that he had accepted a contract to play for the St. Louis Browns for $7,400.[125] By no coincidence, Rickey, Sisler's former baseball coach, was to be the team's new manager.[126]

Dreyfuss immediately filed a complaint, accusing the Browns of "tampering," and further charged that Pittsburgh had unquestioned right to a player under baseball law. The decision was left to Commission Chairman Garry Herrmann, owner of the National League's Cincinnati team.[127] On June 10, 1916, almost four years after the Sisler contract had first come before the National Commission, Herrmann rejected Dreyfuss' complaint, and declared Sisler the property of the St. Louis Browns.[128]

Herrmann's ruling wounded Dreyfuss so deeply that he refused to speak to him for the rest of his life.[129] It certainly didn't make Dreyfuss feel any better as he witnessed George Sisler develop into one of baseball's greatest hitters and finest first basemen of all time. Dreyfuss now became Herrmann's relentless foe and began an unremitting effort to unseat him as chairman of the National Commission, first calling — unsuccessfully — for his replacement at the winter meeting in 1916. Dreyfuss persisted and soon other owners, too, began voicing their displeasure with the Commission. American League owners disliked having two of the three members from the National League. At the same time, National League magnates were upset with fellow owner Herrmann because he sided with his friend Ban Johnson on too many occasions. There was a general consensus that the best remedy was to select a person outside of baseball as Commission chairman.[130] Dreyfuss and Yankees president, Colonel Jacob Ruppert, wanted to replace the Commission with a single Commissioner.[131] "I have advocated a one-man Commission for the last four years," exclaimed Dreyfuss. "This one-man Commission is bound to come — if not this year, surely next. Just mark what I say."[132]

In 1918, another player dispute increased the pressure to reform the National Commission. The row was between the AL's Philadelphia Athletics and the NL's Boston Braves over a player named Scott Perry. As expected, each League president sided with his own league, but this time Hermann also voted with the National League and Perry was ordered to report to Boston. Athletics owner Connie Mack, and Phillies owner Ben Shibe, got an injunction restraining the National Commission from enforcing the order, and Perry remained with the Athletics. The National Leaguers were incensed, with Dreyfuss being the most vocal. He shouted, "Herrmann decides against us, and we have to take it; he decides for us, and the American League goes to court. We need a strong man to head the game, with no connections with any club."[133]

At the next winter meeting, January 16, 1919, the National League voted 6–2 for a one-man Commission headed by a neutral party, while the American League voted 6–2 to continue the existing Commission. The two leagues did agree to search for a new Chairman while Herrmann remained in that office on an interim basis. At the 1920 winter meetings, the National League officially forced Garry Herrmann to make a decision — remain on the Commission or remain owner of the Cincinnati Reds. He chose the latter. Barney Dreyfuss had won half of his fight — the removal of Herrmann — but changing the Commission to a one-man Commissioner, had to wait.[134]

Unfortunately, the two leagues could not agree on Hermann's successor, and as a result, the National Commission had only two members when the Black Sox scandal, the greatest disgrace in baseball history, came to light.[135] Toward the end of 1920, more than a year after it actually happened, front-page newspaper headlines across the country screamed that members of the Chicago White Sox had accepted bribes to control the outcome of the 1919 World Series. This scandal hastened the demise of the National Commission, a transition that many, including Dreyfuss, felt was inevitable.[136]

Under pressure to "do something" following the scandal, organized baseball for a time considered a plan recommended by Albert D. Lasker, a wealthy Chicagoan and stockholder in the Chicago Cubs. According to the Lasker Plan, a reconstituted National Commission would be made up of three nonpartisan members chosen from outside baseball.[137] Names such as ex–President William Howard Taft, and Generals John Pershing and Leonard Wood, were all mentioned. Dreyfuss lobbied for appointing Judge Kennesaw Mountain Landis because of the role he had played in the Federal League dispute.[138]

The most important part of the Lasker Plan was that it gave the committee the sole right to prescribe the rules of the game, and regulate the conduct of major and minor league players, managers, umpires and club owners, even to the point of banning an offending owner from organized baseball.[139] Before long, the three-member committee evolved into a single Commissioner of Baseball with these powers.

Ban Johnson opposed the plan. It would deprive him of much of his authority, of course, but he and his supporters truly felt that men unfamiliar with baseball, regardless of how much success they might have achieved in other fields, could manage the affairs of Organized Baseball successfully.[140]

All the National League owners and those American League magnates opposed to Johnson, were unanimous in their choice of Judge Landis. Finally, even American League owners loyal to Johnson decided that in the interest of baseball it was time to get on with reforming it. On November 12, 1920, fifteen club presidents marched into the federal building in Chicago to offer Landis the job of Baseball Commissioner.[141]

Two months later, on January 12, 1921, Judge Landis accepted the final definition of his powers. As the first Commissioner of Major League Baseball, he was to have complete authority to "investigate, either upon complaint or upon his own initiative, any act, transaction, or practice suspected to be detrimental to the best interests of the national game of baseball." At the last minute Ban Johnson had tried to dilute the authority of the Commissioner by changing the agreement to read that he could merely "recommend" action. Because Dreyfuss had alerted Landis beforehand of Johnson's plan, Landis interrupted the reading of the document and informed the owners that the clause must read to "take" action. "Take it or leave it," said Landis. "You have told the world that my powers are to be absolute. I wouldn't take this job for all the gold in the world unless I knew my hands were to be free." The owners complied.[142]

Barney Dreyfuss was ecstatic. He had been successful in establishing a baseball Commissioner who had no personal stake in the game. He then told *The Sporting News,* "There remains one big step to be taken for the betterment of baseball, and that is the passage of a federal law making baseball gambling a felony. If it is possible to get such a law on the books, the biggest possible advancement will have been made toward keeping the national game pure in the future."[143]

While the club owners had been involved in restructuring baseball, the game was still being played on the field. From 1916, when the Sisler matter had been settled, until 1920, when Landis was given the post of Baseball Commissioner, the Pirates were at best, a mediocre team. They ended in fourth place three times, sixth place once, and in 1917, for the first and only time under the ownership of Barney Dreyfuss, the Pirates finished in the cellar.[144]

Nineteen twenty-one was a disappointing year on the field, although Dreyfuss had added to the team a 27-year-old former Brave, Robert "Rabbit" Maranville, to replace the retired Wagner at shortstop. On August 24, the Pirates were in first place, ahead of John McGraw's Giants by 7½ games. Then they went to the Polo Grounds for a five-game series and lost all five to the Giants, ending the season in second place, four games out.[145] 1921 was a notable year for another reason. On August 5, Pittsburgh's KDKA, the world's pioneer commercial radio station, was the first to air a major league baseball game, describing the action between the Pirates and the Phillies. Although Dreyfuss was convinced that fans would remain at home listening to their radio instead of attending in person, the radio broadcasts heightened fan interest, and attendance actually increased.[146] Dreyfuss introduced another first for the Pittsburgh fans in 1921, announcing that contrary to prior custom, "Fans who attend games at the National League baseball park here may keep balls knocked into the stands without fear of being molested by the policemen."[147]

The following three years, the Pirates finished third twice and fourth once. The Pirate manager these three years was Bill McKechnie, who had earned a reputation of being an astute student of baseball as well as a devout elder of his church.[148] The 1924 Pirate team was another major disappointment to Dreyfuss. It had great talent and on paper it could be considered the best team the Pirates had ever fielded. A Pittsburgh sportswriter called rookie Forest Glenn Wright, who was now playing shortstop, the greatest since Honus Wagner. Rabbit Maranville moved to second, Pie Traynor played third and Charlie Grimm was the first baseman. The Pirates also had two outstanding outfielders in Max Carey and Kiki Cuyler. To win the pennant, the Pirates needed to win two of their remaining three games, all with McGraw's Giants, but Dreyfuss felt confident, for his team had won 13 of its last 19 games. "This time we ought to lick McGraw and make him like it," Dreyfuss told McKechnie. But the Giants swept the series as they had in 1921 and captured the National League flag. The Pirates had to settle for third place, three games behind.[149]

Frustrated by the results of the 1924 season, Dreyfuss decided to revamp his team. He felt that two of his infielders, Charlie Grimm and Rabbit Maranville, spent more of their time playing music and practical jokes than winning ball games. At the annual winter meeting in 1924, he shocked the baseball world when he announced that he had sent Maranville, Grimm and hurler Wilbur Cooper to the Cubs for infielder George Grantham, rookie first baseman Al Niehaus and pitcher Vic Aldridge. Dreyfuss told the press, "I got rid of all my banjo players."[150]

The fans hated the deal because they considered Grimm and Maranville "fun." Cooper was one of the National League's top hurlers, and the players Dreyfuss had received from the Cubs were suspect. Dreyfuss had the last laugh. Not only did his 1925 Pirates win a fifth pennant for him, but the Cubs finished in last place for the first time in their 72-year history.[151] No one on the Pirates had a bad year. Their five starting pitchers won a combined total of 85 games; the lowest hitting average among the regulars was .298; the team scored 84 more runs than the next best team and also led the league in hits, doubles, triples, RBIs, walks, stolen bases, and batting and slugging averages.[152]

The Pirates met the Washington Senators and their star pitcher, Walter Johnson, in the 1925 World Series. Down three games to one, Pittsburgh went on to win the Series by pounding out 15 hits against Johnson. Up to that time, no team had been down three games to one and come back to win the championship.[153]

Because Dreyfuss wanted as many fans as possible to see the World Series in Forbes Field, the Pirate owner built a temporary addition to the left-field section. It accommodated several thousand additional fans that otherwise would not have been able to get into the park. The extra section cost $25,000 to construct and was dismantled after the series. Although the extra seats brought in only $8,000 and the Pittsburgh club could only keep $1,200, Dreyfuss always considered the money well spent.[154]

The Pirates would not repeat in 1926, finishing in third place 4½ games behind the St. Louis Cardinals, who won their first pennant. The 1926 season was the rookie year on the Pirates of one of baseball's greatest stars, Paul Waner. In his first season, he batted .336, hit 35 doubles, and led the league with 22 triples. During Warner's 20-year baseball career, he won three batting crowns and compiled a lifetime batting average of .333.[155]

The Pirates won their last pennant for Barney Dreyfuss in 1927, barely edging out both the St. Louis Cardinals and the New York Giants. The Pirates had four future Hall of Famers in their 1927 lineup, Kiki Cuyler, Pie Traynor, Paul Waner and his brother, Lloyd, who joined the team that year. "Big Poison" Paul Waner led the National League in hitting, RBIs and triples. Lloyd, known as "Little Poison," would have a lifetime average of .316 in his eighteen years in the big leagues. Paul was elected to the Hall of Fame in 1952; Lloyd joined him in 1967.[156]

In the 1927 World Series, the Pirates lost four straight games to the New York Yankees, a club many people considered the greatest team of all time. It included a lineup that became known as "Murderers' Row" with one of the most overwhelming one-two punches in baseball — Babe Ruth and Lou Gehrig. Despite the superiority of the 1927 Yankees, Dreyfuss was deeply bitter about his team's loss, claiming that the Pirates had acted like a defeated club throughout the entire World Series.[157]

Following their 1927 season, the Pittsburgh franchise, one of the most successful in baseball since the turn of the century, went into a decline. It would be 33 years before they could claim another championship. They finished in fourth place in 1928, 8½ games behind the pennant-winning St. Louis Cardinals. It was not only the fourth place finish that galled Dreyfuss, but also the fact that the Cardinal manager was former Pirate skipper, Bill McKechnie.[158] The 1929 Pirates came a little closer to winning, finishing in second place, 9½ games behind the Cardinals, but in 1930, the Pirates finished in fifth place, only six games above .500 and 12 behind the repeat champion St. Louis team.[159]

Barney Dreyfuss was seriously thinking of retiring and anticipated turning the Pirates over to his son, Samuel, who had been the heir-apparent since the day he had graduated from Princeton. The two men enjoyed a close relationship and 36-year-old Sammy was vice-president, treasurer, and business manager of the club. Early in 1931, Sammy became ill, but was diagnosed with simply a bad case of the flu. His condition worsened, however, and on February 19, 1931, Samuel Dreyfuss died of pneumonia, only four days before his father's 65th birthday.[160]

The grief-stricken father was inconsolable. In desperation, he called on the husband of his daughter, Eleanor, to come join the baseball operation. Bill Benswanger, although a longtime Pirate fan, was in the insurance business. Music was his passion, not baseball. But Barney Dreyfuss immediately turned over much of the day-to-day operation of the club to Benswanger, who gave up his lucrative insurance business to help his father-in-law.

Never recovering from the shock of his son's death, Barney Dreyfuss died February 5, 1932. Upon Barney's death, ownership passed to Dreyfuss' widow, Florence, who named Benswanger president. He continued in that position until 1946, when a four-man syndicate that included singer Bing Crosby and real estate tycoon John W. Gilbreath purchased the team. For the first time in almost fifty years, the Dreyfuss family did not own the Pirates.[161]

Upon hearing of Dreyfuss' death, National League President, John Heydler, stated, "I cannot tell how deeply I feel the loss of Barney Dreyfuss. He was the esteemed senior baseball man of the country at the time of his death. Dreyfuss discovered more players than any other man in the game ... his abiding faith in the future of the game continued to the end."[162]

Honus Wagner said, "I played for Mr. Dreyfuss three years in Louisville and eighteen in Pittsburgh. Our friendship warmed through these years, and I feel a great loss at his passing. His generosity was only one of the fine things I remember about Barney Dreyfuss."[163]

The Sporting News said of Dreyfuss, "He fought the expansion of the American League spiritedly, but when he saw the fight was lost, he was the first in his league to greet the new major rival and to appreciate the part it was to play in the development of the National Game." The paper recognized Dreyfuss for originating the World Series in 1903 and credited him with leading the successful fight to replace the old National Commission with Judge Landis as a strong Baseball Commissioner. *The Sporting News* also praised his work in preparing the annual schedules, noting that he was the first and only vice-president the National League ever had.[164]

One sports writer stated that no owner was more progressive in his thinking or more in love with the game than Barney Dreyfuss. "If Charles

Ebbets may be credited with the statement 'Baseball is in its infancy,' then Barney Dreyfuss must be given credit as the sportsman who [nourished] that infant into a lusty giant, a sportsman who wanted to know the score before he learned the attendance figures ... and who was constantly striving for something new and progressive that would improve and advance the game."[165]

That same sportswriter summed up one of the most important characteristics which marked the life of Barney Dreyfuss—the absolute integrity that Dreyfuss brought both to the game of baseball and to his personal life. "Dreyfuss was a man of the highest integrity. His private life was little short of a splendid example. To have succeeded in an honorable business; to have established a prominent part in giving the American people the game closest to its heart; and to have left behind a reputation unsullied constitute the end and aim of all philosophy; the good life which leads to a happy and serene death. All these things Barney accomplished."[166]

3

Helene Britton
The Feminist

Barney Dreyfuss proved that you didn't have to be born in America to be a successful baseball man. Helene Britton proved that you didn't have to be a man to be successful in baseball. Well-versed in the game, Britton was prepared to break new ground when, in 1911, she became the first woman to own and operate a Major League team.

In 1898, Chris Von der Ahe, owner of St. Louis's National League baseball team, the Browns, was so disheartened by the poor performance of his club and the miserable state of his finances, that he placed the team in receivership. In March 1899, Von der Ahe sold the Browns for $40,000 to Helene Britton's father and uncle, Frank DeHaas Robison and Matthew Stanley Robison of Cleveland. The Robisons, who had made their money operating streetcar companies in Fort Wayne, Indiana, and Cleveland, also owned another National League team, the Cleveland Spiders.[1]

When the Robisons took over the St. Louis Browns, they immediately changed the name of the Browns' home field from Sportsman's Park to League Park, the same name as their field in Cleveland. St. Louis's League Park was located at the intersection of Vandeventer Avenue and Natural Bridge Road. Constructed in 1893, the all-wood stands could seat 15,000 in a single-deck grandstand and bleachers in both left and right fields.[2]

The next change the Robisons made was far more radical. The rules of Syndicate Baseball allowed magnates who owned more than one club to transfer players from one team to the other, just as Ebbets had done with Brooklyn and Baltimore and Dreyfuss with Louisville and Pittsburgh. But the Robisons went further. Believing that St. Louis was a better baseball town than Cleveland, they switched almost the entire rosters of the two teams before the 1899 season began. The old Browns players went to Cleveland where they posted the worst record in baseball history — 20 wins and 134 loses.[3] Virtually all the Cleveland players, including three future

HELENE BRITTON — St. Louis Cardinals 1911 to 1917 — Only 32 years old when she became the first woman to own a major league team, "Lady Bea" clearly demonstrated that women could actively participate in a male-dominated enterprise (*Sporting News*).

members of the Hall of Fame — Cy Young, Jesse Burkett, and Bobby Wallace — were transferred to St. Louis. Despite a streetcar strike, an overflow crowd of 18,000 fans crowded into League Park on opening day in St. Louis to see Young and the Browns defeat the Spiders 10–1.[4]

In a final effort to disassociate their club from Von der Ahe's disappointing teams, the Robisons replaced the team's brown socks and caps with red socks and hats, and changed the nickname of the team to the Perfectos, although some fans referred to them as the Red Caps. Legend has it that a female fan, upon seeing the new uniforms for the first time, exclaimed, "Oh, what a lovely shade of cardinal." William McHale, a baseball writer for the *St. Louis Republic,* is credited with being the first to call in print for a change of the team name to the Cardinals.[5] It was not until some years later, when Branch Rickey spoke at a luncheon where his hostess had used a red bird perched on a bat as a souvenir place card, that the nickname "Cardinals" became a "perky bird" rather than a color.[6]

In 1899 the Robisons' rejuvenated team did fairly well, finishing in fifth place in the twelve-team National League. In 1900, the National League trimmed itself to the eight teams that would remain intact until 1953 — Brooklyn, New York, Philadelphia, Boston, Chicago, Cincinnati, Pittsburgh, and St. Louis.[7] The Cardinals finished in sixth place that year.

From 1901 through 1908, the Cardinals continued to struggle, finishing higher than fourth only once and in the cellar three times.[8] The Robisons used five different managers during those years, but the man they really wanted was the player-manager who was later to become the enemy of both Ebbets and Dreyfuss — John McGraw. McGraw came to the Cardinals when the Baltimore club was liquidated, and played for the team in 1900, but refused to manage in St. Louis. In fact, he couldn't wait to leave, playing for the Cardinals only that one season. McGraw hated the St. Louis summers, complaining that, "To win in this heat, a ballclub has to be at least 25 percent better than any other team."[9]

Although the weather may have played a part in McGraw's decision to leave St. Louis, he had a more compelling reason. He had heard rumors that a new major league was being formed by Cincinnati newspaper man, Ban Johnson. McGraw hoped to get a job back east with the new league and did manage for a short time in his old city of Baltimore. McGraw soon moved to the National League, where he stayed with the New York Giants for close to 30 years.[10]

When the American League was founded in 1901, Johnson began to recruit players, especially from the National League. The first and most notable Cardinal to switch leagues was star pitcher Cy Young, who was a major reason the Boston Pilgrims won the first World Championship in

1903. The war between the American and National Leagues was one of the most fascinating events in baseball history, with broken contracts, lawsuits, and players bouncing from one league to the other. The rivalry lasted two years until a truce was reached when the National League accepted the American League as a permanent fixture in major league baseball.[11]

After the 1901 season, the American League folded its franchise in Milwaukee and moved it to St. Louis. The new St. Louis American League team took the old nickname, the Browns, and nostalgically dubbed their home field, located between Grand and Vandeventer Avenues, Sportsman's Park. Not only did the Browns compete for attendance, they also began to raid the Cardinal roster, taking such stars as Jesse Burkett, Bobby Wallace, John Heidrick, Jack Harper, Willie Sudhoff, Dick Padden, and Jack Powell.[12]

This competition was too stressful for Frank Robison, who lost interest in both his team and baseball in general. At the end of the 1906 season, Frank gave all control of the Cardinals to his brother, Stanley Robison. Frank moved back to Cleveland, where he died two years later of apoplexy.[13]

Stanley was a hands-on owner, even managing the team for the final 57 games of the 1905 season. He had fired his manager, Kid Nichols, a future Hall of Famer, in midseason after the two men had had a dispute over one of Nichols' duties.[14]

Unfortunately, Stanley Robison had no more success running the Cardinals than had his brother Frank. Finances were so tight that for two winters Robison slept in an office over the clubhouse. During his five years as club president, Stanley Robison's Cardinals never finished higher than seventh place and averaged 53 games out of first at the end of each season. [15]

After the 1908 season, Stanley Robison began searching for a new manager once again. Former Cardinal player and now Giant manager, John McGraw, heard Robison's appeal and knew that his catcher, Roger Bresnahan, wanted to be a manager. In a three-team swap with the Giants and the Reds, the Cardinals traded three pitchers and an outfielder for Bresnahan, who, in 1909, became the team's player-manager. During the first year under Bresnahan, the Cardinals finished only seventh. Robison brought in new players for the 1910 season to help the team.[16] Despite this, the Cardinals again finished in seventh place.

Even though the Cardinals didn't play well under Bresnahan's leadership, attendance increased. The fiery Bresnahan, with a tough-talking, aggressive demeanor like McGraw's, was a savvy manager whose many run-ins with the umpires amused Cardinal fans. As a result of the upsurge in attendance, the team's finances began to improve. Robison moved out of his office into a luxurious St. Louis hotel suite and began to pay off some of the club's bills. He fully expected his team to compete for the pennant in 1911; but, on March 24, 1911, only days before the start of the season, Stanley Robison died unexpectedly at the age of 54.[17]

While Robison was being mourned, Major League baseball was more concerned about the future of the St. Louis franchise. All of Robison's heirs were women — his sister, sister-in-law and several nieces. Baseball moguls made it quite clear that they did not want women encroaching on their domain. Garry Herrmann, chairman of the National League Baseball Commission and owner of the Cincinnati Red Stockings, stated bluntly that the Cardinals would not be owned or controlled by women. He expected that Robison's female heirs would agree with the other owners in the National League and want to see the club sold.[18]

But, much to the dismay of the other National League magnates, Helene Hathaway Robison Britton, Stanley Robison's niece and Frank Robison's daughter, became major league baseball's first woman owner, inheriting 75 percent of her uncle's baseball club, with the remaining 25 percent going to her mother, Sarah. It was apparent almost immediately that Helene Britton not only intended to own the team, she was going to run it.[19]

When she took over the Cardinals in March 1911, Helene Britton was an attractive 32-year old living in Cleveland with her husband, Schuyler P. (Skip) Britton, and two young children, Frank 9, and Mary, 4. She was an athletic woman who played tennis, loved to shoot and hunt, and was interested in boating and swimming. She also was fond of music, spending many evenings attending amateur musicals with friends and relatives and going to the opera whenever she could. Helene herself played the piano, the mandolin and the banjo.[20] The greatest key to her character, however, was that she was an active suffragette who believed strongly in the right of women to vote and make their own decisions.[21]

As the daughter and niece of baseball owners, she grew up loving the game, even playing it as a girl. She also could keep score like a pro. "My father and uncles talked baseball ever since I can remember. My father insisted that I should keep score. I mastered the details of the game and was able to comprehend the mysterious symbols with which the official scorers at our park designated the plays. But although I learned to know and like baseball, I had ... no notion that I should ever become a major league owner."[22]

In her first statement to the press as the Cardinal owner, she spoke knowledgeably about the Cardinals' recent poor performance, remarking that the St. Louis club had not finished very well for the last few years, "but I think it will soon." As to how Schuyler felt about his wife running a major league baseball team, Helene Britton said that he was rather amused by the situation. Schuyler added that he had confidence in Helene's abilities and did not feel she needed advice on how to look after her interests from any man, least of all her husband.[23]

Helene Britton cautiously began to exert her influence. She retained Roger Bresnahan as manager, but she changed the name of her ballpark from League Park to Robison Field in memory of her late father and uncle. She chose as Cardinal president, Edward A. Steininger, a building contractor who had been a close friend of her late uncle, Stanley. Helene Britton took the title of vice-president, and although she delegated authority to the men in the team's top position, she always took an active part in the decision-making process, exhibiting great self-confidence in whatever she did.[24]

Beginning with the 1911 season, Helene Britton began her practice of attending every home game during the years she owned the team, sitting high in the stands, keeping score of each play of the game.[25]

During 1911, Helene Britton's first year of ownership, the St. Louis Cardinals actually made a run for the pennant. In midseason the team was only three games out of first place. In July, however, their hopes were dashed when the Cardinals were involved in a train wreck in Bridgeport, Connecticut. None of the players was seriously injured, but the team was never the same and ended the season in fifth place with a record of 75 and 74. Even so, it was the Cardinals' best record since 1904, and the first time since 1901 they had finished above .500. The team also enjoyed the best financial year in Cardinal history to that time, attracting 447,768 fans and netting a profit of $165,000, which Helene Britton used to pay off some of the debts she had inherited with the team.[26]

The major benefactor of the team's exceptional showing in 1911 was manager Roger Bresnahan. Helene Britton was so pleased with the results of the season that she rewarded the Cardinal skipper with a five-year contract at a salary of $10,000 a year, a figure many people felt made him the highest-paid manager in baseball. In addition, Mrs. Britton announced that he would receive a share in any future profits of the team.[27] It would not take long for Helene Britton to regret her enthusiasm for Roger Bresnahan.

In December 1911, Helene Britton became the first female owner to attend the annual baseball winter meeting in New York, a tradition she would continue as long as she owned the team. Mrs. Britton had attended baseball meetings before, first with her father and later with her uncle, but she had never sat among the team owners."[28] As baseball's only woman mogul, she stole the sports headlines. All other baseball news was shoved to the back pages of the sports section, as four of the five New York newspapers made her attendance the section's number one story.[29]

Before 1911, the all-male National League owners had conducted their meetings in rooms thick with cigar smoke and foul language. In deference to Mrs. Britton, the men tried to clean up their language and cut back on the smoking, although Lady Bee, as the press began to refer to her, told her fellow owners that "they could burn up all the Havana they wanted to."[30]

She allowed Steiniger, the team president, to cast the actual votes, but she sat in the front row during the meetings. She also sat in the front row each year for the annual club owners' picture. League president Garry Herrmann, one of the most outspoken critics of women owning a baseball team, somehow always managed to sit next to her for the league photograph.[31] As the meetings wound down, Lady Bee, who had also been accompanied to New York by her husband and her manager, gave Bresnahan a free hand to make trades, stating that she intended to go shopping.[32]

At first it appeared that Mrs. Britton's faith in Bresnahan would pay off. The Cardinals began the 1912 season with great optimism, but it quickly turned into one of the most disappointing in the team's history. Manager Bresnahan, the team catcher, broke one of his kneecaps in April, despite being the first catcher to wear shin guards. He caught pneumonia the following month and was able to appear in only 48 games the entire season, catching in only 20 of them. The Cardinals were never in the pennant race, although they were able to finish sixth, ahead of the hapless Brooklyn and Boston teams.[33]

The 1912 season was primarily noteworthy for what happened off the field. Horace Fogel, president of the Philadelphia Phillies, charged that Cardinal manager Bresnahan intentionally benched his best players against the New York Giants in an attempt to help his old team win the pennant. Bresnahan vehemently denied the charges and demanded that the National League clear his name. At the League's annual meeting in December 1912, Bresnahan was exonerated and Fogel was barred forever from baseball.[34]

Bresnahan's most serious problems, however, were with his boss, Helene Britton. The more she came to know her manager, the more she regretted her hasty decision to give him his generous contract. Bresnahan, tutored by John McGraw in the school of rough-and-tumble baseball, often used crude and vulgar language, even in Mrs. Britton's presence. Following the team's poor finish in 1912, Mrs. Britton called Bresnahan into her office, intimating that the team's sixth-place finish might be the result of Bresnahan's poor managing. When she began to suggest some of her own ideas on how the team's play could be improved, her manager became livid, shouting, "I would like to know what the hell any goddamned woman can tell me about baseball."[35] Bresnahan stormed out of the room and the incensed Mrs. Britton immediately phoned James C. Jones, the club attorney who had recently replaced Steininger as president. "I want you to release Roger Bresnahan," she said. "He is not the type of man I want for manager." When Jones advised Mrs. Britton that the manager had been signed for four more seasons, she told Jones: "I do not care if we have to buy up his contract — if we have to pay him in full for four years; I do not want him running my club any longer."[36]

As expected, firing Bresnahan was not easy. In October 1912, Bresnahan hired an attorney to attempt to force the Cardinals to honor his profit-sharing agreement as well as his player-manager contract. The case went to the National League Board of Directors, which recommended arbitration, but neither side could agree on the arbitrators. The Cardinals eventually settled with Bresnahan for an amount reported to have between $10,000 and $20,000. In June 1913, the Chicago Cubs assumed Bresnahan's five-year player contract, and he finished his playing career there in 1915.[37]

Prior to the 1913 season, Mrs. Britton made two changes to her team. First, she hired Miller Huggins, the team's diminutive second baseman, to replace Bresnahan as manager. The thirty-four old Huggins had a law degree, but had decided to play professional baseball. He broke into the major leagues with his hometown Cincinnati Reds in 1904, and was acquired by Stanley Robison in a five-player swap in 1910.[38] His best year with the Cardinals was in 1912 when he hit .312.[39] Huggins had been a favorite of Lady Bee since he joined the Redbirds, and Mrs. Britton knew that he was much more of a proper gentleman than Bresnahan.[40] Many fans opposed the choice. They asserted that Huggins, at five feet, six and a half inches and weighing just 140 pounds, was too small to mete out the physical discipline that some of the Cardinal players sometimes seemed to need. Mrs. Britton, they declared, had been too hasty in getting rid of a dynamic, crowd-pleasing manager, and putting a "little shrimp" in charge. "Just like a woman," they claimed.[41] They also charged that while playing for Bresnahan, Huggins had undermined his manager. Huggins' many supporters, however, pointed out that Bresnahan undermined himself with his explosions against Mrs. Britton.[42] "Hug," as Miller was called, soon became a fan favorite.[43]

The second change Mrs. Britton made in 1913 was to name her husband, Schuyler, president of the team. On the surface, this arrangement seemed to work out well. She had a man in authority she could trust and yet she would remain the decision-maker.[44]

Schuyler Britton was an instant hit with the press, who could not resist the temptation to include some chauvinistic remarks in their articles.

"Instead of sitting in a corner and watching his wife keep score, Mr. Britton will do a little judicious mixing with his patrons, greet them with a smile, learn to know some of them by sight, inquire after their comforts and tactfully listen to their suggestions as to how baseball ought to be run ... here's hoping he will be the real head of the family club."[45] William Reedy, editor and publisher of an internationally circulated St. Louis periodical, regarded Britton as "a generous executive and a man of whom the community could be proud."[46]

The Brittons decided that some novelty at the ballpark would not only increase fan interest but increase attendance at Cardinal games as well. Schuyler Britton announced that on opening day, patrons entering Robison Field would be given free scorecards and all ladies would be presented a flower. He further declared that he intended to build a large scoreboard and add backs to all the bleacher seats. He even suggested placing a roof over the bleachers.[47]

Helene Britton also had some ideas on how to improve fan interest and attendance — attract more women to the ballpark. She believed that while baseball might be a man's game, women were taking an increased interest in the sport, "a healthy and wholly commendable sign."[48] More importantly, she felt that if more women attended games, male attendance would also increase regardless of how the team was performing.

At her urging, Schuyler arranged for a male singer and a band to entertain between innings. The singer selected was so happy to perform before an audience of up to 20,000 people, that he agreed to sing for nothing. One observer noted that the Brittons were turning Robison Field into a "baseball cabaret." The experiment was a success, however, and attendance increased for a while.[49]

Mrs. Britton also proposed that on one day of the week, women should be admitted to games free of charge, making her an advocate of "Ladies' Day" long before the idea became a popular promotion.[50] When the male baseball magnates of the day heard Mrs. Britton's suggestion, they were furious. Led by Pittsburgh's Barney Dreyfuss, they informed her in no uncertain terms that such a practice required league approval unless she was willing to pay the visiting team 25 cents for each woman who attended the game that day. "Possibly the inexperienced 'magnatess' and her advisers— who are comparatively new to league law and procedures, particularly as regards finances— may not have been aware of this very important obstacle to excessive generosity and fraternity. The National League is a co-operative association," Mrs. Britton was reminded.[51]

The Brittons needed every gimmick they could think of to lure fans into the park, because the 1913 Cardinals were pathetic on the field. The team finished in the cellar with a record of 51 wins and 99 losses, and attendance slipped to 203,000. In 1913, the Browns also finished in eighth place, the only time both St. Louis teams came in last in the same year.[52]

The Cardinals' last-place finish in 1913 was only one of Helene Britton's worries. In 1913, the new six-team Federal League was to have more of an impact on her than on either Ebbets or Dreyfuss. The Federal League owners had formed their league simply because they wanted to own a big league team and none of the existing owners would agree to sell. Rebuffed in their attempts to be recognized as the Federals the third major league, the Federals expanded to eight teams, declared *themselves* a major league, and began to woo National and American League players with the promise of higher salaries.[53] Only 18 men actually under contract jumped to the new circuit. The majority of the 81 Federal League players were former major leaguers, including some who wanted to manage a team, such as Fielder Jones, Three Fingers Brown and George Stovall.[54]

With her lackluster roster, Mrs. Britton was not worried that the Federal League was going after Cardinal players. She did have two concerns, though. First, she was afraid that competition from a third major league baseball team in St. Louis might seriously damage her team's attendance and finances, especially given the 1913 Cardinals' last-place finish. In 1914, this fear materialized when Federal League president Jim Gilmore talked two wealthy St. Louisans— Otto Stifel, a brewer, and Phil Ball, an artificial ice plant manufacturer — into backing a third club in St. Louis. Ball named the team Terriers (although the press often used the name "Sloufeds") and hired former Cub pitching ace, Mordecai "Three Fingers" Brown as manager. They played their games at Handlan's Park, old circus grounds centrally located at Grand and Laclede Avenues.[55]

On the field, the 1914 Cardinal season was a happy surprise, with the team finishing in third place, an astonishing leap from the cellar the year before. In fact, Huggin's team had been in the thick of the race until late August, when the "Miracle" Boston Braves came from last place on July 4 to win the pennant.[56] Despite the Cardinals' exciting performance, 1914 attendance increased by only 50,000. The St. Louis Browns also improved in the standings, but their attendance actually dropped. The Terriers had done enough damage to cause both established St. Louis major league teams to lose money in 1914. Making Mrs. Britton's financial situation even worse, her husband had to pay off his promise made prior to the 1914 season, that each member of the team would get a 20 percent bonus if they finished in third place or higher.[57]

During 1914 and into 1915, Helene Britton's other concern was the additional pressure she was getting to put the Cardinals on the market and leave baseball. Since 1911, the National League had been "selling" Helene Britton's Cardinals.[58] The pressure on Mrs. Britton reached a peak after the 1914 season. The National League owners felt that the Cardinals needed to fill so many gaps to compete in the 1915 pennant race, that the distressed club would be a "good buy" for some enterprising syndicate.[59]

At the December 1914 winter meetings in New York, the National League owners, positive that Mrs. Britton had become disenchanted with the administrative aspects of the game, attempted to force the issue once and for all. They even had a lavish floral bouquet placed in her New York hotel room to "soften her up." But as The *Sporting News* noted, she was "not the type of woman who would be bluffed by seven magnates, League President John Tener, and other baseball officials."[60]

Mrs. Britton was well aware that behind closed doors, the other National League owners were plotting to auction her team off to a potential buyer, presumably Phil Ball, owner of the St. Louis Federal League team. As she later told *St. Louis Star Times* sports writer Sid Keener, "I stood toe-to-toe with them and won the fight. They told me my selling the team would be for the good of the game and I completely disagreed. My greatest joys are my two lovely children and I care more for their caresses than for all the ballgames in the world ... but when it comes to seven men telling me what to do and to get out of baseball, well, I just don't get out, that's all."[61]

In reality, at one point, on the advice of her attorneys, Mrs. Britton had decided to sell the team. Delighted, the owners tried to force her to sell on their terms. According to the observations of one newspaper article, "Baseball may not be a game for a magnatess ... but in the meeting room of the Waldorf-Astoria Hotel in New York, Mrs. Britton, calm but determined, stood her ground...and when the other owners attempted a force play, she called in her selling options and returned home still in possession of the Cardinals."[62]

Unfortunately, the National League owners were right about the Cardinals' prospects in 1915. Despite a salary increase that made the Cardinals the highest-paid team in baseball, they had no hitting and finished in sixth place, 18½ games out of first with a record of 72 and 81.[63] The only bright spot in the 1915 season happened on September 10. An unknown 19-year-old with a .277 average who had been brought up from Dennison, Texas, in the Western Association, finished the game at shortstop for the Cardinals. His name was Rogers Hornsby. Before he left St. Louis some years later in one of the most criticized deals in the city's baseball annals, Hornsby posted the highest batting average of any player in the 20th century, led the National League six times in hitting, averaged over .400 three times, and, in 1926, led the Cardinals to the first pennant and world championship in their team history.[64]

Prior to the opening of the 1916 season, the National and American Leagues bought out the Federals, who dissolved their organization in return for a $600,000 payment, ending the war between the leagues. Part of the agreement gave two Federal League Owners, Charles Weeghman and Phil Ball, the right to buy existing major league teams. Weegham bought the Chicago Cubs and moved them into the park he had built for his Federal League team. Ball, the former owner of the St. Louis Terriers, bought control of the St. Louis Browns. On the whole, matters seemed to have worked out rather well. The National League team in Chicago was playing in a better facility and a weak American League franchise in St. Louis was strengthened. More importantly, Helene Britton still owned the St. Louis Cardinals.[65]

Despite the final settlement of the Federal League turmoil, the Cardinals fared even worse in 1916. With a record of 60 and 93, they ended the season sharing the basement with the Cincinnati Reds, and Miller Huggins, once considered a genius manager, was now being severely criticized.[66]

It was again off-the-field events that created headlines concerning the Cardinals between the 1916 and 1917 seasons. In early November 1916, Helene Britton filed suit for divorce in St. Louis while Schuyler Britton was representing the St. Louis Cardinals at the minor league meeting in New Orleans. According to the newspapers, she had sued for divorce in Cleveland in 1911 but the couple had reconciled about the time she became owner of the ball club.[67]

In her 1916 divorce suit, Helene asked for custody of the children, alleging that her husband was "addicted to drink," often brought people who were "loud, vulgar and of ill repute" to her home as guests, cursed and physically abused her, squandered her money, and forced her to support the family.[68] Schulyer Britton learned of the divorce proceedings in the morning papers while on the train to St. Louis. Once he reached town, he disappeared.[69]

Helene Britton called a meeting of the Cardinal board of directors and presented Schuyler's letter of resignation as club president, a document she had been holding since she appointed him. She was then elected president of the Cardinals, making her the first woman president of a major league baseball club.[70] Mrs. Britton reassured everyone that her domestic affairs would not affect the team. Miller Huggins would manage the team in 1917, and except for taking over as president, she planned no other office changes.[71] She did state, however, that with the exception of Rogers Hornsby, anyone on her ball club was for sale or trade.[72]

Just as it had been during the 1914 meeting, the question of whether Helene Britton would continue to own the Cardinals was the focus of the December 1916 major league meeting at New York's Waldorf-Astoria. The attitude of the National League owners had not changed — they wanted and expected her to sell."[73]

If the men in baseball were expecting good news at the winter meetings, they were soon disappointed. Helene Britton declared her intentions to succeed in baseball and to turn the Cardinals around. She also minced no words when she told her fellow owners, "It is not my intention to sell this ball club. I could have sold years ago, but I love the game just like my father and uncle. I could have sold last winter and I could have sold last summer, but I have refused all the offers. It is tiresome to hear all of these reports that I am going to dispose of the club. If there are any flaws in my club, I hope to eliminate the defects, and then, once operating successfully, I know that it will be an easy position for me."[74]

Despite Mrs. Brittons' firm denial that her club was for sale, rumors of offers to buy the Cardinals persisted. The *Sporting News* commented that selling the Cardinals seemed to be one of the most popular winter sports in St. Louis. The most often-heard rumor was that the team would be sold to a wealthy automobile manufacturer, Russell Gardner, for $250,000. Mrs. Britton flatly denied it, stating that while the issue was not money, the club was worth at least $400,000. She also complained about the newspapers making deals for her without her knowledge or consent. "Just because women can't vote in Missouri is no reason they should be dispossessed of their property without having been consulted about it."[75]

Rumors of an imminent sale of the Cardinals continued into early 1917. When pressed for comment, Mrs. Britton replied that she and her manager, Miller Huggins, were too preoccupied with mailing contracts to her team to concern herself with still more rumors about the future of the Cardinals[76]

One rumor concerned Huggins himself. The *Sporting News* reported that Miller Huggins had begun to form a syndicate backed by a group in Cincinnati, Huggins' hometown. Even though Mrs. Britton made her usual denial, the *Sporting News* claimed that Huggins' recent trip to Cincinnati "was not to buy ball players."[77]

Two months later, Helene Britton unexpectedly announced that she had changed her mind. Her domestic troubles and her uneasiness about World War I were part of a combination of factors that entered into her decision. The state of the team was also a big concern — the Cardinals had not been doing well and the team was playing before sparser crowds each year. Mrs. Britton called attorney James C. Jones and manager Miller Huggins to her home and announced that she intended to sell her ball club for $375,000. Speaking from her heart, she simply told them, "Gentlemen, I want to get out of baseball. I guess I have had enough. I want you to be the first to know it, in case you should be interested in buying the club yourselves."[78]

Because Mrs. Britton had always liked him and had informed him of her intentions first, Huggins felt he had the inside track for the team. Delighted, he replied to Mrs. Britton, "I'll get a buyer, or take it on a verbal option." He immediately went with scout Bob Connery, the man who had discovered Rogers Hornsby, to Cincinnati, where the two men interested the wealthy Fleischmann yeast family into backing them. Both Julius and Max Fleischmann were avid baseball fans and at one time were minority stockholders in the Cincinnati Reds. Julius Fleischmann knew Huggins from the time when the Cardinal manager had been playing semi-pro baseball in the Catskill Mountains where Julius had once owned a club. Huggins was prepared to present his proposition to Mrs. Britton when he read in the newspapers that the Cardinals had already been sold to a stock company of St. Louis fans and enthusiasts organized by attorney James C. Jones.[79]

Huggins, who had had no idea that Jones was interested in buying the Cardinals, was sorely disappointed to learn that Mrs. Britton had sold the team to Jones without waiting to hear from him. This disappointment was one of the reasons that Huggins left the Cardinals after the 1917 season to manage the New York Yankees.[80] He went on to become one of baseball's outstanding managers.[81]

Mrs. Britton sold both the Cardinals and the real estate at Robison Field to Jones and his syndicate of baseball enthusiasts for her asking price of $375,000. Of this amount, $25,000 was to go the law firm of Jones and Hocker, their fee for arranging the deal, but there was so much difficulty later in collecting the funds needed to complete the purchase, that Jones waived the lawyers' payment. Despite the difficulty in raising the money, baseball analysts consider the purchase of the Cardinals one of the most lucrative deals in baseball history. Four years later, the real estate alone, approximately 20 acres in northwestern St. Louis, was sold for $200,000 and became St. Louis's Beaumont High School.[82]

Rather than a group of wealthy men, Jones attempted to put together a "stockholders' army" to own the Cardinals. For a minimum of $50 up to a maximum of $10,000, anyone could purchase stock in the team. While this stockholder consortium was unusual, it was not unprecedented. The old National League St. Louis Browns, before they became the Cardinals, were financed that way at one time.[83]

One of the results of Helen Britton's sale was the establishment of what would become a tradition in St. Louis and other major league cities. The plan, called The Knot Hole Gang, was an attempt to curb juvenile delinquency and to encourage people to buy Cardinal stock. Insurance man W. E. Bilheimer suggested that everyone who bought a $50 share would receive a free bleacher seat to give to a needy child. The free admissions were eventually handled by the club, which channeled them through benevolent organizations such as the Boy Scouts, the YMCA, and various religious youth groups. Though the original plan changed over time, the Knot Hole Gang remained an institution in St. Louis for many years.[84]

The sale of Helene Britton's Cardinals to a local St. Louis group also resulted in Branch Rickey's joining the organization. Soon after the purchase was completed, Jones called together seven of the city's top sports editors and baseball writers to get their advice on who should run the team. Each man was given a slip of paper, asked to write one name on it and drop it into a hat Jones passed around the room. When the slips were opened, the same name had been written on each one — Branch Rickey. Jones immediately offered Rickey, who was then with the St. Louis Browns, the presidency of the Cardinals. Rickey breached his contract with the Browns to accept the Cardinals' offer.[85] The *Sporting News* praised the selection of Rickey calling it a "big acquisition for the Cardinals and the National League."[86] Rickey went on to organize a farm system for the Cardinals, which many think was the basis for the winning Cardinal teams over the next 30 or more years.

In April 1917, Mrs. Britton received her first payment from the new ownership and in exchange, liquidated all the team debt before turning over the club. Helene Britton cleared $225,000 from her St. Louis baseball property.[87]

She immediately left town and, with a few exceptions, dropped out of the national public eye. In August 1918, the *New York Times* announced her engagement to Charles Sulyard Bigsby, an electrical appliance distributor and widower. The marriage ended with Bigsby's death in 1935.[88]

At the age of 71, Helene Robison Britton Bigsby passed away on January 8, 1950, in the Philadelphia home of her daughter, Mary R. Britton. Her son, Frank D. Britton, of Highland Park, a Philadelphia suburb, and four grandchildren also survived her. Her body was returned to her native city of Cleveland, where she was interred in Lake View Cemetery, along with three major leaguers— Charles "Heine" Berger, David Pope, and Ray "Chappie" Chapman, baseball's only fatality — and the first owner of the Cleveland Indians, Charles W. Somers.[89]

Although Helene Britton owned the Cardinals for only six years, she left her mark on major league baseball. As the first woman to own a major league team, she was a pioneer in a field dominated by men at a time when women were often considered intellectually inferior and not even allowed to vote in most places. She always conducted herself like a "lady" by the standards of the time, but she made her own decisions, defended her rights and showed that women could understand a "man's game" as well as they did. She paved the way for all women in business, but especially for future women baseball owners.

4

Clark Griffith
The Persuader

Baseball Hall of Fame member Clark Griffith was one of a select few to distinguish himself as a major league player, manager, and owner. A man who spent more than 65 years in baseball, Griffith was recognized as a founder of the American League and the major influence that kept the game alive through not one, but two world wars.

Clark Calvin Griffith was born in Clearcreek, Missouri, in 1869. His father died in a hunting accident when Clark was only two years old, and by the time he was ten, Clark had become a professional trapper to help his mother support the family. When Clark was 13, he contracted malaria, and the family moved to Bloomington, Illinois, where he recovered his health. Griffith began his baseball career as a pitcher with Bloomington of the Central Interstate League where he won 10 and lost only four games. A scout from Milwaukee of the Western Association saw him pitch and immediately bought his contract. Griffith pitched only one year in Milwaukee, posting a record of 27–7 in 1890, and meeting Jimmy McAleer, Milwaukee's leadoff hitter, who was to have an important effect on Griffith's career.

By 1891, Clark Griffith was pitching in the majors for the St. Louis Browns of the American Association. Charles Comiskey, who would be even more crucial in Griffith's life, was the Brown's manager and first baseman. After winning 14 games for the Browns in 1891, Griffith was traded mid-season to the American Association's Boston team.

The first in a series of career setbacks occurred at the end of the 1891 season when Griffith simultaneously developed a sore arm and the American Association disbanded, leaving the National League the only major league in baseball by 1892.[1]

Because of his sore arm, Griffith soon found himself back in the minors with Tacoma in the Northern Pacific League. At this time, America was in the midst of what would be the worst depression until the 1930s. It

CLARK GRIFFITH — **Washington Senators 1912 to 1955 — A winning pitcher and successful manager as well as one of the founders of the American League, Clark Griffith used his persuasive powers and his close relationship with many U.S. presidents to preserve professional baseball during two world wars (National Baseball Hall of Fame Library, Cooperstown, NY).**

was not totally surprising that the Northern Pacific League soon collapsed, leaving Griffith stranded in Tacoma.

His situation improved when he received a telegram from Missoula, Montana, asking him to play in the semipro "outlaw" Montana State League, an association which would pirate players wherever it could.[2] The townspeople of Missoula had promised Griffith that if the players would come there, they would get the same salaries they had received at Tacoma. Griffith was able to talk all of his Tacoma teammates into joining him in Missoula, the first known instance of Griffith's ability to persuade others to follow his lead. It was a gift he would use to good advantage for the remainder of his life.

Griffith spent one year at Missoula and, in 1893, joined Oakland of the tough Pacific Coast League. His record at Oakland was an impressive 30 and 17. Unfortunately, this League became the third to fold under him.[3]

Griffith was unemployed until late August 1893 when he received a wire from his old manager at Milwaukee, James Hart. Hart, who was now president of the Chicago Colts of the National League, desperately needed pitching help and, along with Colts owner Albert Spalding and manager Cap Anson, urged Griffith to come to Chicago.[4]

It was in Chicago that Griffith began to achieve recognition as a great pitcher. He finished the 1893 season there and pitched for the Colts (later to become the Chicago Cubs) from 1894 to 1900, compiling a record of 151 and 94.[5] During each of his years in Chicago, Griffith won at least 20 games; in two seasons, he won 25.[6]

Thin and undersized for a pitcher, Griffith was far from overpowering and relied on his brain as much as his arm to retire opposing players, earning him the nickname, the "Old Fox."[7] He would stall on the mound, unnerving many of the batters he faced, and then strike them out by quick pitching when they weren't ready. Griffith was described as a pitcher who "scuffed, scratched, cut and spit upon every pitch without hesitation. He also threw a screwball, which he claimed he invented."[8] Things changed when he retired as an active player and became an owner, vociferously opposing most of the methods he had employed as a pitcher. For example, in 1920, he became one of the most outspoken opponents of the spitball and called for its abolition.[9] This reversal in philosophy when it suited his purposes proved to be another attribute that would characterize Clark Griffith throughout his life.

During his playing days, Griffith, according to one newspaper account, "reigned supreme as a verbally abusive competitor.... His contemptuous air riled the good hitters out of their composure and few batters came to the plate without being singed by his scathing tongue."[10] Another source described Griffith as the worst umpire baiter who ever lived. One umpire, Tom Lynch, promised that he would bring charges against Griffith if he persisted in using foul language on the field.[11] As with the spitball, Griffith's perspective changed completely when he was an owner. For example, not too many years later, he roundly castigated Ty Cobb for acting much like Griffith did as a player.[12]

Griffith soon became known for employing his verbal skills in a much more productive manner. Although he was a star pitcher of the decade, Griffith's earnings were severely limited by the National League's annual salary cap of $2,400, and he began to speak out against this injustice loudly and often, becoming recognized as a leader of the movement for players' rights. The last union of major league athletes, the Brotherhood of Professional Baseball Players, had fallen apart in 1890 when it tried and failed to create another major league, the Players League. Made up of teams jointly owned by the athletes and a group of backers, the Players League suffered huge financial losses and disappeared after the 1890 season.[13]

Griffith and many other players felt that to successfully challenge the National League, they needed to form another union and back a strong, independent, second major league. Griffith helped organize the new Professional Association of Baseball Players in 1900 and was elected its vice-president.[14]

For many years Griffith had wanted major league baseball to consist of two strong rival leagues. He argued that baseball had suffered from a lack of competition since the old American Association had collapsed, and he tried to persuade his friend, Cubs President James Hart, to break away from the National League and form a competing major league. Hart refused.[15]

While Griffith was conferring with Hart, Ban Johnson, President of the American League (formerly known as the minor league Western Association), was trying to get the National League to recognize his group as a second major league. He was also willing to work with the National League and place teams in former NL cities such as Cleveland and Louisville.[16]

For additional backing, Ban Johnson turned to Charles Comiskey, who had been managing in the minor leagues. Since staffing the new teams was a major concern, Comisky suggested meeting with his friend from St. Louis days, Clark Griffith, who was obviously well-known and respected by his peers and unhappy with conditions in the National League. Griffith agreed to the meeting, but only with the assurance that the end result would be a new major league. The Old Fox told Johnson and Comiskey that obtaining players would be just a matter of time. He advised them to wait until after the National League owners meeting in December, where he and the Players Protective Association (BPPA) intended to petition the magnates for better terms for major league players.[17]

Griffith knew that the BPPA planned to make three demands of the owners: an increase in the maximum player salary to $3,000; uniforms provided by the clubs rather than the players; and elimination of the reserve clause, which bound players to their teams unless sold, traded, or released. He also knew that members of the union had promised they would not sign any contracts with their teams for the 1901 season unless the association officers endorsed the contracts.[18]

As Griffith expected, the National League owners not only didn't agree to any of the players' demands, they literally snubbed the athletes. Griffith immediately wired Comiskey and Johnson, "Go ahead, you can get all the players you want."[19] On the guarantee that Griffith could indeed persuade enough players to "jump" to the new league, Johnson and Comiskey set in motion their plans to establish a rival major league organization. Charles Somers, a Cleveland coal magnate and friend of both Comiskey and Johnson, owned the Cleveland franchise, but agreed to also finance a club in Boston until the league could find another backer. John McGraw, who had been with the St. Louis Cardinals during the 1900 season and held a grudge against the National League, received a franchise in Baltimore after he promised to provide his own backing. Rounding out the eastern division of the league, teams were placed in Philadelphia and Washington, D.C. In the west the four teams included Cleveland; Chicago, given to Comiskey; Detroit, under the management of George Stallings; and Milwaukee.[20] Ban

Johnson became president of the American League and Charles Comiskey was confirmed as owner of the Chicago White Sox. In recognition of Griffith's efforts in establishing the new league, Comisky, with Ban Johnson's approval, appointed Griffith manager of the Chicago White Sox.[21]

Johnson announced that in order to help attract National League players to the new league, he would honor the proposed Players' Protective Association contract, pay hefty salaries, and obliterate the National League's maximum pay policy. It was now up to Griffith to actually recruit the players. Griffith, in a frenzied effort to make good on his promise to Johnson and Comiskey, spent the entire winter of 1900 traveling to every city or hamlet where a targeted ballplayer lived during the offseason. He used his own act of "jumping" in an attempt to woo skeptical players. Employing all of the persuasive skills he had, Griffith successfully acquired 39 of the 40 players he sought.[22] The only one he failed to convince was the star shortstop of the Pittsburgh Pirates, Honus Wagner, who was able to resist only because he refused to talk with Griffith.

In a 1953 interview in *The St. Louis Sporting News,* Griffith recalled his attempt to capture Wagner. "I went to Homestead, near Pittsburgh, and learned that Honus was in a pool hall. I sent word to him to meet me in a hotel. Wagner told my emissary, "I will not see Griff. I do not want to go to the American League. If I let Griff talk to me, I won't be able to turn him down. So, I just won't go and see him."

The year 1901 marked the official beginning of the American League as a major league. In many ways, the American League bore an amazing resemblance to the Players League of an earlier decade. Both brought together an alliance of players, former players and money men who were anxious to become baseball owners. Both emerged, in part, because of player grievances over salaries and the reserve clause. Many of the major stars were disgusted with the old regime and more than ready to join forces with the new league.[23] In fact, 111 of the 185 players in the eight American League clubs in 1901 came from the National League, including such prominent stars as Roger Bresnahan, Jimmy Collins, Lou Crigler, Dummy Hoy, Fielder Jones, Joe McGinnity, John McGraw, Wilbert Robinson and Cy Young.[24] The major difference between the Players League and the newly established American League was that the American League was not a cooperative enterprise: labor and management remained clearly distinct. Two other major differences were that the American League had more substantial financial backing and in Ban Johnson, the new league had an excellent administrator.[25]

Clark Griffith served as player-manager for Charlie Comiskey's Chicago White Sox for two years. During 1901, he not only guided the

Chisox to the first American League pennant, but he also compiled a record of 24 wins and only 7 losses. His won-lost percentage of .774 led all American League hurlers.[26] Winning a pennant for the White Sox gave Clark Griffith the unique distinction of being the first player-manager to win a pennant for a major league team.[27] He later boasted, "I signed players for the other clubs, too, but I managed to sign a championship club for Chicago."[28] The following year, Griffith's White Sox finished in fourth place, eight games behind the pennant winning Philadelphia Athletics.[29]

Griffith had accepted Comiskey's offer to manage the White Sox, but as early as 1900, he had his eyes set on a higher goal — ownership of a major league team. He would later relate, "When I wasn't pitching, they used to have me serve as the club's representative at the gate, keeping track of how many admissions were paid…. It gave me a chance to learn something about the business end of the game and it got me acquainted with all the executives and magnates in the league."[30]

Ban Johnson was determined to prove the power of the American League by invading New York City, which he considered "the richest major league territory extant." In 1903, he transferred to New York the Baltimore franchise which John McGraw had abandoned, and with Comisky's approval, asked Clark Griffith to leave Chicago to manage the New York team. It was christened the Highlanders because its ballpark was at one of the highest points in New York City, but the team would soon become known as the Yankees. McGraw had left Baltimore to become manager of the New York Giants, which considered New York its own stronghold. To keep Griffith and the Highlanders out of New York, the Giants threatened to use political influence to halt the subway and streetcar lines short of their proposed park in the upper Bronx. Griffith retaliated by getting Tammany politicians to buy into the club, effectively taking care of any transportation problems.[31]

By now Griffith was fading as a pitcher, but he was still able to post a record of 14 and 10 in 1903, New York's first season in the American League. That year, Pittsburgh Pirate owner Barney Dreyfuss had scheduled Major League Baseball's first World Series between his pennant winners in the National League and the Boston Pilgrims, pennant winners in the American League. Although the 1903 Highlanders had ended the season in fourth place, Griffith suggested that his team play an intracity series with the New York Giants, in line with what the Chicago, Philadelphia, and St. Louis clubs had agreed to do. Giant manager McGraw and owner Brush were still miffed by what they considered an intrusion of a rival American League team into New York City and contemptuously rejected Griffith's offer.[32]

In 1904, the Highlanders lost the pennant on the final day of the season when 41-game winner Jack Chesboro allowed the winning run to score on his wild pitch. Despite this incident, Griffith still had fond memories of his star pitcher. He recalled that Chesboro was a long ball hitter on a club that Griffith admitted generally lacked power. In the late innings of an important game, Chesboro tripled and Griffith hastily conferred with the next hitter, "Wee Willie" Keeler. Following Griffith's instructions, Keeler, one of the game's all-time scientific batsmen, laid down a perfect bunt, allowing Chesboro to score standing up. The following day Sam Crane, one of the top baseball writers of that era, heralded Griffith for inventing the strategy, born of necessity, which he named the "squeeze play." Crane also credited Griffith as the inventor of the delayed steal.[33]

Griffith served as player-manager of the New York Highlanders from 1903 to 1908. Despite the fact that Griffith was never able to win a pennant for the Highlanders, he was able to help establish them as a solid team in the American League. He won his 240th and final game in 1906, although he made his final mound appearance at the age of forty-five in 1914.[34]

Throughout Griffith's tenure in New York, the owners, the press and the fans berated him, often blaming him for mistakes for which he was not solely responsible.[35] He strongly objected to the advice of New York owners, Frank Farrell and Bill Devery, concerning how to manage the team, and, when interference by the club executives began to infiltrate the clubhouse, he finally quit early in the 1908 season.[36]

Griffith never forgave the Yankees for the unkind and unjust way he had been treated; and, when he himself became a team owner, he did his best to get back at his former team. Between 1923 and 1939, the Yankees won ten pennants, were one of the most financially successful franchises, and had one of the strongest farm systems in the major leagues. At the conclusion of the 1939 baseball season, in an obvious attempt to hurt the Yankees, Griffith successfully persuaded all of the other AL owners to approve a rule prohibiting teams from making trades with the previous season's pennant winner. In defending his proposal, Griffith told his fellow owners, "I'm not aiming at the Yankees, now. Don't get me wrong. I'm aiming at all pennant winners."[37]

There was no doubt that Griffith's second proposal was aimed directly at the New York Yankees farm system. Rather than spend money on building a system of his own, Clark Griffith began to push for legislation that would hurt the Yankees by reducing the number of farm teams within their control. For once, Griffith failed to convince the other owners to go along with him.[38]

After he left the Yankees in 1908, he went to the Cincinnati Reds as a scout. The following year owner Garry Herrmann named Griffith manager of the Reds. Griffith ran the Reds from 1909 to 1911, finishing progressively farther down in the standings each year: fourth in 1909, fifth in 1910 and sixth in 1911. He considered these three years his most unhappy in baseball and often referred to them as his "exile back to the National League." He felt uncomfortable being part of a league he had battled fiercely for years.[39]

During the 1911 World Series, Edward Walsh, a director of the Washington Nationals (the name of the team before they became the Senators), asked Clark Griffith to become the manager. More importantly, Griffith was finally given an opportunity to join the ownership ranks by buying stock in the club. This was what Griffith had been waiting for. He was approaching his 42nd birthday, had pitched in the majors for 16 years, and had been a manager for 11. He was the only one of the three founders of the American League who was not a financial success. Ban Johnson was well paid as league president and Charles Comiskey was amassing a fortune with the White Sox. The incumbent Washington manager, Jimmy McAleer, Griffith's 1890 teammate in Milwaukee, had resigned to move up to the ownership of the Boston Red Sox. Griffith badly wanted to buy into the Washington franchise, but he had no idea where the money would come from.[40]

After resigning as manager of the Cincinnati Reds, Griffith turned for financial aid to the two men he had helped found the American League. Ban Johnson had been urging Griffith to go to Washington to help build up the ailing franchise. But, when it came time to ante up the loan of $10,000 Johnson had originally promised, he reneged. Charles Comiskey also refused to help, bluntly telling Griffith that he was crazy to invest in "that baseball graveyard" at Washington.[41] Determined not to allow the opportunity to pass him by, Griffith scraped together everything he had — $7,000 in cash and $20,000 he raised by taking out a mortgage on his 6,000-acre cattle ranch in Craig, Montana — to become the Washington National's largest single stockholder with 10 percent of the team and the power to run it as he saw fit.

When Clark Griffith took over one of the most dismal ball clubs in major league history, many thought that this was the final chapter in the career of a once-great baseball man. Instead, it was the beginning of a 44-year era in the career of Clark Griffith, whose name was to become synonymous with Senators baseball.[42] From 1912 when he took control of the Senators until his death in 1955, few, if any, sport franchises would reflect the image of one man or one family as did the Senators. Not only was the running of the team a strictly closed family business, but all eight managers during Griffith's ownership were former members of teams Griffith had managed between 1912 and 1920.[43]

Although he was to pitch briefly in three more major league baseball games, for all practical purposes, in 1912 Clark Griffith changed from a major league player into a manager and part owner of a major league baseball team. During his 20-year major league playing career, Griffith had compiled a record of 240 wins and 144 loses, with a career earned run average of 3.31. His winning percentage as a major league pitcher was .619. As a major league manager for 20 years, he posted a winning percentage of .522.[44]

Griffith knew what he was getting into. From 1900 to 1911, the Senators had never finished higher than sixth place. Griffith decided to change his lineup and assemble a team in his own image — small, smart, and quick. He released ten veteran players the first week he took over the club and, by the end of the 1912 season, Griffith had only two players who were over the age of 30. The team astounded the baseball world by finishing that year in second place, not only reaching the .500 level for the first time, but coming within a percentage point of .600. The anchor of the team was the man Barney Dreyfuss refused to consider, hurler Walter Johnson, who won 32 games and led the American League with an earned run average of 1.39. Bob Groom, another mainstay of Griffith's pitching staff, won 24 games that year and both outfielder Clyde Milan and first baseman Chick Gandil hit over .300. A final sparkplug on the team was rookie third baseman, Eddie "Kid" Foster, who played every game in five different seasons and led the league in at-bats four times in his career. Foster had no power, but when it came to bat control, Griffith felt he was even better than Willie "Hit 'em where they ain't" Keeler. If Foster came to the plate with a man on first, Griffith was so confident that Foster would make contact, he allowed the runner to go at will, and was duly credited with introducing a new "run-and-hit" play.[45]

In 1913, the Senators repeated their second-place finish, and Walter Johnson enjoyed the greatest year in his lengthy pitching career — a record of 36 and 7, an earned run average of 1.14, 11 shutouts and 243 strikeouts.[46]

At the end of the 1913 season, two off-the-field events occurred in baseball which deeply rankled Griffith. David L. Fultz, a practicing attorney and former major league outfielder who had played for the New York Highlanders under Griffith, organized major league baseball's third labor union, The Fraternity of Professional Baseball Players. Griffith, the former vice-president of the BPPA, completely reversed his stand on labor unions in baseball and bitterly opposed the fraternity's demands for pay raises and the repeal of the reserve clause, exactly the same issues he had argued for so strenuously less than two decades earlier.[47] Once Griffith began his anti-union stance in baseball, he never wavered in his opposition to players' unions. As late as the 1940s, his Washington Senators were embroiled in a major labor dispute with the American Baseball Guild, which accused him of unfair labor practices and interfering with his players' right to join the union.[48]

The second event which nettled Griffith was the Federal League's attempt to establish itself as another major league. At first, Griffith thought little of the Federal's chances and advised the other owners to allow the league to "run its course."[49] Of course, he could afford to be sanguine. His roster, unlike those of some of his contemporaries, such as Charlie Ebbets, and Barney Dreyfuss, had little to attract Federal League player "raids." Griffith did become concerned, however, when his star player, Walter Johnson, signed a contract to play for the Federal League's Chicago Whales. When Griffith heard the news of Johnson's defection, he immediately went to him and began a lecture on the virtues of loyalty, oblivious to the irony of the situation, given his own background.[50]

Even more ironic was that the Federal League used the same tactics to lure Johnson away from the Senators that Griffith had used to entice players into the American League — offering higher salaries and huge bonuses. The Chicago Whales gave Johnson a $16,000 contract, plus a signing bonus of $10,000. Johnson had received $12,000 from the Senators the previous year. Putting his persuasive powers to work again, Griffith first got Ben Minor, president of the Senators, to match the Whales' salary and then got Johnson to agree to re-sign with the Senators for the $16,000 the Whales had offered. The problem was returning the signing bonus. Johnson had already spent the money and Minor had refused to come through with the extra $10,000. Panicked that he would lose his star hurler, Griffith turned again to Ban Johnson and again was quickly turned down.

But Griffith had another strategy. He knew one baseball man who not only had the $10,000 but also a good reason to fear Johnson's jump to the Federal League — Charles Comiskey. Griffith convinced Comiskey to repay the Whales' signing bonus by shrewdly pointing out that if Walter Johnson were to pitch for the Whales on Chicago's northside the same day the White Sox were playing on the southside, Comiskey's gate receipts would suffer. A smart businessman, Comiskey repaid the Whales $10,000 on behalf of the Senators and Walter Johnson remained a member of the Washington team until his retirement in 1927.

After two consecutive second-place finishes, the Senators dropped to third in 1914, although Walter Johnson had another fantastic year.[51] The

1915 season saw the debuts of two players who immediately became fixtures with the Senators. First baseman Joe Judge played for the Senators 18 of his 20 years in the majors, compiling a lifetime batting average of .298. Future Hall of Famer, Sam Rice, began his career as a pitcher in 1915, but eventually became a starting outfielder for the Senators. In his 19-year career with the team, Rice never hit below .293. It seemed that Rice always made contact, striking out only 275 times in more than 10,000 plate appearances.[52] From 1916 to 1920, the Senators finished in the first division only in 1918, when they came in third.[53]

At the same time that Clark Griffith was struggling to establish a winning team, he initiated something even more important to his team and to baseball as a whole — a close relationship with every president of the United States from William Howard Taft to Dwight Eisenhower. Although it was true that Griffith had the obvious advantage of owning the team in the nation's capital, his own personal charm was also an important factor.[54]

The first president to toss the ball to a Senator player was William Howard Taft in 1910, two years before Griffith became affiliated with the Senators. According to Griffith, Taft had spoken at a woman's suffragette meeting the night before the opening of the 1910 baseball season and the next morning he was still upset over accusations that he was slow to accept women's suffrage. To get out of his bad mood, the President called James S. Sherman, his vice-president, and informed him that the two were going to the ballpark for the Senators opening day game. When Senators manager McAleer saw Taft, he presented the President with a baseball and suggested that he throw out the first ball. Taft, a pitcher for his college team at Yale, was happy to oblige.[55]

In 1912, Griffith, the new owner- manager of the Senators, thought it would be a great promotion to have the nation's president attend every opening game in Washington, and make the tradition of throwing out the first ball a yearly institution. The first thing Griffith did was to talk Ban Johnson, American League President, into allowing the Senators to open every season at home to take advantage of the publicity the President's appearance would provide.[56]

Next, in 1913, he convinced Taft's successor, Woodrow Wilson, that throwing out the first ball was almost as necessary to confirm his presidency as taking the oath of office.[57] Fortunately, Wilson was one of the most genuine baseball enthusiasts of all the nation's chief executives. After he suffered a stroke, he found comfort in baseball and a downstairs room in the White House called "the dugout" was set aside for Wilson to meet daily with his secretary to review box scores and game stories. Whenever

Wilson's health permitted, Clark Griffith would make special arrangements for the President to come to the stadium. The president's car would enter through a designated gate and park by the Senators' bullpen. He would watch the game there while Washington players stood by making sure no foul ball struck the car.[58]

Wilson attended no games in 1914 because of the illness and eventual death of his first wife on August 6 that year; but, the following season, he was on hand in his top hat to perform his duty. He threw the ball to Senator pitcher, Walter Johnson, who responded by pitching a two-hit shutout against the New York Yankees.[59] In 1917, Wilson was unable to attend the season opener because war had just been declared, but he sent his vice-president, William Marshall, in his place.[60]

The involvement of the United States in World War I was to affect all of baseball, including the Washington Senators. There was speculation that baseball might stop during the duration of the war, but early in 1917, American League President Ban Johnson insisted that the game go on, noting that the National League had continued play during the Spanish-American War. A decline in attendance was the only effect of World War I that year, for draft calls did not go out until July and few players were picked. For the next year and a half, owners fought a delaying action with the federal government, maintaining their public patriotism while struggling to keep the game going.

On May 23, 1918, baseball was shocked by Secretary of War Newton D. Baker's "Work or Fight" order that required all able-bodied men of draft age to enlist unless they were doing work considered essential for the war effort. When Washington Senator catcher, Eddie Ainsmith, was drafted in July 1918, Clark Griffith appealed the draft order on three grounds: (1) unlike plants which could convert to making war materials, baseball was a business which could not switch to anything else; (2) ball players didn't have any skills to enter other occupations where they could earn comparable pay; and (3) suspending the national sport would inflict great social harm on the country.[61] Ainsmith became the test case on which the fate of all players eligible for the draft rested.[62]

On July 19, 1918, Baker announced that he did not consider baseball an essential war activity and that not only should Ainsmith be drafted, but that the major league baseball season should end immediately. He added sarcastically that he was sure the American public could find other means of recreation and relaxation.[63]

Griffith was not ready to accept Baker's edict. Using his well-practiced powers of persuasion, Griffith talked Baker into extending the 1918 baseball season until Labor Day, September 2. In exchange, Griffith promised that all baseball players would perform military drills prior to the games using baseball bats instead of weapons. In Washington, young Assistant Secretary of the Navy, Franklin Delano Roosevelt, even led some of the drills.[64]

Griffith was a credible spokesman for baseball because he was a leader in several war efforts. It was the practice throughout both leagues to solicit for Liberty bonds before each game. Clark Griffith took this campaign one step further. Every day around 4 P.M., Griffith would lead a cortege of two automobiles and six buglers to movie theaters, newspaper offices, and other buildings where large crowds congregated to encourage people who might not attend baseball games to buy bonds.[65]

But it was Griffith's Ball and Bat Fund that earned him the greatest recognition. From 1917 through 1919, this fund raised thousands of dollars to purchase baseball equipment for the armed forces.[66] More than 3,000 kits were sent to military camps, each containing a catcher's mitt, a chest protector, a first baseman's glove, three bats, three bases, a dozen balls, a dozen scorecards, and a rulebook. At the time, each set cost approximately $30. General John J. Pershing personally thanked Griffith for his contribution and claimed that not only was the equipment welcomed for its recreational value, but also that by playing baseball, his soldiers had become proficient at throwing grenades. Griffith's Ball and Bat Fund also provided money for copies of *Baseball Magazine* and *The Sporting News.* At one point during the war, *The Sporting News* was rescued from bankruptcy because the American League purchased so many copies for the troops overseas.[67]

When the Ball and Bat Fund shut down in March 1919, the final report showed that a total of almost $144,000 in contributions had been raised.[68] Griffith received plaudits from across the country for creating the fund, but modestly claimed that he had been only its administrator and gave credit to "the great American fan."[69]

By the end of World War I, Griffith realized that he needed to not only reorganize the Senators on the field, he needed to reorganize the ownership structure. His co-owners constantly quibbled with him over player-personnel moves and there was an effort in the boardroom to replace him as manager. There was also friction over the fact that Griffith, normally a tightwad because of his background and the meager revenues generated by the team, wanted to spend money to bolster the club for 1920. The solution to Griffith's problem appeared when his friend, Connie Mack, introduced him to Philadelphia grain exporter William Richardson. With Richardson's backing and additional capital, Griffith rounded up from the Metropolitan National Bank, the two men were able to gain control of 80 percent of the Senators. Richardson gave Griffith full authority over matters of club policy, never interfered with the way Griffith ran the team, and authorized Griffith to speak for both his own and Richardson's holdings.[70]

This ownership arrangement stayed in place for almost 30 years. In December 1949, the Richardson estate sold its 40-percent holdings in the Senators for $550,000 to John James Jachym, a 31-year old ex-Marine who once scouted for Branch Rickey in Brooklyn. Griffith disliked anything having to do with New York and froze Jachym out of the club's operation.[71] Minor stockholders voted the deciding balance of the shares and unanimously re-elected Griffith president in January, 1950.[72] In later years, he would buy enough stock to have controlling interest.[73]

Griffith was installed president of the club in 1920. To signal his new status, the ballpark was renamed Griffith Stadium. It was at this time that the stands stretching from the infield to the foul poles were made into double-deckers, the last significant renovation to the park until lights were installed in 1941.[74]

The Senators ended in sixth place in 1920, the final year Griffith was the field manager. For the next three years, the team had three different managers, all current or former players. One-time Senator shortstop, George McBride, began the 1921 season as manager, but when he was struck in the face by a line drive in August, he had to be replaced by Clyde Milan who completed the 1921 season and piloted the Senators to another sixth-place finish in 1922. Griffith felt that Milan lacked the ability to take charge of his long-time teammates and replaced him at the end of the 1922 season with former Tiger and Senator infielder, Donie Bush.[75]

The year 1922 was important for Clark Griffith and the Washington Senators for a reason which initially seemed unrelated to baseball, but ultimately led to a true baseball dynasty. At the age of 53, Clark Griffith acquired a family. He and his wife, Ann Robertson Griffith, had been married since 1900, but were unable to have children of their own. To help Ann's ailing brother in Montreal, Griffith and his wife adopted the second and third oldest of the brother's seven children. They moved to Washington and became Calvin and Thelma Griffith. Within a year, their natural father died, and Clark Griffith brought the other five Robertson siblings to Washington and set up them up in a separate house of their own.[76]

Calvin Griffith, who had little baseball exposure in Montreal, began to learn the game from an expert. Calvin became the Senators' batboy in 1923 and the following winter he listened while Clark Griffith plotted the world championship of 1924. "He used to have a habit all winter long of sitting down trying to work out deals with other clubs," Griffith said of his foster father. "I was just a kid but he would keep on talking. He would figure out which guys he needed and why we needed this guy. When I went to the ballpark with him he would … point out all the peculiarities of all the ball players to me."[77]

Despite the poor finish of the Senators during the first three years of the 1920s, Griffith gradually inserted some key players into the Senators lineup who would play important roles in 1924 and 1925 when the Senators would win the team's first pennants. The first player was Bucky Harris, who played second base for the Senators from 1919 to 1928 and managed them for many years. The second was Goose Goslin, who began with the Senators in 1921, played with the St. Louis Browns and Detroit Tigers, but ended his career back with the Senators in 1938.[78] Elected to the Hall of Fame in 1968, Goslin reached double figures in home runs in 12 of his 18 years in the major leagues.[79] The third key player was third baseman Ossie Bluege, who debuted in 1922 and played his entire 18-year career with the Senators.[80]

Griffith fired Donie Bush as team manager after the 1923 season and surprised the baseball world by naming 27-year-old Bucky Harris as his replacement. Harris was younger than every other key player on the team except Goslin and Bluege. They combined with stars such as Joe Judge and Sam Rice to propel the 1924 Senators to the first pennant for Griffith.[81] Calvin Griffith credited his father's shrewd trading for the team's success and claimed that the '24 Senators were the cheapest championship team in the history of the game.[82]

The 1924 World Series was historic for a number of reasons. It was the first World Series for both the Washington Senators and pitching great Walter Johnson. It marked the first time in baseball history that a President of the United States and his first lady attended a World Series opener.[83] It also marked the extensive use of the relief pitcher as a major tool in winning a ball game.

Many baseball scholars argue that Griffith's major strategic contribution to the game of baseball was the development of the relief pitcher. While managing the Highlanders, Griffith had yielded to pressure from his owners by pitching his two premier starters, Jack Chesboro and Jack Powell, a staggering 845 combined innings in 1904, thus contributing to their ineffectiveness the following year. Griffith personally finished many games for them, making a career-high 18 relief appearances that year. Griffith also developed the first great relievers, Allan Russell and Fred Marberry, and, along with John McGraw, helped revolutionize baseball with his reliance on the bullpen.[84]

Nowhere was the use of the relief pitcher more successful than in the seventh game of the 1924 World Series. President and Mrs. Coolidge were among the 31,677 fans who packed Griffith Stadium that day. In a ploy designed to nullify the effectiveness of the Giants' great left-handed-hitting first baseman, Bill Terry, Bucky Harris and Calvin Griffith mapped out an elaborate strategy hours before the game. Harris would start right-handed pitcher Curly Ogden, a flop with the Athletics before the Senators claimed him late in the 1924 season. This would force Giant manager McGraw into putting his left-handed hitters into the lineup. Then, in the first inning, Harris would remove Ogden and insert southpaw hurler, George Mogridge, putting the Giants' left-handed hitters at a distinct disadvantage. "If the Giants switch to their right-handed batters after that, I'll switch to Fred Marberry," Harris told his owner. "By that time the Giants won't have any pinch hitters left, if McGraw has shifted with me. The guy I don't want to see in the lineup is Bill Terry [but] even if McGraw leaves him in there . . he doesn't figure to hit our left-handers."[85]

The tactic seemed to backfire as the Giants led 3–1 in the sixth inning. But the Senators tied the score and the game went into extra innings. Walter Johnson, normally a starting pitcher, came in as a reliever and despite a couple of serious threats, hurled scoreless ball into the 12th inning. In the bottom of the 12th, with two out, Giant catcher Hank Gowdy tripped over his mask chasing an easy foul pop-up, giving Muddy Ruel another chance. Ruel took advantage of Gowdy's misplay and doubled. Walter Johnson then reached first base on an error by Giant shortstop Travis Jackson; Ruel held second base on the error. The next batter, Earl McNeely, hit a grounder to third baseman Fred Lindstrom that looked like an easy, inning-ending out. At the last second, however, the ball seemed to hit a pebble, bouncing over the third baseman's head, scoring Ruel. It gave the Washington Senators the World Series victory in 1924, the only one in franchise history.[86]

Bucky Harris won his second consecutive pennant for Clark Griffith in 1925, but although the Series again went seven games, this time the Senators lost to the Pittsburgh Pirates. The Senators went into the 1925 World Series with two 20-game winning pitchers, Walter Johnson and the recently acquired 36-year-old Stan Coveleski. 1925 was to mark the final season in which Johnson would win 20 or more games and only the second time in his 19-year major league career that another 20-game winner on the same staff would aid him.[87]

From 1926 to 1932, the Senators finished in the first division six of the seven years. Their only second division finish was in 1929 when they ended the season in fifth place.

The high point of the Washington Senators team after 1925 was the acquisition of shortstop Joe Cronin in 1928. Cronin had failed to impress the Pittsburgh Pirates the two previous years. With the Senators, however,

Cronin emerged as one of the prime power hitters in the American League. He drove in 100 or more runs five consecutive years and hit .346 in 1930. He would play in the majors from 1926 to 1945, become a manager, general manager and president of the American League. In 1956 Cronin was elected to baseball's Hall of Fame after compiling a lifetime batting average of .301 and a winning percentage as manager of .540.[88]

Bucky Harris managed the Senators until 1928, when Griffith fired him. According to Griffith, Harris committed two sins. First, he slowed down perceptibly in the field. Second, after Harris married the daughter of a United States Senator, and Harris' teammates felt he had become increasingly distant from them.[89]

Walter Johnson had retired in 1927, but Griffith brought him back to manage the Senators in 1929. Griffith fired Johnson in 1932, and remembering his success in hiring a young Bucky Harris as manager a few years earlier, hired 27-year-old shortstop Joe Cronin, to run the team. Cronin, as new manager, presented his boss with a wish list of three pitchers. Within two days at the winter meetings in New York that December, Griffith had acquired all three—Earl Whitehill from the Detroit Tigers, Jack Russell from the Cleveland Indians, and Lefty Stewart from the St. Louis Browns. This trio of pitchers produced 49 wins and 14 saves for Cronin, and the 1933 Senators won the pennant with 99 victories, the most in the history of the Washington franchise.

In addition to the players Griffith had acquired during the winter, Alvin "General" Crowder was the pitching star with a league-leading record of 24–15. Whitehill aided him with 22 wins of his own. The Senators had a brilliant defensive infield with Joe Kuhel at first, Buddy Myer at second, Joe Cronin at short and Ossie Bluege at third. The most outstanding Senator player in 1933 was outfielder Heinie Manush, a future member of the Hall of Fame, who finished second in hitting, led the league with 221 hits, and racked up the league's third best numbers (behind Foxx and Gehrig) for total bases.[90]

The Giants were once again the Senators' opponents and there was no pebble incident this time. Led by three outstanding pitchers, Carl Hubbell, Hal Schumacher, and veteran Cuban Dolph Luque, the Giants wrapped up the Series in five games. Mel Ott hit two home runs and finished the series with a .389 batting average to lead all Series batters. Heinie Manush could not even come close to his season average of .336 and had only two hits, both singles. Franklin Delano Roosevelt attended Game Three in the special Chief Executive's box at Griffith Stadium, but it did little to help the Senators in what would be their last ever World Series appearance.[91]

Nineteen thirty-four was a horrible season for the Senators as they plunged to seventh place after their previous pennant. It was to be Cronin's last year with the Senators, for at the end of the season, Griffith sold his young manager to the Boston Red Sox for shortstop Lyn Lary and $225,000. Griffith had long ago earned a reputation for being a parsimonious baseball executive and his sale of Cronin seemed to prove the point. Unlike Barney Dreyfuss, who only traded, never sold, players, Griffith lived up to his reputation as a miser with his willingness to sell almost anyone if it worked to his advantage. Griffith justified his sale of Cronin, who had married Griffith's niece, Mildred, by stating that he was only trying to save Cronin from nepotism charges.

Charges of nepotism where other family members were concerned, however, didn't seem to bother Griffith in the least. By the 1940s, Griffith's adopted son Calvin was his father's close associate on almost all baseball matters; Calvin's sister Thelma worked in the front office; and Griffith's nephews, Sherry, Billy and Jimmy Robertson were all being groomed for executive positions with the club. Later, retired Washington pitcher Joe Haynes, who had married Griffith's adopted daughter, Thelma, would also become a vice-president of the club.[92]

Griffith brought Bucky Harris back to manage the Senators in 1935. This time, he stayed until 1942, but he was able to lead the Senators to only one first division finish, fourth place in 1936. The club never got closer to first place than 20 games out. Despite the poor showing of the Senators in the standings, there were a few bright spots during Harris' second stint as Senators' manager. Buddy Myer won the 1935 league batting championship, outfielder George Case led the American League in stolen bases five consecutive years, and on July 4, 1936, the Senators attracted their largest crowd ever as 35,563 fans witnessed a holiday doubleheader.[93]

Unlike the Yankee owners, whose extensive farm system helped provide the talent that kept the team competitive year after year, Griffith was too much of a penny-pincher to establish a viable farm system for the Senators. For many years Griffith's "farm system" was made up of a two-man scouting department. One scout was Joe Engel, a former player who pitched for the Senators between 1912 and 1920. He also spent two seasons with the Cincinnati Reds and the Cleveland Indians.[94] Engel was responsible for discovering Joe Cronin and Ossie Bluege.

The more important of the two scouts, however, was Joe Cambria, a long time operator of minor league franchises with a somewhat obscure baseball background. His business relationship with Griffith was simple. He sold players to Griffith cheaply and on a conditional basis, giving Griffith first rights to any of his personnel. Eventually, this relationship developed into a scouting job for Cambria. One of his finds was speedster George Case, who played 1,208 games for the Senators and led the league six times in stolen bases, while compiling a lifetime batting average of .282. Cambria also recommended Mickey Vernon, who would spend 15 of his 20 years in the majors with the Senators. He was the top hitter in the American League twice: in 1946 with a .353 average and in 1953 with an average of .337.[95]

Cambria's real value to Griffith was his diligence in tracking baseball talent in Cuba and other parts of Latin America. Because he had no authority to spend Griffith's money and his scouting ability was questionable, Cambria did not mingle with the other big-league scouts in the Double A leagues, preferring to stick to the sandlots and the lower minor leagues. Ultimately Cambria discovered Cuba, where relatively talented players would sign for meager salaries.[96] Although this appeal to his pocketbook may have been the underlying reason, Clark Griffith's decision to open the doors of baseball to Latin American players became another of his major contributions to the game. It also opened the eyes of competing teams to a rich pool of untapped Latin American player talent, leading the way eventually to the signing of some of baseball's most dominant stars.[97]

Griffith already knew something of the potential of the Cuban market. When he managed the Reds in 1911, he agreed to let Cuban outfielder Rafael Almeida try out for the team. His countryman, Armando Marsans, came along as Almeida's interpreter. After watching the two Cubans on the field, Griffith remarked: "I like his interpreter better." He signed both and Marsans later became one of the best Cuban players in the big leagues.[98]

Most of the Cubans who played for Griffith were unremarkable. They were included on the Senators' roster simply because they came cheaply to the increasingly thrifty Griffith. For example, in 1935, Griffith put Cambria's Cuban discovery, Bobby Estalella, in the lineup. Estalella played 15 games at third base that year, compiling a .314 batting average and becoming an instant fan favorite. The problem was his lack of fielding ability, which made him a liability for not only the Senators but for other teams for which he played, including the St. Louis Browns and the Philadelphia Athletics.[99]

Probably the best of the Latinos to wear a Washington uniform was pitcher Camilo Pascual, who was scouted by Cambria and began his major league career with the Senators in 1954. Unfortunately, Griffith died before Pascual could develop into a star pitcher, who went on to win 174 games in an 18-year career.[100]

World War II was to increase the importance of Griffith's Latin American players, since Cubans remained exempt from draft registration until

1945.[101] Unfortunately for Griffith, the Selective Service directive on April 10, 1945, required Cubans to register for the draft within 10 days or lose their visa status, putting a crimp in Griffith's plans to employ large numbers of them on his team.[102]

Griffith had been instrumental in helping preserve baseball during the First World War, and he is rightly credited with saving it again during WWII. The nation was in turmoil after Pearl Harbor, and many were questioning the morality of putting able-bodied young men on a baseball field rather than in the Armed Forces. It was Griffith's personal connections with the White House that allowed him to negotiate on behalf of organized baseball to continue the game.

From 1912 on, Griffith had established a relationship with each President. He would make at least one annual visit to the White House to present the Chief Executive with a gold pass.[103] With some Presidents, he had an even closer rapport. Franklin D. Roosevelt was an ardent baseball fan who enjoyed slugfests rather than pitchers' battles. He loved to bet on games with his aides and Cabinet members, and he often would call Clark Griffith for pre-game advice. "Griff, tell me about these pitchers," he would demand. Because FDR had contracted polio at the age of 39 and was unable to walk, Griffith erected a special ramp for him to reach his box. Roosevelt realized that elaborate security arrangements had to be made to accommodate him, and he once told Griffith, "I'd come out more often, Clark, but I'm such a nuisance."[104] The President often referred to himself as the Senator's "mascot" because he seemed to bring them good luck when he attended games.[105]

Although President Roosevelt was a baseball fan, he was no fan of Commissioner Kenesaw Mountain Landis. Landis, in turn, was a staunch conservative who loathed President Roosevelt's liberal politics. He had on a number of occasions referred to FDR as "that bastard in the White House." Despite their political differences, Landis swallowed his pride and an exchange of letters in January 1942 temporarily eased the tension between the two men.[106] The key piece of this correspondence was a handwritten note from Roosevelt known as the "green-light" letter, which came about in large part through behind-the-scenes lobbying efforts of Clark Griffith and Roosevelt's political ally, Robert E. Hannegan. Roosevelt told Judge Landis that he personally felt that it was in the best interest of the country to keep baseball going because it gave people employment, allowed them to enjoy some recreation, and helped them relax after work.[107] The green-light letter constituted the federal government's official stance on baseball for the remainder of the war years.[108]

George Case, who joined the Senators in 1937, credits Griffith with a major role in keeping baseball alive during the war. "He spent considerable time imploring Roosevelt to continue baseball and kept getting assurances from the White House baseball would continue — but there wouldn't be any favors to baseball players."[109]

Of course, each team hoped that it would not lose too many players to the Selective Service System. During the war, each major league team had a club executive specifically charged with keeping players out of the draft. Clark Griffith wanted a promise that not more than one or two major leaguers would be drafted per club, and none if teams agreed to drills supervised by military personnel, like the drill Roosevelt led during the First World War.

In addition, Griffith was not above discussing some of his own players with draft officials at power lunches. While no one could prove that Griffith got preferred treatment from Roosevelt, big league owners were quick to notice that Washington players didn't seem to receive draft notices as regularly as members of other teams.[110]

In his green-light letter, the President also suggested that baseball schedule more night games. Griffith had urged FDR to endorse weekend and night baseball for the benefit of war workers in Washington and nationwide.[111]

Clark Griffith's efforts to obtain more night games at Griffith Stadium during WWII was another example of his ability to support a position he had at one time vehemently opposed. Clark Griffith once said, "Fans attending [day] games not only see good baseball but also benefit from being out in the fresh air and sunshine...." He also questioned the effect on play, expressing doubts that batters and fielders would be able to see the balls, "with the glare and shadows of powerful lights."[112] According to Clark Griffith, night ball was "bush league stuff and just a step above dog racing."[113]

The Cincinnati Reds, led by their new general manager, Larry MacPhail, introduced night games to the major leagues on May 24, 1935. Griffith and the other American League owners were united in their opposition. Commented Griffith, "The National League has become a burlesque circuit."[114]

But Griffith soon began to realize that night baseball might be a way to curb something he detested even more — Sunday double headers that permitted fans to see two games for the price of one. He now proposed to the other AL owners, "I [still] feel that night baseball will take its toll on the ballplayers.... However, I would be willing to vote for a limited number of night big league games to take the place of Sunday double headers."[115] He added that he had no intention of installing lights at Griffith Stadium, but "I have no objections to my ball club playing at night elsewhere. It may be the coming thing, though I don't believe so. To me, baseball always will be a daytime game."[116]

On May 16, 1939, Connie Mack's Philadelphia Athletics defeated the Cleveland Indians 8–3 in ten innings in the first AL night game.[117] It had taken four years for the American League to follow the National League's lead and the endorsement was limited. Will Harridge, American League President, allowed only seven home night games per team.

Now Griffith was upset for another reason. The former opponent of night baseball shocked reporters by stating that seven games per year were not enough to make installing lights at Griffith Stadium a paying proposition. "It isn't a good investment, and I have the figures to prove it. In the first place, it takes three years to get your money back. That's just for the cost of equipment and doesn't include the juice that's going into these things, maintenance or anything else."[118]

On May 28, 1941, the Senators became the last American League team to install lights and now Griffith was enthusiastic about the results. One day, the temperature in the nation's capital was 97degrees as Griffith took off his coat and tie, flung them across the antlers of the moose head on his office wall and excitedly told reporters who had gathered there, "We've lost nine in a row, but I venture to say we'll have at least 25,000 fans out tonight."[119]

With lights in his stadium, Griffith now made an even greater effort to increase the number of night games each team would be allowed to play. The green-light letter was a start, and with Hannegan's help, Griffith soon talked the President into declaring the Senators a "special case" during the war because they played their games in a city of wartime bureaucrats. Washington was given the right to play 21 night games, while other teams got only 14.[120] The one restriction was that Griffith had to get permission from the visiting club. Although some managers opposed the increased number of night games, the owners had the final say, and no club owners objected to heftier checks from playing at night.[121]

Griffith also had a strategic reason for wanting more night games. He loved to sign knuckleball pitchers such as Dutch Leonard, Roger Wolff, Johnny Niggling and Mickey Haefner, whose effectiveness at night was far superior to their daylight performances.[122]

When Bucky Harris finished the 1942 season with the franchise's worst winning percentage (.411) since 1911, Griffith replaced him with Ossie Bluege, the ninth straight manager who had played for the organization. With a relatively good team, which included Mickey Vernon at first base, Gerald Priddy at second, and a solid outfielder, Stan Spence, the Senators pursued the Yankees all year. Had they not lost Harlond Clift, their third baseman who had become disabled with the mumps, the Senators might have pulled it off; but, they ended the season in second place, 13½ games out of first.[123]

After their second-place finish in 1943, the Senators plummeted to the basement in 1944, the first time they had ended in the cellar since 1909 and the first time ever since Griffith was running the organization.

The tradition of opening the baseball season with the President or his designee throwing out the first ball overcame even the death of President Roosevelt shortly before the beginning of the 1945 season. On opening day that year, the Senators took the field wearing black armbands as House Speaker Sam Rayburn tossed out the ball.[124] They played respectably, finishing in second place again, a game and a half behind the Tigers.

The Senators managed to stay in the first division in 1946 ending in fourth place, but events mostly unrelated to team performance during 1945 and 1946 were more noteworthy for Griffith.

In 1913, although only a team owner for a year, Griffith had brought about a change in baseball that is still in effect today. Prior to 1913, only players on the pennant winners shared the revenue from the World Series. Griffith felt that it was unfair that the players on the other teams got no financial reward, particularly those on teams that finished second or third. He convinced the other owners to agree to include players on the top four teams in the league in the winnings.[125] World Series revenue is still shared today, but when each League had just eight teams, finishing in the first division was more than a matter of pride; it meant getting part of World Series profits.

In 1945, Griffith was able to bring about another significant change in the operation of the game, when his plan to change the waiver rule governing the release and movement of players was adopted. Griffith's plan established a single waiver fee and mandated that a major league club could withdraw a player from the list only once, instead of many times. This eliminated the practice of some clubs sending out waiver lists every ten days, often putting every player on their rosters on the list. The most important feature was that Griffith's plan gave each team in that league an opportunity to claim a player off the waiver list, with the teams selecting according to their position in the standings at the time the player went on the list.[126]

In 1946, more than 30 years after the Federal League war, Griffith had to fight off a second rival league. Jorge Pasqual, a multi-millionaire liquor distributor, formed the Mexican League and was promising higher salaries to lure players from both Cuba and the United States to his League. In a ceremony in Havana where Griffith was honored by the Cuban government for his contributions to the advancement of baseball in Cuba, Griffith took the opportunity to warn the Cubans against Pasqual, reminding the crowd, "Baseball cannot harbor contract jumpers and unreliables. Cuba must do away with the menace of the Mexican outlaw league, which persuades your boys and our boys to jump contracts and obligations they owe to Organized Ball."[127]

What Griffith failed to remind them was that in 1900 when Ban Johnson was organizing the American League, Griffith did exactly what Pasqaul was doing now — asking players to void their contracts and jump to a new league. Griffith had also been very active in "raiding" Cuba to secure talent for his Senators.[128]

Another memorable event of 1946 was Griffith's introduction of a promotion that was to become a staple of the game. One of the reasons Griffith was reputed to be notoriously tightfisted was the poor performance of his teams throughout his ownership, which usually resulted in poor gate receipts. Like owners before and after him, Griffith tried many promotions throughout the years to increase attendance and help him make more money.

Griffith was the first to use professional on-the-field entertainers, hiring former players Nick Altrock and Germany Schaefer as clown coaches. Renowned baseball clown Al Schacht later replaced Schaefer on the coaching team. In 1934, Griffith signed a pitcher from the House of David team so that he could claim the only bearded major league player. When his biggest gate attraction, star pitcher Walter Johnson, was in his heyday, Griffith was adept at juggling Washington's pitching rotation to ensure that Johnson pitched every weekend.[129]

In 1946, the Senators' attendance was even lower than usual at the beginning of the season, because the team started out so poorly that year. By Mother's Day, it looked like they were headed for last place. To capitalize on the drawing power of Bob Feller, considered one baseball's premier pitchers, the Washington Senators scheduled an exhibition game against Feller's Cleveland Indians. Griffith borrowed a photoelectric-cell device from the nearby Aberdeen, Maryland ordinance plant with the intention of having Feller throw the ball through the device prior to the game to measure the speed of his pitch. Griffith then mounted a massive advertising campaign that attracted an estimated 20,000 additional fans who came just to see how fast Feller could throw. Griffith did not tell Feller what he had planned until he got to the stadium. When Feller found out that he had to throw 30 pitches before the game, he balked because he was scheduled to pitch that night. But Griffith offered the Cleveland hurler

$700 and Feller agreed. His speed was timed at 98.6 m.p.h. This device, of course, was the forerunner of today's "speed gun."[130] Feller became the first pitcher clocked by a form of speed gun while pitching on a mound.[131]

For Clark Griffith, however, the most significant event in 1946 was his election to Baseball's Hall of Fame, honoring him for all of his contributions and his many years of baseball leadership.[132] He was 77 years old and still actively involved in running the Senators organization.

In 1947, Jackie Robinson officially became Major League baseball's first African-American player, although it was rumored that many of the Cuban players Griffith signed, including Bobby Estalella, were more African-American than Cuban.[133] In 1938, Clark Griffith had been the first member of baseball's official family to publicly discuss the possibility of including African-Americans in the game. Many expected Griffith to be the owner who signed the first African-American player, but there were several reasons why he held back.

Concern for the well being of the Negro ball player may have been one of the reasons. In an interview with the Washington *Tribune,* a Negro weekly, Griffith expressed the belief that "colored players would take their places in the major leagues along with those of other races." He also realistically predicted, "A lone Negro in the game will face caustic comments. He will be made the target of cruel, filthy epithets. I know the time will come when the ice will have to be broken, both by the organized game and by the colored player who is willing to volunteer and thus become a martyr to the cause."[134]

A second reason was that Griffith was uncertain how fans in the segregated city of Washington would accept racial integration on the ball field. Washington's African-American population in the 1940s was large, and he was sure that African-Americans in the community would come to the games but he feared that white fans might boycott the team if "too many" African-Americans attended.[135]

Although he did not publicly admit it, Griffith had a third reason in hesitating to employ African-American players on the Senators. When the Senators were on the road, Griffith rented his ballpark on a regular basis to an African-American baseball team, the Homestead Grays. While the Senators were fielding second division teams, the Grays were attracting large crowds, and Griffith could count on an annual income of $50,000 from the Grays. Some years that amount of money was the difference between solvency and bankruptcy for Griffith.[136]

In fact, the Washington team was one of the last in the American League to sign a black ballplayer. Pressure to integrate generated protests by fans, reporters, and political action groups in Washington as well as other cities. Griffith usually dismissed these demonstrations as "a committee of

Commies." Even when more moderate groups and the local Washington papers questioned the Senators' racial policies, Griffith generally responded, "Nobody is going to stampede me into signing Negro players merely for the sake of satisfying certain pressure groups."[137] Griffith eventually signed Carlos Paula, an African-American outfielder from Havana, who played for the Senators from 1954 to 1956.[138]

A seventh-place finish in 1947 meant the end of Ossie Bluege as manager of the Senators. To replace him, Griffith again hired as manager a former Senator, Joseph Kuhel, a one-time first baseman. In 1948 Griffith made undoubtedly the worst trade in his career when he sent Mickey Vernon and star pitcher Early Wynn to the Cleveland Indians for first baseman Ed Robinson and pitchers Joe Haynes and Eddie Kliemann. Haynes was a mediocre player, but the husband of Griffith's niece. Trading future Hall of Fame hurler Early Wynn for Haynes outraged Washington fans. Thelma's Deal, as the transaction became known, was ridiculed around the league. To make matters worse, the playing ability of another member of the Griffith family was also becoming the target of fans' ire. Sherry Robertson, Griffith's nephew, had been touted in his days in the minors as a steady hitter, but he managed only a career average of .230 in his 10-year stint in the majors.[139]

The team closed out the first half of the century exactly as it had begun five decades earlier with two of the poorest seasons in franchise history. The Senators lost 97 games in 1948 and 104 in 1949. It was no surprise when Clark Griffith, weary of manager Kuhel's poor showing, fired him at the end of the 1949 season.[140]

In 1950 Bucky Harris was back to manage the Senators for five more years, his third tenure as Washington manager. This gave him a franchise record of 18 seasons as manager of the Washington Senators. During his last five years as manager, Harris had very little success and the team never even made it into the first division in any of those years.[141]

Again, it was an event unrelated to the team's performance that was most notable for Griffith in the early fifties. Ever since his days as a player, Griffith had detested the National League. He had begun his major league career pitching for Cap Anson's Cubs and also managed in the National League from 1909 to 1911, but Griffith always considered himself an American Leaguer. It was therefore a major concession when Griffith announced that beginning in 1951, Griffith Stadium's scoreboard would be enlarged to include scores of National League games as well as those in the American League. As *The Sporting News* humorously commented, "Truly, the millennium approacheth and men might yet live in amity."[142]

During the fifties, Griffith's adopted son, Calvin, became Executive

Vice President and assumed most of his father's duties, but Clark Griffith was still an active owner almost until the day he died. The last major fight of his baseball career was his unsuccessful attempt to halt the transfer of the St. Louis Browns to Baltimore.

On October 19, 1955, Clark Griffith was admitted to the Georgetown University Hospital for treatment of neuritis. However, he suffered a massive stomach hemorrhage three days later. Despite fighting gamely to recover, he died on October 27, just a month before his 86th birthday.

Calvin Griffith was at his bedside and gave this capsule summary of Griffith's career: "He had a wonderful life and a peaceful death. No man could ask for more."[143]

The eulogies of Clark Griffith lauded his many contributions to the game of baseball, notably his integral role in founding the American League and his introduction of players from the Caribbean into the majors. They also praised his relationships with eight presidents of the United States that had helped sustain the game of baseball through two World Wars and demonstrated that baseball was indeed the national game of the United States.

Clark Griffith probably gave his own best eulogy during a conversation with a sports writer in Florida the last year he went south with his team for spring training. Watching a bunch of kids play baseball, Griffith commented, "If you had started playing baseball as I did when I was seven and you still love the game at 85, you'll understand what it has meant to me."[144]

5

Walter O'Malley
The Prospector

Although Clark Griffith was credited with making baseball America's national game, it was Walter O'Malley who truly made baseball a nationwide game. Ironically, the man who was to change major league baseball so dramatically was not even affiliated with the game until he was almost 40 years old and was brought into the Brooklyn Dodger organization strictly as a financial advisor.

Walter Francis O'Malley was born in New York City October 9, 1903, the son of Edwin J. O'Malley and Alma (Feltner) O'Malley. His father's family was from Mayo County, Ireland, known for its tradition of charm, joviality, and tightfistedness. The elder O'Malley was originally a dry goods merchant, but through his political connections, Mayor John F. Hylan appointed him a city Commissioner of Public Markets.[1] In this position, Edwin J. O'Malley became associated with the power brokers of Tammany Hall, and this friendship would be very useful to his son, Walter.

O'Malley attended high school in New York City and military school in Culver, Indiana, where he played first base on the school baseball team and also ran the school newspaper.[2] He was raised in a "comfortable middle class" manner in Queens and Long Island and recalled being "frightfully spoiled."[3]

In college, however, he quickly achieved success on his own. At the University of Pennsylvania, where he majored in engineering, he also played polo, served on the undergraduate council on athletics, was elected class president in both his junior and senior years, and graduated first in his class in 1926. One of his classmates at Penn remembered O'Malley as a born politician and promoter. "He built the strongest political machine ever on the campus."[4]

After graduation from Pennsylvania, O'Malley attended Columbia University Law School until the stock market crash wiped out the O'Malley family's finances. Walter switched to night classes at Fordham University Law School while working during the day. He received his law degree from Fordham in 1930.[5]

The following year he married his childhood sweetheart, Kay Hanson, the daughter of a former judge and a next-door neighbor of Walter's parents in Long Island.[6] Kay had been diagnosed with cancer of the larynx before the engagement. In one of the first successful operations of its type, Kay had her larynx removed, leaving her unable to speak. Walter insisted on marrying her anyway, reassuring his father, "She's the same girl I fell in love with."[7] They were married for nearly 50 years and had two children, daughter Terry, born in 1934, and son Peter, born in 1938. Peter would succeed his father

WALTER O'MALLEY — Brooklyn Dodgers 1943–1957; Los Angeles Dodgers 1958–1979 — Walter O'Malley knew that major league baseball would be a veritable gold mine on the West Coast. His move expanded the game's geographic boundaries, which led directly to more major league markets throughout the U.S. and into Canada (National Baseball Hall of Fame Library, Cooperstown, NY).

and run the Dodgers until 1997 when the team was sold to Rupert Murdoch.

O'Malley's first job after law school was assistant engineer with the New York subway system. He then began working for a drilling engineer, Thomas F. Riley. Soon O'Malley and Riley formed a partnership, and thanks to O'Malley Sr.'s connections with Tammany Hall, the firm of Riley and O'Malley received contracts for geological surveys from the Board of Education and the New York Telephone Company. After the partnership dissolved, Walter O'Malley started W. F. O'Malley Engineering Company. As the effects of the Great Depression began to be felt on a wide scale, O'Malley lost a number of contracts and decided to give up engineering and practice law.[8] "A lot of professional people were selling apples on street corners at the time," O'Malley noted. "I was fortunate in building up an active [legal] practice, handling mostly bankruptcies."[9]

O'Malley was not physically attractive; he was rather stout with heavy features. In fact, one author described O'Malley as looking like Charlie Ebbets when he grew old.[10] But early in life O'Malley exhibited the traits that were to make him successful and quite wealthy. Walter O'Malley was fun-loving, charming and very persuasive. He worked hard, and he was willing to take risks. Because of his family background, he possessed great political acumen[11] and skillfully used his Tammany Hall connections to buy ownership interests in a number of thriving companies, including the Long Island Railroad, the Brooklyn Borough Gas Company, and the New York Subway Advertising Company. O'Malley also had remarkable financial and legal skills. As an attorney, he represented some of the nation's largest banking enterprises, a clientele which ultimately brought about his association with the Brooklyn Dodgers. [12]

In 1933, O'Malley met George McLaughlin, president of the Brooklyn Trust Company, and sold Mc Laughlin on a multiple-mortgage deal which proved very profitable for the bank. From that point on, McLaughlin took a great interest in O'Malley and his career.[13]

Ten years later, McLaughlin was attempting to liquidate the insolvent Ebbets family estate. His bank held a $500,000 mortgage on Ebbets Field and a loan of $200,000 made for general team operations. The mortgage was past due and real estate taxes had yet to be paid. McLaughlin, an ardent Dodgers fan, didn't want to foreclose on the stadium, so he sought help from a mortgage expert: Walter O'Malley.

Prior to that time, O'Malley had considered baseball "a sort of hobby." He attended both Dodger and Yankee games and in his younger days had been a New York Giant fan. "The Dodgers were merely another client," explained O'Malley. "I was asked to reorganize the club and pull it out of the doldrums. We were coming out of the Depression and so much real estate was under foreclosure. I had to find a method of recognizing the mortgages on the team's properties." O'Malley pioneered a plan which reorganized over $100 million of those mortgages and removed the threat to Ebbets Field.[14]

O'Malley soon discovered that the Dodgers organization was a financial nightmare. Concession receipts, which made up 10 percent of the gate, were loaded uncounted into ordinary duffel bags and dumped into a vault in a downtown Brooklyn bank. He witnessed one executive going to the ticket office cash register, "taking a handful of bills and heading to the racetrack." O'Malley told Mc Laughlin that matters were so bad that, "The only way I can get something meaningful done is if I myself become a director of the team."[15] Acting for the Brooklyn Trust, McLaughlin named O'Malley a director and also head of the Dodgers legal affairs.[16] The 40-year-old O'Malley was moving up in the world.

As the ballclub's attorney, O'Malley remained in the background, while Dodgers president Larry MacPhail struggled to improve the team. MacPhail had recently turned the Cincinnati Reds around and McLaughlin hired him as Dodgers president in 1938 with the expectation that he could repeat his success in Brooklyn. Among the first things MacPhail did was to refurbish and install lights in Ebbets Field at a cost of $200,000. He then spent another $50,000 to purchase first baseman Dolph Camilli from the Philadelphia Phillies. The lights and the Dodgers' withdrawal from a three-team compact that had prohibited broadcasting games on the radio in New York outraged the Giants and Yankees.[17] MacPhail's efforts were successful — the Dodgers won the pennant in 1941 — but expensive.[18] O'Malley, who always wanted the best results for the least cost, appreciated the Dodgers' performance on the field, but deplored MacPhail's spending habits.

When MacPhail resigned after the 1942 season to join the army, the Brooklyn Trust Company sold 75 percent of the team's stock to three partners: John L. Smith, president of Pfizer Chemical Company, the wartime supplier of penicillin and a major customer of the bank; Branch Rickey, former general manager of the St. Louis Cardinals, who succeeded MacPhail as Dodger president; and Walter O'Malley, the team's attorney who paid $82,000 for his share. Dearie Mulvey, the daughter of Charlie Ebbets' former partner, Steve McKeever, and Dearie's husband owned the remaining 25 percent.[19] All eleven of Ebbets' heirs were destitute and had to sell their stock in the team.[20]

Walter O'Malley and Branch Rickey never got along. They had a few things in common: they both were constant cigar smokers, excellent speakers, and liked to make money. But their differences were far greater. O'Malley liked an occasional drink and a good off-color joke while Rickey was a teetotaler and hated profanity.[21] Most importantly, they didn't agree on how to run a baseball club.

O'Malley had no experience in the game, but soon made it clear that he expected to have his say. Rickey, in contrast, was a living baseball legend. He had created the modern spring training camp and pioneered the use of the farm system to supply the major leagues with talented players. Understandably, the farm system which Rickey had developed for the Dodgers was his pride and joy; O'Malley considered it a costly but necessary source of raw product.[22]

O'Malley also complained that Rickey was either finding ways to spend money, currying favor with his players, or both. After the 1946 season, Rickey wanted to reward the team for their second-place finish by buying each of them a new Studebaker. O'Malley immediately vetoed the plan.[23]

Rickey and O'Malley also disagreed about the value of the emerging medium of television. Rickey sneered at TV and stated that it would eventually lower attendance and harm minor league baseball. O'Malley quickly saw television as another outlet for baseball and an opportunity to make more money.[24]

To most baseball observers, this conflict between O'Malley and Rickey was really a conflict between baseball's past and its future. Rickey was a man who felt that baseball was a civil religion; O'Malley felt that what really mattered were "balance sheets and dividends."[25]

It soon became apparent that either O'Malley or Rickey had to go, and as a protégé of the Brooklyn Trust Company, O'Malley was clearly in a stronger position. In 1950, O'Malley was finally successful in getting Rickey out. John Smith, the Pfizer magnate, who had held 25 percent of the Dodgers' stock, died. As executor of Smith's estate, the Brooklyn Trust Company granted O'Malley the right to manage Smith's stock, giving him control of 50 percent of the ownership.[26]

O'Malley then offered to purchase Rickey's stock for $346,667, the exact amount Rickey had paid for it. Suddenly, William Zeckendorf, a New York real estate mogul, entered the picture with a rival offer of $1 million. A clause in Rickey's and O'Malley's partnership agreement stated that if either opted to sell his shares and had a genuine offer, the other had first right to buy the stock at the offered price. O'Malley, wanting desperately to oust Rickey and take control of the club, unhappily paid Rickey the $1 million, and was also forced to pay Zeckendorf an additional $50,000 as "compensation for tying up [his] capital."[27] This might have been the only time that any one got the better financially of Walter O'Malley.[28]

On the day he bought Rickey's stock, O'Malley held a press conference and stated that he had "the warmest possible feelings for Rickey as a man.... I do not know of anyone who can approach Mr. Rickey in the realm of executive baseball."[29] His real feelings were undoubtedly more accurately expressed when he complained, "Rickey will probably receive credit for all Dodger successes for years to come, and the incumbent administration only the blame."[30] Despite what he told the press, O'Malley was enraged by the way Rickey had outmaneuvered him. From that day forward there was a rule in the Dodger front office that any employee who mentioned the name Branch Rickey was fined $1.[31]

O'Malley and Rickey may have been feuding in the front office, but the Dodger teams between 1943 and 1950 fared very well. Except for coming in seventh in 1944, the Dodgers finished in the first division the other six years, winning the pennant in 1947 and again in 1949. During this time the Dodgers had on their roster a number of high-quality players, including stars such as Pee Wee Reese, Pete Reiser, Arky Vaughn, Mickey Owen, Eddie Stanky, Carl Furillo, Ralph Branca, Gil Hodges, Roy Campanella, Preacher Roe, Billy Cox, Duke Snider, Don Newcombe, and, of course, Jackie Robinson.

Jackie Robinson was undoubtedly the most controversial player to wear a Dodger uniform between 1943 and 1950. Because Branch Rickey had signed him in 1947, making him the first African-American player in the major leagues, Robinson felt very loyal to Rickey. For his part, O'Malley wanted to rid the Dodgers of every Rickey protégé and supporter, but he realized that no single player had been more responsible for the Dodgers' success than Robinson. During the next five years, the relationship between the two men continued to deteriorate until O'Malley decided to trade him. Robinson preempted the trade by retiring from baseball in 1956.[32]

In his autobiography, Robinson maintained that, "To O'Malley, I was one of those 'uppity niggers.'"[33] O'Malley emphasized that his attitude towards Robinson was based solely on the fact that he was a "Ricky man." Tommy La Sorda, Dodger manager for more than 20 years, differs greatly with Robinson's version. He argues that Rickey, as owner of only 25% of the team, must have had O'Malley's agreement for signing Robinson. "There's no question that Mr. O'Malley should have shared in the credit." After Robinson and other black players joined the team, states LaSorda, "[O'Malley] made them all feel like they were an important part of the organization. He was color blind and treated everybody alike."[34] When Florida's segregation laws barred black players from public golf courses, O'Malley built a course in Vero Beach for his all of his team — black and white — to use during spring training.[35]

To replace Rickey in 1950, O'Malley hired two vice-presidents: Fresco Thompson, who had directed the Dodgers' farm system, and Buzzy Bavasi, who had managed the Dodgers' Montreal farm club. Thompson and Bavasi were O'Malley's type of executives. Bavasi was a street-smart native of New York City, who was at home in a billiard parlor as well as a boardroom. Thompson was a former infielder who had a keen eye for talent. Both enjoyed a drink from time to time and often sprinkled their conversation with four-letter words. To further eliminate Rickey's influence, O'Malley fired manager Burt Shotton, a Rickey confidante, and replaced him with former Cincinnati Reds manager, Charlie Dressen.[36] At last, O'Malley had associates he trusted.[37]

Author Roger Kahn referred to the Dodger teams of 1951 through 1955 as the "The Boys of Summer." During that five-year span, the Dodgers won four National League pennants and one world championship and led the National League in attendance. While O'Malley credited Rickey with building the farm system and hiring star African-American players, it was O'Malley who continued and expanded his team's formidable player-development program.[38]

In 1951, the Dodgers lost the pennant in one of the most dramatic playoffs in baseball history. The Dodgers and the Giants had each won one game in a best-of-three series. In the third game, the Dodgers had a 4–1 lead going into the bottom of the ninth at the Polo Grounds. After the Giants got three hits and made only one out, starting pitcher Don Newcombe was replaced by Ralph Branca. Branca grooved an 0–1 pitch to Bobby Thompson for what became known as "the shot heard around the world," a homerun which gave the Giants the victory and the right to meet the Yankees in the World Series. That pitch also cost Dodger coach Clyde Sukeforth his job for sending in Branca rather than Carl Erskine or Clem Labine. Of course, the fact that Sukeforth was one of the last of the Rickey men didn't help his cause.[39]

The Dodgers won the National League pennant the following two years, but lost the World Series both times to the New York Yankees. The year 1953 marked the fifth consecutive time the Dodgers had lost the World Series to the Yankees.[40]

Since the 1930s, when Casey Stengel was paid for not managing while he finished the final years of a multi-year contract, the Dodgers tried to sign managers to only one-year contracts. Following the 1953 season, Charlie Dressen, who had replaced Burt Shotton in 1950, was offered his usual one-year contract. Dressen's wife, Ruth, however, wrote O'Malley that her husband deserved a three-year contract for winning his second pennant for O'Malley and achieving the best record in club history with 105 wins. O'Malley refused to extend the contract, and, while Dressen hesitated and delayed signing another one-year pact, O'Malley announced that he was replacing Dressen for the 1954 season with Walter Alston, a veteran of the Dodger organization.[41]

Not surprisingly, the volatile Dodger fans were shocked. "WALTER WHO?" screamed New York newspaper headlines. Alston would soon answer that question as he went on to manage the Dodgers from 1954 to 1976, signing one-year contracts each year.[42] Under Alston, the Dodgers finished in second place in 1954 and in 1955 clinched the pennant on September 8, the earliest ever in National League history.[43]

The 1955 World Series marked the sixth Series confrontation between the Yankees and Dodgers in 15 years. After the Dodgers lost the first two games, it appeared as if 1955 would also mark the sixth consecutive Yankees triumph. The Dodgers won games three, four, and five, thanks to the slugging of Roy Campanella, Gil Hodges, and Duke Snider. The Yankees bounced back in game six to tie the series at three games apiece. In the crucial seventh game, the Dodgers shut out the Yankees 2–0, when Gil Hodges drove in the first run of the game with a single in the fourth and the second with a sacrifice fly in the sixth. The Yankees had only one real scoring threat, but Dodger outfielder Sandy Amoros made a spectacular running catch in the sixth that started a double play, allowing Dodger hurler Johnny Podres to win his second World Series game. The Dodgers had won their first World Series title in 55 years.[44]

From the time O'Malley took over the reins as president of the Brooklyn Dodgers, he was able to make the team fiscally sound, showing a financial profit each year, but he constantly thought of new ways to promote his team. Because he was the most influential owner of his day, many historians overlook the fact that O'Malley was also one of the most innovative and promotion-minded moguls.

One of his first projects was to turn his Florida ballpark into an attractive destination for residents and visitors. O'Malley realized that making spring training an enjoyable experience for Dodger fans was not only good public relations but good for business. Under Branch Rickey, the Dodger field at Vero Beach had been a basic rural ballpark with open bleachers. O'Malley replaced the bleachers with comfortable grandstands, planted the slope of the outfield barrier with Bermuda grass and royal palms, and constructed underground streams that formed a pond stocked with trout. He boasted that everything was indigenous except the trout. The cost of reconstructing the training camp was costly but he stated, "I can justify the expense. A lot of my players like to fish. The trout keep 'em [in camp] and out of paternity suits."[45]

In addition to giving fans pleasant surroundings in which to watch pre-season baseball, he promoted spring exhibition games by mixing in experienced players with drawing power along with the rookies trying to make the big league team.[46] He was the first owner to bring both major and minor leaguers to one spring training site.[47] To supplement the radio and newspaper publicity, O'Malley would hire a man to work the Beach hotels, giving out cards advertising the games. Long before spring training gained its present popularity, the Dodgers drew more than 90,000 fans for their spring training games.[48]

In Brooklyn, O'Malley also introduced a number of promotions, always with the idea of ensuring that the average fan could see Dodger games. At every home game, O'Malley held back 12,000 seats to be put on sale the morning of the game. He did away with group plan ticket sales, making more tickets available for individuals. O'Malley also increased the number of Ladies' Days and to help women understood the mechanics of the game, he held baseball clinics for them at local department stores.[49]

Some of O'Malley's most popular promotions involved music in the stadium. O'Malley hired seven men, two of them professional musicians, known as the Dodger Sym-Phony band. They paraded through the ball park during the game, serenading spectators, playing salutes to the Dodgers, and generally razzing the opposing team. And then there was O'Malley's Music Appreciation Night. Fans who brought musical instruments to the game got in free and were encouraged to accompany the mayor of Brooklyn as he sang *Take Me Out to the Ballgame*. Although the mayor officially declared the evening "Music Depreciation Night," people were not offended. Walter O'Malley was bringing fans into the ballpark and they were having a great time.[50]

O'Malley was most innovative in the area of televising baseball games. Despite the fact that Ebbets Field was showing its age in the mid–1950s, it provided a prosperous base for televised games. By 1955, the Dodgers were televising all their home games as well as more than 20 road games, earning the team close to $800,000 from radio and television.[51] For the benefit of viewers who had purchased "experimental" color TVs, O'Malley had red numbers put on the front of the Dodgers' uniforms.[52] O'Malley's most enduring television-related innovation was to establish a televised "Game of the Week" each Saturday during the season, a plan endorsed by the other baseball executives during the 1955 winter meetings.[53] Even baseball fans outside Brooklyn enjoyed following the Dodgers on TV.

Perhaps O'Malley's most unique promotional strategy was to encourage team loyalty by bringing fans and players closer together. At Ebbets Field, an alleyway led to the Dodger dressing room. Although fans could easily see the players as they ran onto the field, a high grilled fence kept fans and players apart. When O'Malley took over, he had windows cut into the fence and designated certain days as "autograph days," allowing the fans to reach out and get the signatures of their favorite players. O'Malley also asked each player to spend some time at the windows to talk to the fans.[54] Ironically, this closeness was one of the major reasons Brooklyn fans felt betrayed when the team left town.

Even while O'Malley was promoting games at Ebbets Field, he was well aware of the physical shortcomings of the stadium. According to O'Malley, "The aisles are too narrow. The stairs are too steep. Poles obstruct the views [and] we need twice as many seats. The girders holding up the whole thing are rusting away."[55] With space for only 700 cars, parking was a major problem. "Fewer people were riding the subways," O'Malley recalled, "because they were riding in automobiles — and we couldn't park them."[56]

Although he often denied it, O'Malley was concerned about the changing social composition of Brooklyn and the area surrounding Ebbets Field. It had once been an elegant community, but it began to deteriorate when its inhabitants started moving to the suburbs. Slums were spreading and O'Malley worried that this would affect attendance.[57]

As far back as 1947, when he was still a minority stockholder, O'Malley had commissioned an engineering firm to design a new stadium with a revolutionary dome. He told the engineers, "Imagine a park with no poles, escalators taking the fans to their seats, plenty of parking, restaurants and train stations right in the park. Then, to end worries about rain, we put a dome over everything."[58] Of course, people rejected "O'Malley's Pleasure Dome" outright, making derisive jokes and laughing about his "absurd" notion.[59] They didn't realize that he had designed the stadium model that was to go up in city after city within the next 20 years.

Domed stadium or not, O'Malley knew he needed a new facility, and he wanted to build it in Brooklyn at a new site — a parcel of land at Atlantic and Flatbush Avenues, around the Long Island Railroad system at the west end of the borough. Although he intended to pay for the stadium himself, he needed the city of New York to condemn the site and then sell him the land cheaply. Lawyer O'Malley knew that under Title I of the 1949 Federal Housing Act, any business presently operating on the Atlantic-Flatbush site could be relocated and the land made available to the Dodgers. Engineer O'Malley had a plan to completely rejuvenate the area with a new railroad terminal, a new market, free-flowing traffic, and a new stadium.[60]

In March 1955, Walter O'Malley rounded up his cronies from Tammany Hall and along with some prominent Republicans, pushed a bill through the New York General Assembly creating a Brooklyn Sports Center Authority.[61]

Even before the Sports Center Authority undertook the complicated business of condemning the land, O'Malley began to raise the capital he needed as his share of the venture. In 1953 O'Malley sold Ebbets Field for $3 million to a real estate operator named Marvin Kratter and signed a lease promising that his Dodgers would play there for three more years.[62] Later, some pointed to this action as the first sign of his "real" intention to move out of New York.

To get the Brooklyn site he wanted for his new ballpark, Walter O'Malley had to negotiate not with Mayor Robert Wagner, but with Robert Moses, sometimes dubbed, "the single most powerful figure in twentieth-century New York City government."[63] Officially Moses was the Commissioner of Parks, but in reality, he also controlled highways and urban projects as well. He opposed a baseball field in downtown Brooklyn because he felt that despite O'Malley's traffic design, the streets could never handle all the cars the stadium would bring.[64] When Moses pushed alternate sites including "a lovely parcel of land in Flushing Meadow, at the site of the old World's Fair in Queens," O'Malley is purported to have replied, "If my team is forced to play in Queens, they will no longer be the Brooklyn Dodgers. Going to Flushing Meadow is no different, in a sense, from going to Jersey City or Los Angeles. As long as you're going to move, what difference does it make whether you move five miles or 5,000 miles?"[65] O'Malley soon learned that Moses would not allow him to acquire the land he wanted.[66] Those who felt that O'Malley was sincere in wanting to stay in Brooklyn could rightfully blame Moses as the real villain who forced him out.

At the winter baseball meeting in 1955, Walter O'Malley told the other owners that it looked like he was not going to get "the only practical site in Brooklyn" and that now "we have to look elsewhere."[67] To back up his words, he announced that in 1956, the Dodgers would reschedule seven home games from Ebbets Field to Jersey City, New Jersey — one against each National League rival. O'Malley promised that without a new stadium, he would play even more games outside Brooklyn in 1957.[68] Some saw the handwriting on the wall. New York City sportswriter Roscoe McGowen wrote that the major effect of the Jersey City move was to wake people up to the fact that baseball in Ebbets Field was probably in its final seasons and, "Unless O'Malley succeeds in getting the site he wants — at Flatbush and Atlantic Avenues—for his new stadium, it is as definite right now as anything can be that there will be no stadium and no Dodgers in Brooklyn."[69] Arthur Daley, writing in the *New York Times,* warned, "If O'Malley can't resettle in Brooklyn, he'll move to Queens or Long Island or — who knows? — California."[70]

During the winter baseball meeting in 1956, O'Malley and his old friend, Chicago Cubs' owner Phil Wrigley, began negotiating a deal for O'Malley to buy Wrigley's AAA Pacific Coast franchise in Los Angeles, in exchange for the Dodgers' AAA team in Fort Worth, Texas. The burning question now was whether the Dodgers would really leave Brooklyn for the West Coast.[71]

Despite a cloudy geographic future, the Dodgers continued their stellar play on the field. 1956 turned out to be one of the team's most exciting years with the pennant winner not determined until the last game of the regular season. The Dodgers went into the final weekend one game behind the Milwaukee Braves. A three-game sweep of the Pirates combined with the Braves losing three straight to the St. Louis Cardinals, gave the Dodgers the pennant. Heroes of the 1956 Dodgers included Don Newcombe, whose 27–7 record earned him both the Cy Young and Most Valuable Player Awards; Clem Labine, who won ten games and saved 19; and Duke Snider, who clouted 43 homers and drove in 101 runs. Carl Furillo delivered a number of clutch hits in September. One of the Dodgers' most pleasant surprises was former Giant pitcher Sal Maglie, who compiled a record of 13–5 and whose 1.38 ERA led all National League pitchers. Many local civic groups, concerned that the team might not remain in Brooklyn, tried to convince O'Malley of their support by increased attendance — 166,000 more than the previous year.[72]

The Dodgers were pitted against the Yankees again and although Brooklyn had finally defeated them in 1955, the 1956 World Series was a return to the old pattern. Like the Dodgers the previous year, the Yankees lost the first two games, then won the next three and split the remaining two games. The highlight of the 1956 World Series was Yankee hurler Don Larsen's perfect game — a feat still unique in World Series play.[73] It was also the final year of Jackie Robinson's career.[74]

After the Dodgers lost the series to the Yankees, O'Malley went to Los Angeles to close a secret deal to move his team. Los Angeles had been shopping around for many years for a major league baseball team and had had an avid prospect in Clark Griffith. O'Malley, however, beat the Old Fox to the West Coast and shook hands on an agreement which would bring his Dodgers to Los Angeles following the 1957 season.[75] His swap of minor league franchises with Phil Wrigley had given him territorial privileges in the city and title to Los Angeles' Wrigley Field. O'Malley then traded this ballpark to the city of Los Angeles for the site where he intended to build a new stadium.

The move had to be approved by the other National League magnates, but any objection they might have had was removed when Giants owner Horace Stoneham announced that beginning in 1958 he, too, would move his team out of New York and join O'Malley on the West Coast. Until O'Malley persuaded him to come to California, Stoneham had intended to move his Giants to Minneapolis where he had a farm club. "I wasn't the one who convinced Stoneham to leave New York," maintained O'Malley, "He had already made that decision. What I did was talk him out of a move to Minneapolis and convince him that San Francisco was better."[76]

O'Malley needed Stoneham to move with him because the National League had insisted that more than one team had to be on the West Coast in order to accommodate the league's travel schedule. The owners approved the move for both teams. Although it was almost a year later, October 8, 1957, that the Dodgers officially announced they were going to Los Angeles, it had long been public knowledge that 1957 was the Dodgers final year in Brooklyn.[77]

In their last season in Brooklyn, the Dodgers won only 84 games and ended in third place, their lowest finish since 1948. The final game played in Ebbets Field took place on September 24, 1957, when 6,702 fans watched Danny McDevitt, a rookie southpaw, shut out the Pirates 2–0.[78]

When O'Malley announced he was taking the team out of Brooklyn, Dodger fans called him every name they could think of and invented a few new ones. According to them, he was a "Gaelic Machiavelli," a cold schemer who would cast aside any loyalties in order to make a dollar. The general consensus was that O'Malley was "lured by the glint of gold in California, and oblivious to the loyal, broken-hearted fans they left behind them."[79]

Approximately 25 years later, Peter Golenbock interviewed Brooklyn residents about their reaction to the move. The memories were still fresh and sharp. One fan told Golenbock that his friends wanted to kidnap and shoot O'Malley. They figured if O'Malley were dead, the Dodgers wouldn't move. Another blamed O'Malley's greed. "Greed was the whole thing. O'Malley feathered his nest. They gave him half of Los Angeles for nothing, and the bum, he got the money, but what did he do to us?" Still another fan and his friend tried an experiment. The two men each wrote on a napkin the names of the three worst human beings who ever lived. When they compared lists, they found the same three names in the exact same order: Hitler, Stalin, and Walter O'Malley.[80]

The entire borough of Brooklyn vilified O'Malley, but Horace Stoneham's announcement of the Giants' move to San Francisco sparked little emotion (except from fans who blamed O'Malley for both moves.)[81] O'Malley had his own explanation. "I think most of the writers realized that Horace's position was untenable in New York. It was almost impossible for him to operate successfully."[82]

What O'Malley didn't say was that he didn't have the credibility of Horace Stoneham, whose family had owned the Giants since 1919. The sportswriters and fans could excuse Stoneham for moving a team that faced certain bankruptcy in Manhattan; they couldn't forgive O'Malley, who was prospering in Brooklyn, for separating the team from the borough that loved them.[83] This bond is probably the most significant reason to explain the animosity that persisted for decades against O'Malley. The Brooklyn Dodgers had become the single most important symbol in giving Brooklyn its distinctive identity and when the Dodgers moved westward, the borough's baseball fans felt that O'Malley had injured them personally.[84] Years later, Carl Furillo summed it up when he said, "It seemed the whole team belonged to Brooklyn."[85]

When Walter O'Malley brought his Dodgers to Los Angeles, he redrew the map of baseball and made the National League true to its name. Before 1958, the Major Leagues consisted of 16 ballclubs, all located in the Northeast and Midwest, close enough so that the teams could travel by railroad. With two teams on the West Coast, air travel became a necessity. While some of the other owners chastised O'Malley for upsetting the geography of the game, the Dodger owner claimed that he was simply taking baseball where the population was migrating. Of course, he was right. By the end of the 1960s, six Major League teams were playing ball on the West Coast.[86]

In addition to redefining baseball geographically, O'Malley also redefined baseball as a business. The Dodgers were certainly not the first team to pull up stakes. Both the St. Louis Browns and the Boston Braves had earlier moved their teams to other cities, but these clubs were losing money. The Dodgers, however, were extremely profitable. Furthermore, they had become baseball's cultural icon with a loyal following, not only in Brooklyn, but wherever Dodger television was broadcast. O'Malley saw the limitations in Brooklyn and knew that California would offer more opportunities for him to increase the team's profits. Sports columnist Red Smith wrote of O'Malley, "It had always been recognized that baseball was a business, but if you enjoyed the game you could also tell yourself that it was also a sport. O'Malley was the first to say out loud it was all business."[87]

The relocation of the two New York teams also eliminated the possibility of the Pacific Coast League developing into a legitimate third major league. Instead, the Dodgers and Giants controlled the two most prosperous cities in the PCL and forced out three PCL franchises: the San Francisco Seals, the Los Angeles Angels and the Hollywood Stars.[88]

The main reason O'Malley was willing to move to Los Angeles when others before him would not, was that he had overcome the lack of a suitable park for major league play. O'Malley had negotiated a deal that benefited both the Dodgers and the city of Los Angeles. In return for O'Malley building his ideal Dodger Stadium there, the city gave him more than 300 acres of conveniently located, city-owned ground and agreed to spend millions of dollars grading it and millions more constructing connecting roads and freeways to accommodate the city's automobiles.[89] The site was Chavez Ravine, named after its original owner, an early Angeleno named Julian Chavez. Before it was transformed into one of the great sites in baseball, Chavez Ravine was a barren area of hills and gullies, home to a small community of Hispanics. The city had taken it for a federal housing project that never came to fruition and the federal government returned it to the city with instructions to use it for a public purpose. Los Angeles had tried to get rid of the property for years, looking without success to entice developers who could come up with viable plans.[90]

For his part, the site met all of O'Malley's specifications. He first saw Chavez Ravine during a layover on the Dodgers' trip to Japan after the 1956 World Series. It possessed what he had wanted in Brooklyn — great accessibility to highways which converged nearby, and ample room for parking, which would not only attract fans to the game but would be another source of revenue for the Dodgers.[91]

O'Malley was absolutely sure of one thing. He was going to build a privately financed stadium, the first since Yankee Stadium in 1923. He stated over and over that he did not intend to seek public money to construct his new stadium. Time and again, he repeated what he had said when he sought a new stadium in Brooklyn, "I don't want to be a tenant in a political ballpark. I want to own my own ballpark and run it the way I think it should be run."[92]

In October 1957, a 29-member contingent arrived from Brooklyn ready to begin business as the Los Angeles Dodgers. The group included O'Malley, front office officials, radio and television announcer Vin Scully, and a few members of the Dodger baseball team. At an impromptu press conference, O'Malley indicated that he was ready to set up headquarters, begin work on the Chavez Ravine project, and, most importantly, find a suitable site to play until Chavez Ravine was ready.[93]

Los Angeles' Wrigley Field was too small for the crowds O'Malley intended to attract, and he ultimately decided that the Dodgers would play their home games in Memorial Coliseum. Home field for UCLA Bruins football and Los Angeles' NFL team, the Rams, it was a stadium far more suited for football than baseball. In fact, the Coliseum could hardly accommodate baseball. Right field was 440 feet from home plate, while left field down the line measured no more than 250 feet. Left-center started at 320 feet before it extended into a much longer distance. Commissioner Ford Frick ordered O'Malley to construct a second screen eighty feet behind an existing one in left field and to have the second screen serve as the home-run boundary. California law, however, forbade such an additional structure because of the large number of earthquakes prevalent in the Los

Angeles area, and Frick was forced to accept Memorial Coliseum for what it was—including some center field seats that were 700 feet from home plate.[94] National League players began to dub the Coliseum O'Malley's Chinese Theatre. One newspaperman wrote that it was "the only ballpark that can hold 94,000 fans but only two outfielders."[95]

The Dodgers played in the Coliseum from 1958 to 1961. Their first year on the West Coast was a disaster. "The Boys of Summer" were getting older and the Dodgers finished the season in seventh place with a record of 71–83, the worst since 1944. Before the year even began, catcher Roy Campanella had been paralyzed from the shoulders down in an offseason automobile accident. One-time pitching ace Don Newcombe lost his first six decisions and was traded to Cincinnati. Carl Erskine won the first game the Dodgers played in Los Angeles, but could win only four more games the rest of the year. Dodger stars Duke Snider, Gil Hodges, Jim Gilliam, and Carl Furillo all had mediocre seasons. Team leader, shortstop Pee Wee Reese was relegated to a utility role and ended the season with a batting average of .224, and announced his retirement shortly after. Despite the poor showing, the Dodgers season attendance was 1,845,556, over 800,000 more than they drew in Brooklyn in 1957.[96]

The Dodger brass of general manager Buzzy Bavasi, farm system chief Fresco Thompson, and scouting supervisor Al Campanis, along with manager Walter Alston, generally preferred to fill the roster with players from the Dodgers elaborate minor league farm system. After the 1958 season, however, they traded for two seasoned outfielders—Wally Moon and Rip Repulski. Repulski contributed little, but Moon hit .302, with 19 homers and drove in 74 runs. Although a left-handed batter, he was able to hit to the opposite field and made excellent use of the short left field wall. Snider, Hodges, and Maury Wills all had comeback years, and with Don Drysdale's 17 victories, the Dodgers ended the season in a first-place tie with the Milwaukee Braves.[97] This created the third tie-breaking playoff in National League history, all of them involving the Dodgers. Unlike the disappointments of 1946 against the Cardinals and again in 1951 against the Giants, the Dodgers won the playoffs in 1959, defeating the Braves by winning two consecutive games.[98]

The Dodgers met the Chicago White Sox in the 1959 World Series. They were drained after being forced to win two playoff games just to qualify for the World Series while their opponents had breezed to an easy pennant with three dominant pitchers, Early Wynn, Bob Shaw, and Billy Pierce. Thanks to the heroics of Dodger pitcher Larry Sherry, who won two games and saved two others, the Dodgers defeated the White Sox in six games, thus claiming the second World Series flag in club history and the first ever to be won by a West Coast team. Each of the three games played at the Coliseum drew more than 92,000 fans.[99]

The last two years the Dodgers played in the Coliseum were important chiefly for the players who would be the foundation of the franchise for most of the 1960s. Carl Furillo had been released following the 1959 World Series and the other two outstanding hitters, Snider and Hodges, were on the decline. Frank Howard, Ron Fairly, Willie Davis, Maury Wills, and Tommy Davis would take their places. Johnny Roseboro was Campanella's successor behind the plate. Pitching standouts included Don Drysdale, Johnny Podres, reliever Ron Perranoski, and the incomparable Sandy Koufax. Koufax had been on the Dodger roster since 1955, but it was not until 1961, his seventh year in the majors, that the southpaw proved he could win consistently enough to earn a place in Baseball's Hall of Fame. The Dodgers finished fourth in 1960 and second in 1961.[100]

Walter O'Malley's new ballpark, Dodger Stadium, finally opened in 1962, six months behind schedule. The delay had been caused by a political ploy unknown to Tammany Hall-bred Walter O'Malley, but dearly beloved in California — the referendum. On December 1, 1957, the city clerk of Los Angeles announced that opponents of Dodger Stadium had gathered enough signatures to place the Chavez Ravine agreement on referendum, giving Los Angeles voters the right to uphold or invalidate the city's contract with O'Malley. On June 3, 1958, the electorate was scheduled to vote on the stadium issue, known as Proposition B. A "yes" vote would uphold the contract while a "no" vote would nullify it. Walter O'Malley was shocked by the whole procedure. "I was completely unaware of the thing," admitted a surprised O'Malley. "We never had such a thing in New York."[101]

Proposition B passed with a narrow margin of victory of 26,000 votes out of 676,000 cast. The victory for O'Malley was greatly aided by heavy support from Los Angeles' African-American voters, who remembered that the Dodgers were the organization that broke baseball's color line.[102]

In planning Dodger Stadium, O'Malley discarded his image of a domed park and took as his inspiration a local attraction. O'Malley had visited Disneyland shortly after moving to Los Angeles and came home raving about it. "You just have to see that place — the presentation of it, the restrooms, the food."[103]

Dodger Stadium was a beautiful park designed only for baseball. The stadium was reputed to have the best hot dogs, the coldest beer, and ample parking.[104] Because of the way Dodger Stadium was constructed, patrons were able to drive directly to the appropriate level, color coded to match the color of their tickets, and emerge at the level where their seats were located. Escalators were provided for fans who wanted to move between levels.[105] O'Malley spent more than $1 million on landscaping, planting olive and palm trees in the parking lots and installing a Japanese garden in center field.[106]

By the time the new ballpark opened, the total cost had reached $22 million. To finance the construction, O'Malley got a low-interest loan from Union Oil Company, giving the company exclusive rights to advertise on the ballpark scoreboard. Union Oil also received the broadcast rights for 10 years.[107]

The first game ever played at Dodger Stadium took place on April 10, 1962, with the Cincinnati Reds defeating the Dodgers 6–3 before a sellout crowd of 52,564.

Large crowds were the norm at Dodger games because O'Malley did not rely solely on the novelty of a major league team to draw fans to the stadium. One of the methods he used was a change in his television policy. In Brooklyn, O'Malley pioneered the televising of most of his team's home games. In Los Angeles, however, he reversed that policy, restricting telecasts to a minimum and usually only when the Dodgers played the rival San Francisco Giants.[108]

O'Malley actually intended that Dodger games not be broadcast on free TV, but instead wanted them only on pay television. In later years, variations of this scheme would be widely used and enormously profitable. In the 1950s, however, California, through another referendum, banned paid televising of sports events. Although O'Malley retaliated by offering the fewest number of televised games of any club, he still made money from his television contract.[109]

Television was only one way O'Malley promoted his team in Los Angeles, adapting some of his Brooklyn strategies on a grander scale and introducing some new ideas. He had Straight-A games for top students, community nights, and numerous giveaways where the Dodgers distributed truckloads of free merchandise, including T-shirts, caps, helmets, and bats.[110] Former Dodger players staffed the Dodgers speaker's bureau. For an annual fee of $5, members of the Dodger fan club received a large number of souvenirs and notices of more promotions.[111]

His family-oriented approach to filling the stadium exemplified promotional genius based on a profitable balance sheet with volume as the key. O'Malley kept ticket prices low (box seats were priced at only $3.50 for 18 consecutive years) and he started his night games early. According to O'Malley, "The future of all sports has to do with building a grassroots following, starting with youngsters going to games with their parents." Low admissions, early game times, and O'Malley's strategy of having the fewest number of free water fountains at any park meant good business at concession stands, where revenues far exceeded ticket income.[112] Buzzy Bavasi once stated, "If we let everybody in for nothing we'd still make a profit."[113] According to O'Malley, baseball at Dodger Stadium operated on the Las Vegas principle: it isn't what it costs you to get in; it's what it costs you while you're there.[114]

Although there was nothing new about season tickets, O'Malley strongly promoted their sales. Soon 12,000 seats, or close to 25 percent of the capacity at Dodger Stadium, were sold in advance. Season tickets assured the Dodger owner $3 million to $4 million up front, no matter how the team fared in the standings.[115]

In reality, the team's performance alone would have attracted large crowds to the games. The mid–1960s were Walt Alston's most successful period as Dodger manager. The man who had once been mocked as "Walter Who?" won pennants for O'Malley in 1963, 1965 and 1966. In 1963 the Dodgers swept four straight games in the World Series against their still bitter rivals, the New York Yankees.[116] In 1965 the Series went the distance, but the Dodgers defeated the Minnesota Twins when Sandy Koufax pitched a 2–0 shut out in game seven.[117] In 1966 the Baltimore Orioles swept the Dodgers in four games.[118]

Nineteen sixty-three was the year when Sandy Koufax began establishing himself as the truly dominant pitcher of his decade. He started slowly, but once he caught fire, he was the most unhittable southpaw ever to face National League batters. During the four-seasons from 1963 through 1966, Koufax's record was 97 wins and only 27 losses.[119]

After their first-place finish in 1966, the Dodgers came in eighth in 1967 and seventh in 1968. The team did not have to look far to discover the reason for their tumble. Koufax's appearance in the 1966 World Series had been his last in the Major Leagues. He received the Cy Young Award during the offseason and soon after announced that he was being forced into early retirement because pain in his pitching arm made it impossible for him to go on.[120]

There were also changes in the front office. Buzzy Bavasi left the Dodgers to head up operations for the new Padres team in San Diego. A few months later, Fresco Thompson died, leaving only Al Campanis to represent the old regime. Campanis assumed many of the duties of general manager, but Bavasi's departure and the death of Thompson accelerated the rise of Walter O'Malley's son, Peter, in the organization.[121]

Nineteen sixty-nine was an historic year for both baseball and the Dodgers. It marked Walt Alston's 15th year as manger of the Dodgers as well as baseball's centennial year. It also marked the greatest baseball expansion in big-league history.[122] Many historians credit the growth and expansion to Walter O'Malley's initial move westward.[123] In addition, O'Malley, who was an acknowledged leader among the other owners, exerted his influence several times to shape this movement.

Major-league expansion actually began in 1962. O'Malley's move out of New York, taking with him the city's other National League team, triggered an attempt to create a third Major League, the first since the Federal League wars ended in 1916. New York Mayor Robert Wagner established a four-man civic group for the purpose of luring an existing major league team from another city. Bill Shea, one of New York's most influential attorneys, was a member of the group. Shea had been a law clerk in the Brooklyn Trust Company at the same time as Walter O'Malley. When the head of the Brooklyn Trust chose O'Malley to oversee the operation of the Dodgers, Shea was offended and jealous. And when O'Malley moved the team to Los Angeles, Shea was incensed. He was determined to replace the Dodgers.[124]

In May 1959, Commissioner Ford Frick announced that neither the American nor the National League planned to expand, therefore eliminating the possibility of a new team in New York. Shea's efforts to entice an existing major league team to move to New York were also unsuccessful, so he decided to start a new league. To give the organization credibility, he announced that O'Malley's old nemesis, Branch Rickey, would be working with him. According to the 1960 census, at least six metropolitan areas had larger populations than four existing major league cities. These six were now targeted as prime candidates for the proposed third league.[125]

In July 1959, Shea unveiled his Continental League, stating that it would place franchises in New York, Houston, Minneapolis-St. Paul, Toronto and Denver. Reporters were skeptical about the possibility of finding enough major-league caliber players to fill the teams' rosters. Shea answered, "No one heard of an atomic scientist fifteen years ago. Now they're coming out of the woodwork. You can't tell me that a nation of 160,000,000 people can't produce two hundred more big league players."[126]

Walter O'Malley was key in thwarting the plans of Rickey, Shea, and their Continental League. Some big-league owners were worried only about competition from the proposed new league; Walter O'Malley was also concerned that if the AL and NL tried to fight Shea and Rickey, they would generate anti-trust action against the Major Leagues. O'Malley advised the other owners that compromise was a much better solution and persuaded them to agree to add two teams to each league for the 1961 or 1962 seasons.[127] The American League added the Angels in Los Angeles and put a new team in Washington, D.C. to replace the Senators, which Calvin Griffith had moved to Minnesota. Both new AL teams began play in 1961.[128]

O'Malley tolerated the newly formed Angels, owned by cowboy film star Gene Autry, because they provided another source of revenue for the Dodgers. Without a park of their own, the Angels were forced to rent Dodger Stadium for their home games and O'Malley was delighted to host them. He added $200,000 to the Dodgers' coffers for every million customers the Angels drew.[129] Autry built their own stadium in Anaheim after the 1965 season.[130]

Two new teams were also added in the National League — one in Houston and the other, headed by Shea, in New York City. Both NL teams began play in 1962.[131] Ironically, New York City's Shea Stadium was built on the same site in Queens that Robert Moses had tried to make the new location of Walter O'Malley's Dodgers.[132]

In 1969, a second round of expansion began that enlarged major-league membership to 24 teams. The American League added one team in Seattle and another in Kansas City. The league also changed to a two-division format. The National League at first threatened to "go to war" over the actions of the Junior Circuit, but, eventually, the National League voted to follow the American League's lead by adding teams in San Diego and Montreal in 1971. O'Malley encouraged his colleagues to move their timetable up to 1969 to match the AL. Each league now had playoffs between its two division winners for the league pennant and the right to compete in the World Series.[133] Despite O'Malley's decisive role in creating two 12-team leagues, he admitted on a number of occasions that he would have preferred having three eight-team leagues truly divided geographically with one in the East, one in the West, and one in the Mid-West.[134]

O'Malley actually advocated taking expansion beyond North America when he suggested that at least two cities in Japan were ready for the majors with the necessary stadium, player talent, economic backing, public enthusiasm, and great support from the press. "Japan has an abundance of talent, an area in which we in the United States are short," said O'Malley. "They can field one or two teams right now that can beat at least half our teams."[135] O'Malley did not live to see the contributions of Japanese and other Asian baseball players in both the National and American Leagues.

During the first ten years of divisional play, from 1969 to 1979, the Dodgers had a remarkable record in the National League West. They won their division in 1974, 1977, and 1978, and finished in second place five times. Their worst finish was fourth in 1969.[136] In 1974 they tied their high of 102 wins, but were defeated in the World Series in five games by the Oakland Athletics. It was the first World Series played entirely on the West Coast.[137] In 1977, Ron Cey, Steve Garvey, Dusty Baker, and Reggie Smith each hit 30 home runs and helped lead the Dodgers to another pennant, but the New York Yankees defeated the Dodgers in the World Series four games to two. This was the Series in which Reggie Jackson established his reputation as "Mr. October" with a record of five home runs, including three in successive bats in the final game.[138]

Nineteen seventy-eight was the year the Dodgers finally realized O'Malley's prophecy of attracting three million fans during the regular season.[139] It was also the last year the Dodgers would appear in the World Series under Walter O'Malley's ownership. Like many previous World Series, the Dodgers were defeated by the Yankees, this time in six games. The Yankees lost the first two games but won the next four establishing another World Series first.[140]

Despite his lack of a baseball background, shortly after he took control of the Dodgers, Walter O'Malley was elected by the other owners to the major league's five-man Executive Council, a position of power he occupied for 28 years.[141]

As a leader on the Executive Council, O'Malley was, as writer Leonard Koppett called him, " a smooth politician who shaped decisions on weighty matters like expansion, divisional playoffs,... and labor contracts with the Players Association."[142] He was so skillful in his leadership that Ted Turner, who often clashed with O'Malley, once stated, "I think it's true that he has a lot of influence on the other owners and the commissioner, but I think they look up to him out of respect for his experience and success. He has certainly never tried to force anything on me."[143]

O'Malley had strong feelings about many issues that affected the structure and play of the game and was always willing to speak out for what he felt most benefited baseball.

One of baseball's most controversial issues was the reserve clause which, in the early 1970s, was tested in court by Curt Flood. O'Malley stated that he definitely considered the reserve clause necessary for baseball's solid foundation, although he admitted the Dodgers would probably benefit if it were repealed. "If there were no reserve clause," confessed O'Malley, "then many of the best players would want to play here.... Selfishly, we would benefit by removal of the reserve clause. Realistically, there would be such imbalance that the game couldn't exist."[144]

O'Malley also put the game ahead of his own interests when it came to exorbitant bonuses being paid to bright young prospects. In the mid–60s, when the major-league average salary was $19,000 a year, "bonus babies" were being offered $100,000 merely for signing a major-league contract. Unable to compete, the poorer baseball franchises suggested an annual player draft similar to the one used by both the National Basketball Association and the National Football League. Most Dodger executives were opposed to this plan since their team employed the most scouts and benefited most from a wide-open signing policy. Buzzy Bavasi recalled that he urged O'Malley to oppose such a player draft, but O'Malley sided with the poorer franchises, reminding Bavasi, "an annual player draft is good for the game."[145]

O'Malley knew exactly where he stood on free agency, saying that his team's policy on signing free agents could be summed up in one word: Never. When one of his own pitchers, Andy Messersmith, filed for free agency, O'Malley spread the word that the other magnates were not to go after him. O'Malley's authority over his fellow magnates was so great that not one other owner made the ex–Dodger an offer, until Atlanta's Ted Turner broke ranks and signed Messersmith to a $1 million, three-year contract.[146]

O'Malley's foresight benefited baseball and all professional sports in another way: he provided the impetus that made sports management a special academic discipline. In 1957, O'Malley first began advocating formal educational programs for people who wanted to work in professional baseball. Nine years later, in 1966, Dr. James G. Mason established the first masters degree program in sports management at Ohio University. That single master's program soon expanded to more than 190 institutions that prepare sport managers and administrators on the undergraduate and graduate levels.[147]

O'Malley also looked out for the future of the players and is credited as the baseball owner who devised the player pension plan.[148]

O'Malley's political experience taught him that organizations that speak with one voice work best and he demanded unity in his clubhouse. He expressed this belief in a most unusual way in 1972. That year the Players Association, which had become the players' collective bargaining unit, conducted the first strike in the 20th century. Twenty-one of the 25 Dodger players voted to strike. At the end of the season, O'Malley released the four who had voted with management against the strike. He later explained that he would have preferred all of his players to oppose the strike, but since they hadn't, O'Malley considered the four who voted to be potential clubhouse troublemakers and he got rid of them.[149]

But it was O'Malley's power over the office of baseball commissioner that earned him the unofficial title of the most influential man in baseball of his time. When Walter O'Malley first headed the Dodgers, Ford Frick was Baseball Commissioner, serving from 1951 to 1965. Even during Frick's tenure, many argued that Walter O'Malley was the real commissioner, the *eminence grise*.[150] In 1965, writer Arthur Daley stated that O'Malley ruled baseball in all areas, except those where television interests prevailed.[151]

Colonel William D. Eckert succeeded Frick as commissioner. Suggested by General Curtis LeMay, Eckert was not known in baseball circles, nor had he ever distinguished himself militarily. Cynics viewed the election of such a weak commissioner a strategic victory for O'Malley and predicted that in no time Eckert would be under O'Malley's thumb. Eckert was so ill-suited to the job that he couldn't even handle the administrative duties of commissioner, which were eventually taken over by a four-man cabinet selected by the owners. On the night of December 6, 1968, realizing his lack of support, Eckert resigned.[152]

Walter O'Malley was responsible for Bowie Kuhn's election as baseball's next commissioner in 1969 and again in 1976. In 1969, after Eckert submitted his resignation, two factions were deadlocked over his successor. The followers of Walter O'Malley promoted Chub Feeney of the New York Giants, while another group backed Mike Burke of the New York Yankees. As a compromise, O'Malley suggested 42-year-old Bowie Kuhn. Kuhn, who had earlier represented the major league owners in some of their dealings with the ballplayers, was unanimously approved on an interim basis and then in August 1969, was given a seven-year contract.[153]

Many of O'Malley's associates and critics felt that O'Malley backed Kuhn as commissioner because Kuhn would follow O'Malley's lead.[154] When rumors proliferated that Walter O'Malley, rather than Bowie Kuhn, was running baseball, Bill Veeck was the first owner to publicly concur. "Walter O'Malley is the true commissioner of baseball, not Bowie Kuhn. Kuhn does what he is told."[155] On another occasion Veeck stated, "[O'Malley] was instrumental in getting Mr. Kuhn in as commissioner and you usually go home with the guy who brought you. The commissioner calls him all the time. He never calls me."[156]

The designated hitter rule was a good example of how O'Malley related to Kuhn. Partly because he didn't like the strategy and partly because he especially disliked Charlie Finley, the man who proposed it, O'Malley was adamant in opposing the DH. He convinced the other National League owners to block it in the NL. In 1972, the American League voted to adopt the designated hitter rule and, although the National League had voted it down, Baseball Commissioner Bowie Kuhn had the power to impose or prohibit it in both leagues. O'Malley did not wait for Kuhn to rule but sent him the message that, "If you impose it on the National League, you will have the damndest lawsuit on your hands you ever saw." Kuhn backed off.[157]

O'Malley was personally responsible for the re-election of Kuhn to a second term as baseball's commissioner. Kuhn's first seven-year term was to expire in August 1976 and the rules required that the owners consider rehiring him 12 to 18 months before that. During his first term, Kuhn had angered a number of owners, particularly Charles Finley of the Oakland Athletics. By June 1975, Finley was leading a "Dump Bowie" movement that had the support of some owners and many players. To be re-elected, Kuhn required a 9–3 vote in each league. Since O'Malley continued to be one of his strongest backers, Kuhn had the National League's support. But Finley and Baltimore's Jerry Hoffberger were strongly anti–Kuhn and both the Yankees and Eddie Chiles of the Texas Rangers announced they would also oppose Kuhn's re-election. On the day following the All-Star Game, the American League voted 8–4 to retain Kuhn — one vote short of the number Kuhn needed. O'Malley managed to delay the joint meeting of the two leagues and persuaded the Rangers and the Yankees to change their votes. When the two leagues got together, the vote in the American League was 10–2 and with the National League voting for him 12–0, Kuhn's contract was renewed for another seven years.[158] Some baseball observers claimed that Kuhn spent his second term defending the policies established by the O'Malley-dominated Executive Council.[159]

Both O'Malley and Kuhn denied the stories that Kuhn was under O'Malley's control. Kuhn asserted often that he had always been too mulish to be controlled by anyone. "I try, not with invariable success, to treat other people with respect. So it was with Walter. Old enough to be my father, he had not only my respect but my admiration and affection as well."[160] "I've been very careful over the years," O'Malley once stated, "especially with Commissioner Kuhn, not to recommend anything. If he wants my opinion, I don't hesitate to give it to him, but he's not the type … you should tell what to do."[161]

In 1970, Walter's son Peter O'Malley became club president when Walter O'Malley announced his retirement. Turning most day-to-day Dodger business over to Peter, Walter O'Malley assumed the newly created post of chairman of the board and continued to exercise a considerable amount of power until his death in 1979.[162]

Throughout the early and mid–70s, O'Malley attended most Dodger games, but illness was beginning to drain him by the end of 1978. He missed the World Series in 1978 between the Dodgers and the Yankees because he was having lung surgery at Our Lady Queen of Angels Hospital in Los Angeles. On April 23, 1979, he submitted his resignation as a member of baseball's Executive Council, and four months later, on August 9, 1979, Walter O'Malley died of congestive heart failure at the Mayo Clinic in Rochester, Minnesota. He was 75 years old. His wife, Kay, his childhood sweetheart, had died at the family home less than a month before Walter O'Malley passed away.[163]

Sports Illustrated, commenting on O'Malley's death, noted that the Dodger owner had dominated the inner councils of baseball and added, "It was probably a good thing that he did. Most owners treat their teams as toys, or as investments that fit in nicely with their tax setups. But baseball was O'Malley's only business and he worked like hell at it."[164]

County Supervisor Kenneth Hahn, the first official in Los Angeles to speak to O'Malley about moving his team to California, ordered flags lowered and the Olympic torch in the Coliseum lighted in his memory. "His warm Irish humor with his sound business judgment, combined for the best in professional baseball. He is one in a million and can't be replaced."[165]

Bowie Kuhn, who visited O'Malley shortly before he died, issued a short statement that probably summed him up best, "He was as great an executive talent as I ever saw, or think that I am apt to see. While baseball was his medium, his skills would have flourished in any walk of life."[166]

6

Bill Veeck
The Populist

During his long baseball career, Bill Veeck, Jr., owned three different major league teams; but, in his heart, his head, and his work, he always thought of himself first as a fan. The promotions for which he is most remembered all had the goal of making baseball an enjoyable experience for the fans. Of equal importance, Veeck was a savvy businessman who knew how to have fun while he was doing what he did best — selling the game of baseball.

Many owners entered baseball from other careers, but Bill Veeck, Jr. was in the game virtually from birth. The son of Grace and William Louis Veeck, Sr., Bill Jr. was born in Hinsdale, Illinois, February 4, 1912. His father was a sportswriter on the Chicago *Evening American,* using the pseudonym "Bill Bailey." Veeck Sr. was a satiric writer who took great pleasure in criticizing the Chicago Cubs, owned by chewing gum tycoon, William Wrigley. Bill Veeck, Sr., once wrote, "My infant son can throw his bottle farther than this team can hit."[1] Wrigley grew tired of reading Veeck's barbs in the *Evening American,* and after an especially stinging criticism, the irate Wrigley asked Veeck Sr., "If you know so much, why don't you run the team?" Veeck accepted the challenge and was so successful that Wrigley named him the club's president in 1919, a position he held until his death in 1933.[2]

When Bill Veeck, Jr., was eight years old, his father took him to spring training and three years later allowed him to work part time mailing out Ladies' Day tickets. He was a stock room boy, sold peanuts and scorecards, worked with the ground crew, and cleaned up the park.[3] Bill Veeck is also credited with overseeing the construction of the Cubs' hand-operated scoreboard, the largest hand-operated scoreboard at that time.[4] Veeck learned many facets of the game simply by working for his father, but more importantly, he observed how to successfully run a major league baseball team.[5]

Bill Jr. had completed three semesters at Kenyon College in Gambier, Ohio, when his father died in 1933. He immediately returned to Chicago for a fulltime job with the Cubs, where he learned even more about the operation of a baseball club. At various times, he worked with the team's advertising agency, operated the commissary, supervised ushers and ticket sellers, and conducted tryout schools for high school players. He even worked in the concession stands. Seven years later, in 1940, he became club treasurer and assistant secretary. At night he attended Northwestern University where he studied accounting, engineering, and business law, knowledge he put to good use as he bought and ran his teams.[6]

Bill Veeck and owner Phil Wrigley differed greatly on how management should promote the Cubs. Veeck tried to convince Wrigley to become a pioneer in promoting night baseball. Phil Wrigley, the last major league owner to install lights, wanted no part of night baseball.[7] Both men agreed, however, on adopting "Beautiful Wrigley Field" as a marketing slogan. Wrigley asked Veeck to plant trees in the aisles of the bleachers, but the wind kept blowing the leaves off. Several sets of trees later, Veeck planted the ivy which today gives Wrigley Field its distinctive appearance.[8]

Although Veeck had always dreamed of someday owning the Cubs, he and Wrigley parted ways in 1941 when the Cubs began selling bleacher seats in advance, a practice Veeck bitterly denounced as an affront to regular fans. When he left the Cubs in 1941 he cited personal conflicts between "baseball men" and "gum men."[9]

Soon afterwards, Bill Veeck and Charlie Grimm, a first baseman his father had brought to the Cubs from Pittsburgh in 1925, purchased the Milwaukee Brewers, the Cubs' farm club in the American Association. With very little capital, Veeck arranged the purchase by putting together a syndicate to assume the team's debts, using just enough of his own money to have controlling interest.[10]

The original Brewers were an American League team, which moved to St. Louis in 1901 to become the St. Louis Browns. In 1902 Milwaukee received an AA franchise and also called the new team the Brewers. The team was in deep financial trouble, and Bochert Field, where the team had played their home games for 40 years, was dirty and rundown. Always an advocate of a spotless and inviting park, Veeck cleaned and painted the stadium. To increase attendance, Veeck introduced Milwaukee fans to the innovative marketing schemes and promotions which were to become hallmarks of his baseball career.[11]

BILL VEECK—Cleveland Indians 1946–1949; St. Louis Browns 1951–1953; Chicago White Sox 1959–1962 and 1976–1981—Bill Veeck, "the people's owner," was ostracized by his peers throughout his career, but ultimately was recognized as one of baseball's most knowledgeable, astute, and innovative owners (National Baseball Hall of Fame Library, Cooperstown, NY).

Veeck put into practice what he wrote in the first of his three autobiographical books, "All I have ever said is that you can draw more people with a losing team plus bread and circuses than with a losing team and a long, still silence." He could often be found sitting in the stands mingling with patrons, a practice he would continue with all of his teams. But, in addition to enjoying the fans' company, Veeck wanted their opinions. His son, Mike, explained this practice. "It was just his way of doing market research."[12]

Spectators came to the ballparks because of Veeck's promotions as much as they did to see a ballgame. Fans were awarded gifts such as cakes of ice, stepladders, a duck and three uncaged pigeons. Cow-milking contests, pig races, and countless other competitions were constantly being held. At least one jazz band entertained spectators at each game. Veeck and Grimm even formed their own band at one point.[13] In addition to give-a-ways, Veeck also tried to accommodate his fans. He began scheduling some games in the morning to allow swing-shift workers from local industrial plants to attend the Brewers games.[14] At these morning games, Veeck would serve free cereal and coffee, and Veeck would attire his ushers in nightshirts.[15]

Veeck had not been in Milwaukee long before he began to alienate members of the baseball establishment. They were taken aback by the number and nature of his promotions, but they were most offended by his willingness to challenge the rules, as in the adjustable fence incident. Even though the distance from home plate to right field at Bochert Field was only 265 feet, it didn't help the Brewers' weak hitters. Veeck constructed a 60-foot chicken wire extension on top of the fence to turn the opposing teams' short home runs into long singles. By the second year of his ownership, the Brewers had vastly improved, so Veeck devised a system for raising and lowering the fence, depending on the hitting prowess of the visiting teams. When other teams complained to league officials, Veeck was ordered to stop using the fence, but he was able to show that there was nothing in the league rules to prohibit this practice. The league changed the rules the following day.[16]

Veeck's promotions may have caused organized baseball some concern. But they seemed to have an amazing effect on the Brewers both on the field and at the gate. From eighth place the first year of Veeck's ownership, they jumped to second place in the American Association in 1942 and won pennants in 1943, 1944, and 1945.[17] In 1941, the entire season's attendance totaled 73,000. Attendance for the following year increased to 273,589, the highest in minor-league baseball. Veeck's original debt of $85,000 was reduced to $17.[18] In 1942 *The Sporting News* named Bill Veeck minor league executive of the year.[19]

In December 1943, Bill Veeck enlisted in the U.S. Marine Corps and was sent to the South Pacific. Early in 1944, the recoil of an anti-aircraft gun crushed his right foot. He later admitted, "It was my own carelessness."[20] Because he left the hospital too quickly, his injury was never able to heal properly. In 1946, doctors were forced to amputate part of his leg. He was to have many more operations and would wear a wooden prosthesis the rest of his life.

He returned to the United States in mid–1945 and sold the Brewers franchise at the end of the season. Veeck had married Eleanor Raymond, a childhood sweetheart from Hinsdale, in 1935 and this marriage produced three children. His wife, a former circus elephant trainer, once stated that she was wrong in thinking that when she married Bill, she was through with circuses. Veeck hoped that selling the team and concentrating on his home life might salvage their shaky marriage.[21] With money from the sale of the Brewers, he bought a ranch in Arizona and retired to Tucson with his family.

By 1946, he was restless. His long-time friend, Harry Grabiner, who had been in the Chicago White Sox front office at the same time Veeck was with the Cubs, was also retired. Both men yearned to return to baseball. First Veeck and Grabiner tried to buy the White Sox, but the Comiskeys weren't selling.[22] Veeck next considered the Pittsburgh Pirates and the Cleveland Indians. He chose the Indians because he felt the Cleveland economy was stronger, the city owned a stadium that could hold more than 80,000 fans, and Cleveland appeared a better stage for the myriad of promotional stunts he had in mind to improve attendance.[23]

In order to buy the Indians, Bill Veeck put his business and law knowledge to good use. This was a time when wealthy people were in a 91-percent income-tax bracket and eager for legal tax breaks. The 42-year-old Veeck pioneered the use of a creative piece of financing called a debenture-common stock group. This venture allowed investors to put up money partly to buy stock and partly as a loan to the organization; the money paid back became nontaxable loan repayments, rather than taxable dividends.[24] On June 23, 1946, five years to the day after his Milwaukee purchase, Veeck & Co., a ten-man syndicate headed by Bill Veeck that included meat-packing executives, a motion picture executive, a bank president, film star Bob Hope, and former baseball great, Hank Greenberg, bought the Cleveland Indians for a reputed $1.6 million. Veeck owned 30 percent of the stock and control of the team, in return for his services and $250,000 of his own money.[25] Rudy Schaefer, Veeck's general manager at Milwaukee, was given the same duties in Cleveland.[26]

"The team looked hopeless," said Veeck, "so I bought it."[27] The Indians had not won a pennant since 1920 and had drawn only 289,000 fans for the first half of the 1946 season. League president Will Harridge, anticipating that Veeck would use some of the same antics which brought him notoriety in Milwaukee, warned Veeck that his stunts in Milwaukee were not appropriate for the major leagues. To some degree, Veeck heeded Harridge's warnings but advised the American League president that "Entertainment softens the pain of losing." Although he initially tried to tone down his efforts in Cleveland, Veeck did promote his club.

Veeck immediately won over the Cleveland fans with his quick wit, energy, curly blond hair, boyish good looks, and his casual attire. (Veeck never wore a tie, and was often referred to as "The Sport Shirt" by his critics and the press.) They soon found out that he was also eminently fair and truly respected his fans and his players. Veeck wandered through the crowd on his crutches and, as he mingled with the fans, a man patted him on the back and proclaimed, "This is the best darned thing that ever happened to this town."[28]

His first move was to improve the fans' access to the team by setting up a 10-line switchboard directly connected to team offices and removing the door of his own office. Next, Veeck demanded that his vendors sell larger hot dogs and more peanuts per bag when he discovered that fans were not getting enough for their money.[29]

Finally, to show his faith in his ability to raise attendance, Veeck abandoned the small ballpark where the Indians had played their weekday home games, and moved all home games to spacious Municipal Stadium. And the fans responded. When the 1946 season concluded, the Indians had topped the one million mark in attendance; and two years later, the team drew more than 2.6 million, a major league record for fourteen years.[30]

Veeck always felt that it was in Cleveland where he had his most success. What made his promotions unique — and successful — was the element of surprise. Veeck showed the other baseball moguls that imagination and surprise were superior to bland planned promotions.[31] Rudi Schaeffer succinctly summed up Bill Veeck's promotional skills. "Back before Bill stirred up the pot, the biggest promotion in the major leagues was to open the gates and say we're playing at three."[32]

Unlike other club owners, Veeck generally didn't advertise his promotional days, but preferred to wait until the fans came to the park before letting them in on the secret. On one occasion he gave away jackets to the first ten thousand fans entering the park. Another time he staged a race between the speedy Cleveland base-stealer, George Case, and world-famous sprinter Jesse Owens. Veeck encouraged people to think that any time they came to see the Indians play, that game could be special.[33]

In order to draw more women to the ballpark, Veeck immediately revived Ladies' Day, used often by his father in Chicago but discontinued in Cleveland for many years. He refurbished rest rooms, gave away nylon stockings which were still scarce following World War II, and had orchids flown in from Hawaii.[34] He installed a supervised nursery in the stadium so mothers could come out and root. "If husbands want to come," said Veeck, "I'll provide wife-sitters."[35] He encouraged all local radio stations to broadcast the games and invited all the mayors in Ohio to one night game as his guest. Between seasons, he toured the state to bring the Indians to the attention of towns outside Cleveland. Veeck was also the first American League owner to post National League results on his scoreboard as a service to the customers.[36]

For the 1946 and 1947 seasons, when the Indians were still a struggling team, Veeck signed two clowns to entertain the fans. In pre-game shows, Jackie Price would throw and catch a ball backwards or catch or throw standing on his head. He also could simultaneously throw three baseballs to three players, standing far apart.[37] At the suggestion of manager Lou Boudreau, Veeck hired Max Patkin to liven up the game itself. A good minor-league prospect before sustaining an arm injury in World War II, Patkin had developed a humorous coaching routine he delivered from the first-base coaching box whenever the manager put him in a game where the outcome was already determined. Wearing a baggy uniform, he would stand on his head, run through a multitude of absurd signs, and occasionally lose his pants.

Not everyone enjoyed his routines. Washington owner Clark Griffith complained that Patkin disrupted his players' concentration. Veeck quickly reminded Griffith that he had hired clowns Nick Altrock and Al Schacht on his coaching lines, making it hypocritical for him to object to Patkin now. When the 1947 season ended, Veeck figured he would have a much better team the next year and shipped Patkin and Price to entertain minor league crowds for the remainder of their contracts. [38]

Veeck's promotions were not very popular with the baseball commissioner, the press, or most of the other owners. They regarded Veeck as a dangerous maverick who had little respect for the traditions of the game and underminded the integrity of baseball. "However," noted Veeck, "I never noticed any of the owners,... looking quite that insulted when I handed them their share of the receipts."[39]

The team that Veeck inherited when he purchased the Indians in mid-season 1946 was not very good, finishing in sixth place, 36 games behind the pennant-winning Boston Red Sox.[40] In 1947, the Indians improved slightly, moving up to fourth, 17 games behind the New York Yankees.[41]

Veeck knew that the most important thing for his fans was a winning team. "If your ball club can win games, your patrons will go for anything you give them as an added attraction, and the nuttier it is the more they'll go for it. But if you have a bum team, all the sideshows in creation won't get them out, and keep them coming out."[42]

To give the Cleveland fans this winning baseball team, Veeck made a number of trades. In the autumn of 1946, in one of his biggest deals, Veeck acquired slugging second baseman Joe Gordon from the New York Yankees in return for hurler Allie Reynolds, and in a second trade with the Yankees, he sent Cleveland second baseman Ray Mack and catcher Sherman Lollar to New York for outfielder Hal Peck and pitchers Gene Bearden and Alan Gettel. Veeck then traded outfielder Gene Woodling to Pittsburgh for veteran catcher Al Lopez.[43]

In 1947, his best trade was one he did not make — he did not send popular player-manager Lou Boudreau to St. Louis. Boudreau had told Veeck that he needed a change of scene because he had managed the club too long, but the fans and press in Cleveland protested so vehemently that Veeck ultimately gave the skipper a new two-year contract. Veeck, however, not Boudreau, chose the coaching staff for 1948 season: Mel Harder, Bill McKechnie and Muddy Ruel.[44] Veeck was also enlarging his team's farm system and was operating a revolving door policy with his team roster. He jokingly commented, "We've got three teams: one here, one coming and one going."[45]

Near the end of the 1947 season, Bill Veeck became the first American League owner to break the color barrier. The Dodgers, of course, had made Jackie Robinson the first African-American player in the Major Leagues earlier that year. Bill Veeck claimed that he thought about signing a black player on the Milwaukee team as early as 1943, but had not. Possibly from a sense of regret, or possibly because he was annoyed that Branch Rickey was now getting credit for integrating baseball, he wrote in his 1962 autobiography, *Veeck — As In Wreck,* that he had planned to purchase the Philadelphia Phillies in 1943 and stock the club with top-notch Negro League players. According to his story, both Baseball Commissioner Judge Kenesaw Mountain Landis, and National League President Ford C. Frick, blocked his plans.

Three members of the Society for American Baseball Research (SABR) exhaustively researched this story and concluded that Veeck had fabricated it. "It is," claim the authors, "simply a case of historians wishing to believe Veeck's tale to be true."[46]

Whatever he had intended to do earlier, Veeck did sign Larry Doby, a second baseman from the Newark Eagles of the Negro National League, to a contract with the Cleveland Indians on July 5, 1947.[47] Veeck was determined to choose a player who would contribute to the long-term, rather than the short-term, interests of the Indians. Black sportswriters and other Negro League observers repeatedly told Veeck that Larry Doby was the logical choice.[48]

After signing Doby, Veeck met with the Indians players. "There were a couple of grumbles," recalled Veeck. "It was only the fringe players who had objections and I think it represented an economic threat to them. " Veeck told the dissenters that if they didn't accept Doby, they could play ball elsewhere. When three players refused to shake Doby's hand, Veeck traded them.[49]

In his first season, Doby was a poor second baseman and did little in his 32 at-bats, compiling only a .156 batting average.[50] Nevertheless, both Veeck and Boudreau felt that Doby had potential. Veeck decided to convert Doby into an outfielder and hired Tris Speaker, considered by many one of the greatest center fielders of all time, to teach Doby how to play the outfield. Indians coach Bill McKechnie and Hank Greenberg, one of the Indians' partners, also helped and encouraged Doby.[51]

With the benefit of this expert coaching, Doby finished the 1948 season with a .301 batting average, and played a prominent role in leading the Indians to the pennant and World Championship.[52]

Cleveland began the 1948 season by winning six straight games. The Indians, Athletics, and defending champion Yankees were neck and neck in early July when Bill Veeck made another controversial addition — pitcher Leroy "Satchel" Paige. Paige was the most famous pitcher in Negro League history; Cardinal star Dizzy Dean once called him the greatest pitcher he had ever faced. Boudreau opposed the move until Paige had a secret try-out at Municipal Stadium. After 15 minutes, Boudreau responded, "Sign him."[53] At the purported age of 42, Paige entered major league baseball for the first time.

Many sportswriters, particularly J. G. Taylor Spink , editor of *The Sporting News*, blasted Veeck for exploiting Paige. "To bring in a pitching rookie of Paige's age is to demean the standards of baseball in the big circuits." Said Veeck, "I signed Paige because he is the best man available to help us win."[54] But the best answer came from Paige himself as he demonstrated his still considerable pitching skill. "I demeaned the big circuits considerable that year," Paige said many years later. "I won six and lost one."[55]

By August, the 1948 pennant race had narrowed to a contest between the Boston Red Sox and Cleveland Indians. On September 26, with the Red Sox and Indians tied for first place, 76,772 fans watched Cleveland's Bob Feller win a five-hitter, giving the Indians a one-game lead. The Indians went into the final day of the season needing one more victory to clinch the pennant. Before another packed house in Cleveland, Detroit's Hal Newhouser defeated the Indians 5–1, while the Red Sox beat the Yankees 10–5.

For the first time in American League history, a one-game playoff was needed to determine the league champion. Behind the pitching of Gene Bearden, with Boudreau as one of the stars, Cleveland won the game and their first pennant in 28 years.[56]

The Indians faced the Boston Braves in the 1948 World Series, and although the Braves outhit the Indians and tied them in runs scored, most of the Braves' runs came in game five when they outlasted the Indians 11–10. The Indians, spreading their runs more evenly, defeated the Braves in the 1948 World Series, four games to two.[57] History was made when Satchel Paige became the first black pitcher to appear in a World Series game.[58] At the end of the season, *The Sporting News* named Bill Veeck major league executive of the year.[59]

Many baseball writers call 1948 the "Miracle on Lake Erie." Veeck helped explain why his Indians had been so successful that year. "I built an exciting ball club, several of my players had outstanding years, the city was starved for a pennant-winning team and I am one of the few owners who knows how to cultivate and entertain the guests— not bad for a team that operates in one of baseball's smallest markets and that in 1946 was still so penurious that it demanded the return of all foul balls hit into the stands."[60]

In fact, one of Veeck's most imaginative promotions occurred during the Indians' outstanding 1948 season. On September 9, 1948, factory night watchman Joe Earley and his wife, June, were reading a letter to the editor of the *Cleveland Free Press.* suggesting a Bill Veeck Night to honor the Cleveland owner for revitalizing the city. Earley wrote back to the *Press,* tongue in cheek, proposing that since Veeck had sponsored special nights "for everyone from Elks to Eskimos, why didn't the Indians hold an appreciation night for a fan, good old Joe Earley?"[61]

Eventually the letter reached Veeck's desk. Veeck liked the idea of honoring one fan who would represent all the fans who had helped his Indians set an all-time attendance mark that year. Local merchants volunteered to help Veeck honor Earley, who was completely unaware of the plans. Joe Earley knew only that because of his letter, he had been invited to Municipal Stadium as Veeck's guest to watch the Indians meet the Chicago White Sox. He hoped that in addition to his guest passes for that game, he might receive a couple of passes to a future game.

On September 28, 1948, the stage was set. Normally the Indians could expect a crowd of 35,000 fans for a game with the White Sox, but the pennant race and "Good Old Joe Earley Night," brought out more than 60,000 fans (many entering on free passes.) Earley was showered with gifts, both silly and genuine. He received a cow and a calf, two dogs, a swaybacked horse, a goat, a pig and eight piglets. Along with the livestock was a Model-T Ford, complete with a backfiring motor and fenders that fell off like a "circus" car.

On a more serious note, Veeck addressed the gathering and announced, "The things we're doing for Joe just typify the feeling of the Cleveland Indians baseball club for all you fans." He then awarded Earley a brand-new yellow Ford convertible, a year's supply of gasoline, phonograph records, lamps, an easy chair, a gold-plated lifetime pass to any American League contest and Veeck's personal check for $1,000.

General Manager Rudi Schaeffer always felt that the Earley promotion was Veeck's best. "It was a natural phenomenon ... so spontaneous. Compare it to what they do today. They give away a bat or ball, and it's called a promotion. To me, that's not a promotion, that's a giveaway. A promotion is something you generate out of thin air and make fly."[62]

In 1949, Bill Veeck was greatly disappointed when the Indians failed to repeat their pennant-winning performance, finishing in third place, eight games behind the New York Yankees. They did manage to draw another 2.6 million fans. Even if Veeck could not give his fans a pennant, he could still entertain them. Once the Indians had been mathematically eliminated from the pennant race, Veeck staged a mock funeral and buried the 1948 championship flag in Municipal Stadium before a home game with the Detroit Tigers. Veeck, wearing his usual sport shirt along with a stovepipe hat, drove the coffin bearing the flag to the flagpole in center field and stopped behind the wire fence. Rudie Schaffer read last rites from *The Sporting News* and the coffin was lowered into a grave, covered with flowers, and marked by an imitation tombstone inscribed "1948 Champs."[63]

Despite all Veeck's frivolous and promotions, he was one of the most knowledgeable men ever associated with baseball. He wrote widely about what was right with the game and what could be done to improve it. In the late 1940s, Veeck wrote a piece for *Look* magazine containing a number of suggestions for baseball. First, Veeck felt that the game moved too slowly. To speed it up, he wanted relief pitchers ready to enter games more quickly, and an end to arguments with the umpires. To encourage more children to play baseball, he urged adults to become involved and help sponsor teams. Most of all, he wanted baseball to improve the way "the product" was packaged. "Our attitude is that we've put a team on the field so we're entitled to sit back and rake in the sheaves. If any other business I know of cultivated the same merchandising philosophy, it would achieve bankruptcy in 30 days." His final point went far beyond baseball and expressed much of his basic philosophy. "No sermon from a pulpit can be as eloquent as a baseball team composed of every race, creed, and color, playing together in unity and harmony."[64]

After the 1949 World Series, Veeck's first marriage ended and, to raise the money he needed for his divorce settlement, he sold the Indians for $2.2 million to a syndicate headed by his protégé Hank Greenberg, and Ellis W. Ryan, an insurance executive.[65]

At about that time Bill met Mary Frances Ackerman, a onetime drama student who was a press agent for the Ice Capades. After dating for approximately two weeks, Bill proposed to her. They were married in the spring of 1950 and were to have six children.[66]

Bill Veeck did not remain out of baseball long. In 1951, attracted by another team that needed help, he, St. Louisans Mark Steinberg and Sidney Salomon, plus a group of backers from his Cleveland purchase, formed a new syndicate and bought the St. Louis Browns for $1.5 million from owner Bill De Witt. As part of the deal, Veeck also got Sportsman's Park, the home field of both major league teams in St. Louis.[67]

Shortly after he purchased the Browns, Veeck reassured St. Louis fans that he did not intend to move the team. "I have come here to accept a challenge and the Browns are it. Let me assure you that we have no plans to disturb the Cardinals either. This city is big enough to support two major league teams."[68] Veeck later admitted privately that he doubted St. Louis could support two major league teams and that he fully intended to drive the Cardinals, the city's favorite team for the past 25 years, out of town.

Veeck knew that he faced a tough assignment in building up the Browns, one of the most pathetic teams in major league baseball. Since they had entered the American League in 1902, the Browns had finished in the cellar eight times, in the second division 38 times and won their only pennant in 1944, when World War II had depleted baseball talent. They played so poorly in 1950, the year before Veeck bought the team, that owner Bill DeWitt hired a psychologist to hypnotize them into improving their play. The psychologist left after a few weeks with the Browns deep in the cellar with a record of 8–25.[69]

In 1950, the team drew only 247,131 fans and by July 1951, the Browns seemed headed for their usual dismal finish both on the field and at the gate. At the time of Veeck's purchase, the Browns' record stood at 21–49 and they were 23½ games out of first place.[70] After watching his new club play, even Veeck was forced to admit, "They were the worst looking collection of ballplayers I've ever seen," he said. "It hurt to look at them."[71]

The press quickly wanted to know how Veeck was going to improve them. "I don't expect I can get much help from other American League clubs and I have talked to them all." He also told them that he didn't plan to add any black players except for Satchel Paige. "There are not too many good Negro players left—fellows who can measure up to major league standards," he pointed out. "The younger crop is a couple of years away." Bill Veeck would soon learn that St. Louis was the most segregated city in Major League Baseball during the 1950s. Black players on visiting teams were forced to stay in black hotels, which were not air conditioned during the broiling St. Louis summers. Veeck complained to the local chamber of commerce, "[Black] baseball players are not coming to the Browns if they cannot get meals and hotel lodgings like all the other ballplayers," but except for a rare moment in 1952, when officials of the Chase Hotel allowed Satchel Paige to attend a team dinner, Veeck's plea went unheeded.[72,]

While he was trying to build a better team, Veeck was also employing the same strategies in St. Louis that had worked for him previously: a sense of humor, accessibility to the fans, and promotions. He and Mary Frances went on barnstorming tours to build up fan support for the Browns. Veeck would begin his pitch by apologizing for the poor play of his team, then adding, "We got rid of half of our players and we mean to get rid of the rest as soon as possible. Our secret weapon is to get a couple of Brownies on every team and louse up the League."[73] As he had done in Cleveland, he would answer the telephone at Sportsman's Park himself. Not long after he took over the Browns, a fan called asking what time the day game started. "What time can you get here?" Veeck responded.[74]

At home games, Veeck circulated among the crowd, often sitting and talking with the fans. He was particularly interested in women's opinions; their most common complaint was that the ballpark needed a good cleaning. Veeck got the fire department to bring in a hook and ladder unit to hose the place down. When a woman asked Veeck why he did not list the first names of the players on the scorecards, he had them put there the following day. He also began the practice of sending free tickets to the parents of all newborn babies in St. Louis.[75]

On July 4, 1951, Veeck hung a huge banner outside the ballpark, "Open For Business Under New Management." Between games of the holiday doubleheader, Veeck treated the fans to a gigantic fireworks display and supplied free beer and soda to the 10,932 in attendance. He rehired comics Jackie Price and Max Patkin to entertain the fans and Millie the Queen of the Air slid down a tightrope that stretched from right field to third base.[76]

Two of Veeck's most memorable stunts were held five days apart in August 1951. On August 19, the Browns played a doubleheader against the Detroit Tigers, attended by 18,000 people, the largest crowd at a Browns' game in four years. It was billed as a celebration of both the 50th anniversary of the founding of the American League and a birthday party for the Brown's radio sponsor, Falstaff Brewery, but Veeck's penchant for surprise was the highlight. After the usual Veeck between-game entertainment—jugglers, bands, acrobats, and dancers—the fans watched groundskeepers wheel out an oversized birthday cake. Out popped three-foot, seven-inch, 26-year-old theatrical midget, Eddie Gaedel, wearing a Browns' uniform with the number ⅛ on his back. The fans roared but the entertainment was far from over.

As the Browns batted in the bottom of the first, Bernie Ebert, the field announcer, declared, "Batting for Frank Saucier—No. ⅛—Eddie Gaedel." The midget came out swinging a small bat. Umpire Ed Hurley hurried to the Browns' dugout to protest, but Manager Zach Taylor showed him Gaedel's contract, which officially added the little man to the roster. Reluctantly, Hurley allowed Gaedel to bat.

Tiger pitcher Bob Cain wanted to lob the ball underhanded, but Hurley insisted he throw normally. Gaedel walked on four straight pitches. Just to prevent Gaedel from getting carried away at the plate, Veeck had warned him to keep the bat on his shoulder. "I've got a man in the stands with a high-powered rifle, and if you swing at any pitch, he'll fire."

When Gaedel reached first base, Jim Delsing was sent into the game to pinch run. After the game Gaedel told reporters, "For a minute I felt like Babe Ruth." American League President Will Harridge, who insisted Gaedel be released immediately, eventually agreed to include his appearance in baseball's official record.

According to Veeck, the origin of the stunt was not a James Thurber story as many believed, but rather a conversation with former Giants manager John McGraw, who spoke of a hunchback batboy named Eddie Morrow that McGraw had always wanted to send to the plate.

Just five days after Gaedel's appearance, Veeck held Grandstand Managers Day. About 1,100 fans were chosen to sit behind the dugout and indicate by boos, applause, and "yes" and "no" cards what they wanted the Brownies to do. Manager Zach Taylor relaxed in street clothes behind the Browns' dugout, puffing on his pipe and reading a newspaper. Two coaches held up large signs asking the grandstand managers whether to bunt, steal, pinch-hit, etc. Majority ruled. Unbelievably, the Browns defeated the Athletics that night 5–3 to end a five-game losing streak. Veeck announced that he would disband the group because it was best to "quit while you're ahead."[77] Zach Taylor resumed his managerial duties and the Browns proceeded to lose five of their next six games.[78]

Although Veeck's antics brought more fans to the ballpark in 1951, the team still ended at the bottom again with a 52–102 record, 46 games behind the first-place Yankees.[79] There were only two high points on the field that season: Ned Garver's 20 wins, the first time since 1924 that a pitcher had won 20 games for a last-place team;[80] and rookie outfielder Bob Nieman's two home runs his first two times at bat. They were his only home runs in 1951.[81]

Even if Veeck despaired of his team's play, he could always find pleasure in baiting Fred Saigh, the St. Louis attorney who owned the Cardinals. Veeck made every Saturday game Ladies' Day, as he had done in Milwaukee and Cleveland, and challenged Saigh to do the same thing. To taunt him and the Cardinals further, Veeck painted "Sportsman's Park, Home of the Browns" in huge letters on the most prominent outside wall of the ballpark and decorated the inside of the park with Brownie memorabilia.[82]

In 1952, Veeck further irked Saigh when he hired popular ex–Cardinals Harry Brecheen as pitcher-coach, shortstop Marty Marion as player-coach, Dizzy Dean as radio announcer, and Rogers Hornsby as manager. Veeck had long admired Hornsby even though his father had fired him as manager of the Cubs 20 years earlier. Hornsby lasted only 50 games before Veeck realized he had made a mistake and replaced him with coach Marty Marion.[83]

Unfortunately, Marion could do no better than raise the Browns one notch in the 1952 standings where they finished 31 games behind the Yankees.[84] One bright spot in the Browns' miserable season was the pitching of Satchel Paige, who posted a record of 12–10, with 10 saves and a 3.07 ERA.[85] The other was the Browns attendance of 518,796 fans for the season, more than in their 1944-pennant winning year. Their rivals, the Cardinals, drew fewer than a million fans for the first time since the end of World War II.[86]

If Cleveland was the high point in Veeck's career, St. Louis was undoubtedly the low. First, the other American League owners took actions to slash his already meager revenues as punishment for trying to cut into their profits. Veeck was already an outsider among his fellow owners, who felt that his promotions made them look "stuffy" and forced them to spend time and money to compete with him.[87] He irritated them further when he proposed a draft of minor-league players that would have distributed talent more evenly, making the weaker clubs more competitive.

Veeck became a complete pariah when he proposed that visiting teams share in local radio-television money since, as he pointed out, they provided half the show. After the American League club owners voted down Veeck's revenue-sharing plan 7–1, the Browns' owner refused to allow the televising of games in which the Browns were the visiting team. The other seven teams retaliated by changing the schedule for 1953 to eliminate all night games in St. Louis, a financial blow for Veeck.[88] Why did he make such a rash demand, he was asked later. "This was absolutely necessary," replied Veeck, "for if the Browns had been able to get a bigger cut of the gate and some of the television dough, we would probably still be in St. Louis and I still believe my argument was sound."[89] Ironically, the owners adopted a version of Veeck's minor-league plan just nine years later, and when TV revenues began to widen the gap between wealthy and poor teams, owners did agree to split national TV dollars equally among all clubs.[90]

But Veeck's final blow came not from the American League owners, but from the local National League team. Fred Saigh was indicted for income-tax evasion and sold the Cardinals to St. Louis-based Anheuser-Busch Breweries. Veeck knew that as a ball club, the Browns were not good enough to challenge the solidly entrenched Cardinals. As he later recalled, "The Browns never reached the point where they were a winning team, let alone a pennant contender. This hurt us tremendously in our effort to develop new fans, especially from out of town, where Cardinal superiority was reflected in the expansion of their radio network."[91] He also recognized the power of August Busch. "The Busch name is a solid tradition in St. Louis history and his unlimited capital makes him the ideal man for the community."[92]

Veeck announced that he intended to move the Browns out of St. Louis.[93] For 24 hours, he seriously considered going to Los Angeles but ruled it out because the only available place to play there was the oddly shaped Coliseum.[94]

His final two choices were Milwaukee, now the top farm club of the Boston Braves, and Baltimore, an independent International League team ever since the old Orioles had become the New York Yankees in 1903. Braves owner Lou Perini beat Veeck to Milwaukee when he announced that in 1953, he would move his major league squad there from Boston. This relocation ended 50 years of geographic stability in baseball.[95]

The picture looked bright in Baltimore. Jerry Hoffberger of the National Brewing Company in Baltimore offered Veeck $300,000 for the rights to sponsor the Browns if they came to Baltimore. As required, Veeck asked the American League owners for permission to move.[96] The other AL owners then played their cruelest trick on him. After assuring Veeck that he would get their approval, in Tampa in March 1953, they voted 6–2 to oppose his move to Baltimore. It was too near the opening of the season for such a drastic change, they claimed; yet, the very next day, the National League owners voted 8–0 to give Perini permission to transfer his team to Milwaukee immediately.[97]

In 1953 Bill Veeck was broke. Before the season began, Veeck hocked everything he possessed, including his Arizona ranch. He was forced to sell his best players in order to get through the year so that, hopefully, he might be able to move to Baltimore in 1954. Although it wasn't a smart business move, he sold Sportsman's Park to August Busch because the mortgage was in default and Veeck couldn't even pay for the park's upkeep. The Browns had no income from television or even from radio.[98]

To no one's surprise, the 1953 Browns once again finished in the cellar, winning only 54 games while losing 100.[99] One of the few highlights of an otherwise dreadful season occurred on May 6, when pitcher Bobo Holloman, in his only season in the major leagues, tossed a no-hitter against the Philadelphia Athletics in his first start. It was the fourth and final no-hit game in St. Louis Browns history. Only 2,473 hardy fans turned out on a chilly, rainy evening, and they received rain checks for their fortitude.[100]

Not that it really mattered what Veeck or the Browns did. A clique of

American League owners was determined to drive Veeck out of organized baseball. Del Webb of the New York Yankees headed this group, which included the Senators, Red Sox, Tigers, Athletics and Indians. They wanted the Browns to move to Baltimore but only in exchange for Veeck's agreement to sell out.[101]

Facing bankruptcy and receivership, on September 29, 1953, Veeck agreed to sell his syndicate's entire holdings to a Baltimore-based group led by Mayor Tommy D'Allesandro. The ball club, renamed the Baltimore Orioles, moved into the recently renovated Memorial Stadium where they remained until 1993 when Oriole Park at Camden Yards was opened.[102]

Once Veeck's sale of the Browns had been completed, he packed his suitcase but told reporters, "My departure does not mean that I am leaving baseball. In fact, like a bad penny, I'll probably turn up again somewhere." Veeck was sure that most of the American League owners were hoping it would not be in their league.[103]

Baseball magnates patted each other on the back. By forcing Veeck to sell the Browns and leave baseball, they had accomplished three objectives. First, Boston and St. Louis, which could each support only one major league team, now had that team — the Red Sox in Boston and the Cardinals in St. Louis. Second, the major leagues now had teams in Milwaukee and Baltimore, two former minor-league towns. And, finally, the close-knit major league magnates had rid themselves of Veeck, their most troublesome outsider.[104]

Many baseball historians were saddened by Veeck's departure from baseball. They claimed that Bill Veeck was the only major league baseball owner who realized that more and more people were seeking family entertainment they could enjoy together, and that baseball had to be promoted like any other entertainment.[105]

Although he would not return as an owner until late in the decade, Bill Veeck was not out of baseball. For a while, he worked for P. K. Wrigley, owner of the Chicago Cubs and the minor league team, the Los Angeles Angels of the Pacific Coast League. Veeck's job was to explore the possibilities of bringing major league baseball to the West Coast. " Major league baseball is definitely coming to the West Coast," Veeck stated, "sooner than most people think. Of that I feel certain."[106]

On February 3, 1955, Bill Veeck submitted his resignation to P.K. Wrigley, announcing "The work is done. We have developed a practical and workable plan to bring major league baseball to Los Angeles and San Francisco. It is now up to one of the major leagues to get up its collective nerve and expand into this wonderful new territory, with profit to itself and immeasurably greater prestige for the great game of baseball."[107] It was more than two years until Walter O'Malley took up that challenge. Although he certainly deserves credit for putting the plan in action, Bill Veeck should also be credited for laying the groundwork.

Between 1954 and 1959, Veeck tried to buy the Detroit Tigers and the Philadelphia Athletics. Both times, he felt, the Yankees were behind his losing bids. "The Yankees," he said, "hastened my departure from baseball and retarded my return."[108] In 1959, Bill Veeck returned to major league baseball, by becoming the majority partner of a consortium that bought the Chicago White Sox. It included his friend, former Detroit Tigers' star Hank Greenberg, and Chicago banker Arthur Allyn. He also got back at the Yankees when his White Sox won the pennant later that year. The White Sox were owned by Charles Comiskey's children: Chuck, with 46 percent, and his sister Dorothy Rigney, with a controlling 54 percent. Veeck and his syndicate purchased Dorothy's share for $2.7 million. Veeck had acquired not only his third major league team, but also a series of lengthy lawsuits and the perpetual enmity of Chuck Comiskey.[109]

No sooner had Veeck purchased the Chisox, than he began to make changes. "Comiskey Park is like a dungeon," he said. "So we tore down a few useless pillars and ripped out everything that hung overhead that loomed over you. We wanted to get away from that dungeonlike atmosphere to one of cleanliness and airiness." He painted the entire park white, inside and out. He established contact with the radar watchers around Chicago to get early warning of approaching storms so ushers could hand out plastic rain capes to fans in areas exposed to rain.

Veeck quickly learned that women disliked Comiskey Park. To change this attitude, Veeck stationed ushers immediately inside the gates to approach any woman who appeared confused and to escort her personally to her seat. He redecorated and cleaned up the once-offensive restrooms. He installed new lighting, full-length mirrors and various levels of vanity tables and placed cloth towels in the washrooms instead of paper towels "just to get a little class." He gave away roses, admitted mothers to the ballpark free on Mother's Day, and, on certain Sundays, gave away green stamps, instead of cigars or beer. Veeck's efforts paid off as the number of women attending White Sox games tripled. The overall White Sox attendance for 1959 doubled from the previous year to 1,423,144.[110]

In addition to setting an attendance record in 1959, Veeck's White Sox won their first pennant since 1919, the year of the "Black Sox Scandal." The 1959 White Sox were not a power-hitting team. In fact, they had the fewest homeruns (97) of any team that year, as well as the second-lowest team batting average. (.250) They did have speed, however, and the team was dubbed the "Go Go Sox" as they led the league with 113 stolen bases. Shortstop Luis Aparicio and center fielder Jim Landis combined for 76 of the 113 steals. In addition to speed, the Sox had one of the league's leading defensive second basemen in Nellie Fox, who led all American League second basemen with a .988 fielding average and also hit .306.[111] Fox's play that year earned him the Most Valuable Player Award in the American League.[112]

The 1959 White Sox also had solid pitching led by 18-game winner Bob Shaw and 22-game winner Early Wynn.[113] Wynn, a future Hall of Famer who was to chalk up 300 victories, had come to the White Sox from the Cleveland Indians in 1958 in a trade for Minnie Minoso. Wynn's 22 victories in 1959 earned him the Cy Young Award that year.[114]

The White Sox won their 1959 pennant by five games over the second-place Cleveland Indians and 15 games over the hated third-place New York Yankees, who had captured nine pennant flags between 1949 and 1958. In the NL, the Dodgers had won their first major league pennant since leaving Brooklyn, beating Milwaukee in a playoff game. The Dodgers went on to defeat the White Sox in the World Series in six games.[115]

During the 1959 season, Veeck's White Sox played an exhibition game with their crosstown rivals, the Chicago Cubs, before a crowd of nearly 30,000 fans. That same year, the Dodgers and Yankees played before more than 90,000 fans. "Just think," said Veeck, "neither of these games meant anything in the standings yet people turned out in droves because they wanted to see something different. My daddy first suggested interleague scheduling back in 1922 and I've been for it ever since," declared Veeck. He suggested that each club play a series with every team in the other league.[116]

Nineteen fifty-nine was also the year when Veeck put the names and the numbers of the Chicago White Sox players on the backs of their uniforms. Veeck admitted that he got the idea from watching a basketball game in Minneapolis one winter where the teams had the players' names on warm-up jackets. "But not on uniforms," added Veeck. "It occurred to me that baseball people didn't use names on their uniforms because they were afraid that it would louse up their program sales."[117] Once Veeck originated the practice, other owners copied him. Bing Devine, GM of the St. Louis Cardinals, was the first in the National League to do so.[118]

In 1960 the White Sox finished in third place, but White Sox fans probably remember 1960 primarily for Veeck's exploding scoreboard. The scoreboard cost Veeck $350,000, but he felt that White Sox fans enjoyed it more than any other promotion.[119] Personally, he felt that it was his best stunt. The scoreboard erupted into electric bedlam every time a White Sox player hit a home run. By simply pushing a button, the operator could bring forth a raucous din of foghorns, shrieks, sirens, and the sounds of battle. The 32-second performance also included rockets and blazing lights. Veeck stated that the idea for the scoreboard originated in a play, *The Time of Your Life*, by William Saroyan, in which the jackpot on a pinball machine went off with a barrage of roaring cannons and waving American flags.

The visiting teams, of course, were not amused by Veeck's new toy. On one occasion, Cleveland Indians outfielder, Jimmy Piersall, well-known for his violent temper, threw a baseball into the scoreboard after a game. This time, Veeck was not amused. He told Chicago sportswriter Jerry Holtzman that if Piersall ever pulled that stunt again, "We'll use our rocket launchers on him and we'll put him into orbit."[120]

White Sox manager Al Lopez felt that opposing teams would take the board in stride. "Veeck isn't doing it to rile anyone. He just wants to give the fans some added fun. It's nothing new," continued Lopez. "In St. Louis an eagle flies whenever a Cardinal player hits a home run." The flamboyant Veeck told his critics, " All my life, I've heard of gadgets which did everything but whistle Dixie. Well, I finally got the perfect squelch to those wise guys. This board of mine … even whistles Dixie."[121]

The same year Veeck introduced his exploding scoreboard, the *Sporting News* announced its plans to award a trophy to honor the best relief pitchers in each league. Veeck applauded this plan as a step in the right direction and felt that this award would help upgrade the salary scale of the relief pitcher. Veeck also suggested a change in the scoring rules regarding winning and losing pitchers. "The practice of almost always awarding a victory to the pitcher of record is an injustice," said Veeck. "Sometimes a succeeding relief pitcher is much more effective, but the system says that in all but exceptional cases, the pitcher of record when his team takes the lead should get the win. Obviously the relief pitcher often does not receive credit for an outstanding performance."[122]

Veeck also expressed his views on the quality of umpiring in the major leagues that year by installing what he called an "Eye-in-the-Sky" camera. Said Veeck, "As soon as we began using the camera — which takes a thousand frames a second, and can show every step of a close play — there wasn't one heated argument or big boner. Lethargic umpires knew they were being double-checked." To avoid even more "bad umpiring," he also proposed that umpires go to spring training like the players and called for an official umpiring school. Of course, he also suggested that his camera be installed in more parks.[123]

The 1961 White Sox ended the season in fourth place. In increasingly ill health, Veeck nonetheless did his best to keep the fans entertained. In 1959, Veeck hired his famous midget, Eddie Gaedel and three other little people to drop out of a helicopter dressed as Martians and surround the diminutive Chisox double play combination of Luis Aparicio and Nellie Fox. The "Martians" told the crowd they had arrived to help the duo in their fight against the "giant earthlings."[124]

In April of 1961, Veeck called on Gaedel for the last time. Fans at Comiskey Park had complained that the vendors blocked their view of the game, so he hired Gaedel plus seven other midgets to sell peanuts and soda in front of the box seat section. By that time Gaedel was suffering from high blood pressure and an enlarged heart.[125] Two months later, he was badly beaten in a street mugging in Chicago and died of a heart attack. Bob Cain, the former Tiger pitcher who walked him in St. Louis, flew with his wife to Chicago to attend Gaedel's funeral. "I felt I owed my respects to him and his mother. I'll never forget the little man who affected my life so much."[126]

After the 1961 season, Veeck's leg caused him constant pain. It had been amputated at the knee during World War II, but doctors told him the rest of his leg had to come off, too. They also told him that he had enlarged blood vessels in the brain that required complete rest. In 1962 Veeck sold the White Sox to Arthur Allyn, Jr., the son of one of his partners.[127]

This time, Veeck would have no official connection with the game of baseball for close to 15 years. After the sale of the White Sox, Veeck moved to an estate on Maryland's Eastern Shore, regained his strength, and wrote the first of his three books with ghostwriter Ed Linn. By 1965, he once again was offering advice to improve major league baseball. He called for both offensive and defensive platooning of players, a permanent pinch-hitter for pitchers (a precursor of Finley's designated hitter), and a wider home plate. To speed up the game, Veeck suggested changing from four balls and three strikes to three balls and two strikes (another issue Finley would try to institute), and allowing a batter to walk without the pitcher actually delivering four balls. "The result will be continuous action and more excitement," said Veeck. Four years before expansion and divisional play, Veeck predicted that baseball would wind up with two leagues of 12 teams each, and that the leagues would adopt inter-league as well as inter-division schedules.[128]

Veeck tried to advance his ideas about baseball to anyone who would listen to him, including baseball commissioners. In 1965, when William Eckert replaced Ford Frick as Commissioner of Baseball, Veeck wrote an extensive article in *True* magazine, offering him words of advice. He suggested expanding the American League by adding teams in Oakland and Dallas-Fort Worth, stocked with players from the existing teams. Expansion teams would be allowed only two players each from any one club's active list. He also suggested that the commissioner re-schedule the "Game of the Week" from Saturdays to Mondays and make it the only major league game that day.[129]

During his hiatus from baseball, Veeck thought about the game a great deal. He not only wrote numerous baseball articles and books, he also assembled a little black box full of ideas. "And they're all new," he said. "Everybody's using my old ideas — pyrotechnic scoreboards, names on uniforms, bat days etc." "Actually," Veeck admitted, "my little black box is … a file cabinet in my Maryland home. There's about 1,500 ideas in one drawer, and I'm working on a second drawer now."[130]

There was no question that Bill Veeck longed to return to major league baseball. The Baltimore Orioles seemed the likeliest prospect, but his 1975 attempt to purchase the team fizzled. Veeck's next opportunity came even sooner than he anticipated. Organized baseball was going through an unsettling time in 1975. The Seattle Pilots had moved to Milwaukee in 1970. The city of Seattle retaliated with a $32.5 million lawsuit against major league baseball and demanded a replacement team immediately. Meanwhile, Charles Finley, owner of the Oakland Athletics, had been constantly attempting to move his team out of town, preferably to Chicago. The American League was pressuring Chicago White Sox owner John Allyn to sell his team to a group from the state of Washington that included comedian Danny Kaye. This would solve three problems. First, by moving the White Sox to Washington, Seattle would drop its lawsuit. Second, selling the team would relieve John Allyn's horrendous financial situation in Chicago. He could not meet his payroll and was being sued by his brother, Art. Finally, Charles Finley, who felt that Oakland was not supporting his championship A's, could own Chicago's American League franchise.[131]

Allyn refused to cooperate, announcing that he could not care less about pleasing the American League, Chuck Finley, or the city of Seattle. Instead, he accepted a bid from a new syndicate headed by Bill Veeck. At a league meeting on December 3, 1975, the owners turned down Allyn's sale of the White Sox to Veeck by a vote of 8–3 with one abstention. Even after all this time, Veeck was still not "one of the boys." They thought Veeck's debenture-stock capitalization plan was inadequate and they generally didn't like his way of doing business. They countered with what they thought was an impossible offer. If Veeck could come up with an additional $1.2 million in ten days, they might reconsider their previous vote. Much to their consternation, Veeck met their condition with the help of Jack Brickhouse, the Chicago Cub's announcer, who got Veeck the funds he needed from Canteen Corporation, a Chicago-based sports concessions firm.[132]

Even though Bill Veeck had secured his needed capital, he fell one vote short when the owners voted again. It took an appeal by Detroit Tiger owner, John Fetzer, to save him. "We've got to be men about this," he told his fellow owners. "Look, I don't like allowing a guy in here who once called me a sonofabitch over and over. But gentlemen, we've got to take another vote." On the second vote, by a margin of 10–2, Veeck received the necessary votes to purchase the White Sox.[133] Bill Veeck and his partners paid $8 million for 75 percent of the team stock, while John Allyn retained a 25 percent share.[134]

Veeck, the man who brought in the first black player in the American League, also brought the first African-American into baseball's ownership ranks. In arranging the White Sox deal, Veeck included in the syndicate Chicagoan John Harold Johnson, owner of *Ebony* and *Jet* magazines, as one of the smaller stockholders.[135]

Veeck's first action after the White Sox deal was approved may have caused some of the ten owners who voted for him to have second thoughts. Promising that he would not negotiate secret deals, Veeck and his general manager, Rollie Hemond, set up desks in the hotel lobby and made four trades within full view of spectators.[136] Veeck's fellow owners realized that with Veeck back in baseball, they needed to brace themselves for a shock wave of gags, gimmicks, and promotions sure to please the fans.

After Veeck sold the White Sox in 1961, Comiskey Park had been renamed White Sox Park. Veeck pleased many of the White Sox fans by announcing that not only would the field be known as Comiskey Park, it would also have real grass in the infield again. The previous owners had installed synthetic turf to save money. In typical Veeck fashion, he invited fans to come to Comiskey Park prior to the start of the 1976 season and remove the nylon turf with their bare hands.[137]

Within weeks after buying the team, Veeck began to realize that his timing could not have been much worse. Baseball was entering the era of free agency, where Veeck was going to be at a decided disadvantage.

In the spring of 1975, pitchers Andy Messersmith and Dave McNally, acting on the advice of their attorneys, refused to sign the contracts they had been offered for that year. Rather than holdout, both pitchers played without contracts. When the season ended, the two hurlers asked the Players Association to file for arbitration in their behalf. A three-member panel judged their case: Marvin Miller of the Major League Baseball Players Association, spoke for the players, and John Gaherin had been hired by the owners to represent management. The third member, Peter Seitz, an attorney and professional arbitrator, cast the deciding vote, ruling that by playing an entire season without a contract, the two pitchers had freed themselves from their clubs' reserve rights and were free agents. The 100-year-old reserve clause was dead.[138] Many baseball observers have noted that had Seitz's ruling come before Veeck had completed negotiations for the White Sox, the deal might not have been made.[139]

Under free agency, owners without "deep pockets" soon found themselves desperately trying to compete with the wealthier magnates. Bill Veeck had no income outside baseball and his organization lacked the capital to afford high-priced free agents . Other owners were able to get tax breaks by depreciating part of their players' contracts each year. The White Sox syndicate, which had been organized as a corporation, could not take these write-offs unless the team was profitable. Even with Veeck's promotions, the Sox would never draw the one million fans needed to be in the black.[140]

It was ironic and more than a little sad that Bill Veeck should have been one of the first victims of free agency. From the time when Judge Landis was Commissioner, Veeck had opposed the reserve clause and advocated making players free agents. In his younger days, while attending college night classes, Veeck had studied contract law, particularly the way it related to baseball, and had concluded that the reserve clause was "morally and legally wrong."[141]

Over the years, Veeck did not change his attitude toward the reserve clause. In the 1970 antitrust suit filed by Curt Flood against major league baseball, Bill Veeck testified on behalf of Flood, arguing that changes could be made in the reserve system that would not harm the successful operation of baseball. He offered two alternatives: a "Hollywood" contract under which a club could "reserve" a player's use for a set period of time, usually seven years, and then could renew its option on the player in return for a scheduled raise; and a "football" contract that allowed a player to play without a contract and become a free agent at the end of the season, but his new club would have to pay a calculated cost to his old team for developing the player.[142]

Despite the problems, Veeck's second ownership of the White Sox lasted five seasons, from 1976 to 1980. During those five years, the team's performance and Veeck's pressure to succeed were reflected in the number of managers Veeck employed. When Veeck took over the club, he fired incumbent manager Chuck Tanner and replaced him with Paul Richards, who had originally managed the White Sox from 1951 to 1954. In 1976, the White Sox finished sixth in a six-team division.[143]

Veeck replaced Richards at the beginning of the 1977 season with former pitching great, Bob Lemon, who was named Manager of the Year for his 90–72 record that year. The White Sox finished third in a division that had increased to seven teams.

Veeck fired Lemon midway through the 1978 season and replaced him with Larry Doby. Doby, the first African-American to play in the American League, became the second black manager in baseball.[144] Doby remained the manager for the rest of the 1978 season. Veeck then hired former Cub shortstop Don Kessinger as manager for 1979, but he was in charge of the club for only 100 games when he, too, was fired. Kessinger knew the fundamentals of the game but, because of clubhouse dissension during the 1979 season, Veeck brought in Tony LaRussa. LaRussa managed the White Sox until the middle of the 1986 season, when he went to the Oakland A's.[145] The White Sox finished in fifth place all three seasons, 1978, 1979, and 1980.[146]

Since Veeck didn't have the money to acquire top-notch, high-priced stars through the free-agent market, he was forced to use his creative abilities to get good players. Veeck developed the "rent-a-player" plan, which allowed the White Sox to acquire star performers in the last years of their contracts, fully aware that they would sign with another club when the contract ended. This system helped add key players, particularly during the 1977 season, when Veeck was able to obtain free-agents-to-be Richie Zisk and Oscar Gamble. Zisk and Gamble combined to clout 61 home runs for the White Sox that year. The following year, Gamble signed with the San Diego Padres and Zisk with the Texas Rangers.[147]

In addition to creative player staffing, Veeck gave White Sox fans the kind of promotions with which he was always associated. He hosted a Shakespeare night, nights honoring almost every ethnic group in Chicago, and a so-called Superstition Night, when witches were invited to cast spells on the opposing teams. He reactivated 54-year-old Minnie Minoso as a designated hitter. Although Minoso was only one for eight in the three games in which he appeared, he was now able to brag that he had played in four different decades. Veeck began the tradition of having White Sox announcer, Harry Caray, sing "Take Me Out to the Ballgame," during the seventh-inning stretch, a custom Caray took with him to the Cubs. Although others claimed credit, most baseball observers say that having players take curtain calls after hitting homeruns was Veeck's idea. Not all his ideas succeeded. The White Sox players were embarrassed when they had to don uniforms with short pants, and wore them only in the first game of a double-header against the Kansas City Royals, August 8, 1976.[148]

One of Veeck's last and most disastrous promotions took place July 12, 1979. Billed as "Disco Demolition Night" and devised by a local disc jockey, fans were admitted to the game for 98 cents and a disco record to be burned between games of the double header with the Detroit Tigers. Fifty thousand fans filled Comiskey Park, and 5,000 more rushed the gates and entered the park without paying. Between games, when the disc jockey began destroying thousands of records as planned, youthful invaders, including many who had been smoking marijuana, ran onto the field, creating havoc, destroying property, and overwhelming Veeck's security force. The Chicago Police were called to restore order as firemen valiantly tried to put out the blazes caused by the demolition of the records. Meanwhile, Veeck stood on the field pleading in vain with the crowd, "Please get off the field; please get off the field."[149]

Umpire crew chief Dave Phillips announced that the White Sox would forfeit the second game of the double header because of "inadequate crowd control and damage to the playing field, both of which are the responsibility of the home team." For only the fourth time in American League history, a major league team forfeited a baseball game.[150]

Though Veeck was still a master at creating entertainment and fun at the ball park, during the years from 1975 to 1980, he was not able to offer his fans the kind of winning team he wanted. More importantly, he failed to recognize that attracting the individual fan was no longer enough to make a ball club successful. He missed out on season ticket sales, because he found it distasteful to market to the businesses and corporations that were buying the bulk of the season tickets. Veeck also failed to increase revenues through TV rights, even though the Cubs station WGN was paying him very little and Chicago was one of the top media markets in the country.[151]

Toward the end of the 1980 baseball season, Bill Veeck's health began to fail again. He had chronic emphysema, resulting from smoking four packs of cigarettes a day. What remained of his leg was constantly infected, which required multiple operations. He was also going deaf and he was becoming depressed by both his poor health and the poor play of the White Sox. In August 1980, Veeck announced that he had agreed to sell his team for $20 million to multi-millionaire Edward DeBartolo, who had made his fortune in shopping malls and banks. DeBartolo was the chief stockholder in the Pittsburgh Penguins of the NHL, owned three racetracks and had a son who owned the San Francisco Forty-Niners of the National Football League.

The other American League owners and Commissioner Bowie Kuhn adamantly opposed the proposed sale. They argued that De Bartolo was not a Chicagoan and there was no guarantee he would keep the White Sox in Chicago. In fact, there were rumors that he intended to move the team to New Orleans. Italian-American groups accused Kuhn of ethnic bias, claiming that he and some of the owners feared that because of De Bartolo's ancestry, he had ties to Mafia gangsters and the underworld. Whatever the reasons, on two occasions the American League voted down DeBartolo's bid to purchase Veeck's White Sox.[152]

Veeck was then approached by a local group headed by 49-year-old suburban real estate developer Jerry Reinsdorf and his friend and fellow classmate from Northwestern Law School, Edward Einhorn, offering to buy the team. On January 29, 1981, Bill Veeck and his partners sealed the deal for approximately the same figure De Bartolo had offered. The members of the syndicate, including Veeck, all did well financially, but Veeck despised and resented the new White Sox owners. Reinsdorf perceptively summed up the reason. "We represented something to Bill he didn't like ... we were what he considered corporate types, suits and tie guys."[153]

As usual, Veeck had the last word. "I didn't like the American League owners when I came into the league, and I don't like them going out of it."[154] He added, "Only [Calvin Griffith and I] had our would-be wealth totally invested. All other owners are a corporate entity fed by advertising campaigns and ego trips."[155] When Bill Veeck left major league baseball for good in 1981, more than one-third of the clubs had owners with less than five years in baseball.[156]

Bill Veeck never again set foot in Comiskey Park, but went back to where he had started in baseball — watching the Chicago Cubs at Wrigley Field — only this time he sat in the bleachers. Veeck had a lifetime pass to any major league game, but he preferred to pay his way into the ball park where he had helped plant the ivy on the outfield walls.[157] "By paying," he would always say, "I kept my right to complain."[158]

Even though he had left the game of baseball and his health continued to deteriorate, Bill Veeck still had ideas about on how the game might be improved. He thought that both leagues should have the same rules regarding the DH, either keeping or discarding it together, and he wanted to realign the two leagues into three divisions and arrange regional contests between the leagues.[159]

On January 2, 1986, Bill Veeck died of a heart attack at the age of 71. He had entered Illinois Masonic Medical Center a few days earlier after suffering shortness of breath. His survivors included his wife, four daughters, four sons, six grandchildren and a sister.[160]

Veeck was eulogized by many as a man who truly loved baseball and life. His good friend, Bill Costello, noted these qualities, saying, "He had his strong beliefs and priorities, but he never let them consume him. He always saw the folly that went with the dreams. He lived life and he loved every minute of it."[161] Hank Greenberg, Veeck's longtime friend and frequent partner, praised Veeck's integrity and humanity. "The only owner I ever knew who gave a damn about his players was Bill Veeck."[162] Ken

Holtzman, former star pitcher for the Oakland A's and Chicago Cubs, served as a player rep and met Veeck frequently. Holtzman praised Veeck's vision and stated, "I have never heard a player say anything bad about Veeck."[163]

Despite all the innovations and promotions people attribute to Bill Veeck, it should not be forgotten what a shrewd and knowledgeable baseball person he was. Only three times from 1947 to 1964 did the Yankees lose the American League pennant and all three times a Veeck-related team beat them. Veeck won a World Championship in Cleveland in 1948, and even though he was not associated with the Indians in 1954 when they won the pennant again, it was a team Veeck had built. Veeck's White Sox also took the American League title in 1959.[164]

It was not until 1991, five years after Veeck's death, that the 18-member veterans committee elected him posthumously into the Baseball Hall of Fame. Many sportswriters firmly believed that Veeck should have been inducted while he was still alive, but they also were realists. Jerome Holtzman, a Hall of Fame sportswriter who covered Veeck for the *Chicago Tribune*, said, "I never thought he would get in because he was not popular with baseball people. He always felt they took things too seriously. But he was worthy. He was a skilled operator, a great marketer and a colorful figure."[165]

Tony La Russa, the last person to manage a team for Bill Veeck, spoke for many admirers of Veeck when he said, "He loved the game of baseball but he never forgot the game is for the fans."[166] Veeck once predicted that his epitaph would read, "'He sent a midget up to bat'…. I really wouldn't mind that," he said, "but I'd like it to be cleaned up a bit to read more piously, 'He helped the little man.'"[167] Veeck got his wish. His plaque in the Hall of Fame reads "Bill Veeck, A Champion of the Little Guy."[168]

7

Charles Finley
The Maverick

Charles Finley was like Bill Veeck in two ways: he was a master promoter, and he was an outcast among the other owners who detested him and opposed his ideas whenever possible. Unlike Veeck, who grew up in the game, Finley was formally in major league baseball for only 20 years, but his innovations made the game far more colorful and more accessible to the average fan. Even more impressive, many of his changes to the rules and strategies of play were so logical that they became part of the game, even though they came from Charlie Finley.

Charles Oscar Finley was born February 22, 1918, in Ensley, Alabama, outside of Birmingham. He was one of seven children of Oscar and Burmah Finley. His father worked in the steel mills and Finley remembers his family as being poor but never going hungry. His father once told him, "Son, a man's fortune rests in the palm of his hands. Now get out and use those hands."[1] Charlie Finley heeded his father's advice and worked numerous odd jobs to supplement the family's meager income. He was a born salesman, once winning a medal and a bicycle for selling 12,500 subscriptions for the *Saturday Evening Post.*[2] He bought reject eggs for five cents a dozen and sold them for 15 cents. He even picked grapes and made wine, which he sold to his neighbors.[3] Charlie Finley was also a born maverick. The picture in his high school yearbook was captioned: "He who mischief hatcheth, mischief catcheth."[4]

In 1934, when Finley was 16 years old, the family moved to Gary, Indiana, where his father got a job at United States Steel Works. Finley worked in the steel mills with his father for 47 cents an hour while he attended Gary Junior College and the University of Indiana at night. He completed a course in engineering in three years, but still found time to play first base for the semi-pro La Porte Cubs in the Gary suburb of LaPorte, Indiana. Baseball had been his life's passion since he worked as a 50-cents-a-day batboy for the Birmingham Barons in the Southern Association. Later in life, he would tell anyone who would listen, "I always wanted to be a professional player, but I never had the talent to make the big leagues. So I did the next best thing. I bought a team."[5]

At the age of 19, Finley actually "owned" his first team, the Gary Merchants. He convinced retailers to contribute $25 in return for putting the store's name on a player's shirt. He then purchased sweatshirts for 98 cents and had the names stenciled on, making a hefty profit on each one.[6]

Finley married Shirley McCartney in 1941; the marriage was to produce seven children. When World War II broke out, Finley attempted to enlist, but was rejected by all four branches of service because he had an ulcer. He finally found a way to help his country by taking a defense-related job at the Kingston Ordinance Plant, which manufactured small-caliber ammunition for the government. At night, Finley began selling life insurance for the Travelers Insurance Company and, when the war ended, insurance became his fulltime profession.[7]

Finley shattered all records at Travelers Insurance Company for selling accident policies in a single year, but he paid a price for his success. In 1946, when he was only 28 years old, he developed a hacking cough and a tightening in the chest. His doctor diagnosed an advanced case of pneumonic tuberculosis, a disease that was considered incurable at the time. According to his physician, Charlie's only chance for survival was complete rest. He was admitted to the James O. Parramore Hospital in Crown Point, Indiana, where he remained from 1946 to 1948.[8]

During his 27-month stay in the hospital, Finley had a great deal of time to think about the irony of his situation. He sold insurance for a living; yet, he had no insurance to cover his own disaster. His wife was forced to return to work to keep the family going.[9] He also realized that there were countless self-employed people in his same predicament. They lacked insurance, but since they were not covered by a group plan, they were unable or unlikely to buy it on their own. Physicians, in particular, seemed to fit this description.

When he left the hospital, Finley concentrated on selling insurance to doctors, using his personal experience as a key selling point. The genius of his plan was that he worked through local and national professional organizations, from the Lake County Medical Society, to the American College of Surgeons, creating group plans that offered greater coverage for the individual doctors. Finley earned hundreds of thousands of dollars in commis-

CHARLES FINLEY— Kansas City A's 1961–1967; Oakland A's 1968–1980 — Self-made millionaire Charles Finley was one of the most disliked owners in baseball history, but colorful uniforms and the designated-hitter rule were just part of his legacy to the game (National Baseball Hall of Fame Library, Cooperstown, NY).

sions. He made his first million two years after forming his own insurance firm, Charles O. Finley Company of Chicago. He soon became a millionaire many times over.[10]

Charlie Finley was ready to buy a major league baseball team. During the 1950s, he tried and failed four times. His first attempt was in 1954 when he tried to purchase the Philadelphia Athletics. The Athletics were a team with little talent, playing their home games in an aging ballpark. Connie Mack, longtime owner and manager, had sold off many of his better players. Mack retired in 1950 and, four years later, his son Roy put the team up for sale. Unfortunately for Finley, Arnold Johnson, a business associate of Yankees co-owner Dan Topping, had better connections and more money. Johnson bought the Athletics and immediately moved the team to Kansas City, Missouri.[11]

Finley was also unable to purchase the Detroit Tigers in 1956. In 1958 he entered the bidding for the Chicago White Sox, but Bill Veeck and his associates bought that team. When the American League expanded in 1960, Finley tried to gain control of the Los Angeles Angels franchise. In an effort to counter the group headed by cowboy star Gene Autry, Finley attempted to bring Roy Rogers into his syndicate. However, Autry's group won the bidding.[12] Commenting on Finley's six-year effort to purchase a major league baseball team, one executive stated, "I never saw anybody who wanted to get into baseball so badly. He'd have bought anything."[13]

On March 10, 1960, Kansas City owner Arnold Johnson suffered a fatal heart attack in Florida during spring training. A short time later, Connie Mack's son, Roy, also died. In December, Johnson's heirs sold their 52 percent of the Athletics to Finley for nearly $2 million. Over the objection of her two sons, Roy Mack's widow sold Finley the Mack family shares in the Athletics for a similar amount. After 72 years, the Macks were out of baseball.[14] By Christmas 1960, Charles Finley had finally realized his dream — he owned a major league baseball team.[15] The dream cost him nearly $4 million.[16] At the time he purchased the Athletics, he and Red Sox owner, Tom Yawkey, were the only sole owners in major league baseball.[17]

Although he had successfully purchased the Athletics, the other baseball magnates distrusted him. Joe Inglehart, chairman of the Baltimore Orioles, was given the responsibility of "checking Finley out," and warned his fellow-owners, "Under no conditions should this person be allowed into our league."[18] After Finley had complete control of his club, he was made to feel like an intruder. "The old-time owners didn't accept me then, and I don't think they ever will. I didn't inherit a team. I didn't work my way up through the minor leagues as an executive. At the first major league meeting after I had bought the Athletics and Gene Autry had bought the Angels, [Commissioner] Ford Frick ... didn't even have the courtesy to introduce either of us to the National League owners."[19]

In fairness, there were a number of reasons why Finley was ostracized. The rather attractive 6-foot, 200-pound Finley was hard to like. He was loud, opinionated, duplicitous, caustic, brash, foulmouthed, and insensitive. According to sports columnist, Jim Murray, he never let anyone forget that he was a self-made millionaire, inserting into every conversation his slogan: " Sweat Plus Sacrifice Equals Success.[20]

One of Finley's first moves after he purchased the Kansas City team was to change its name from the Athletics to simply the A's. Finley explained that the name Athletics was too closely associated with the losing clubs of former Philadelphia owner Connie Mack.[21] Not that the current team didn't deserve the association. In 1960, the Athletics finished last, winning only 58 games while losing 96. In fact, in 27 seasons in Philadelphia and Kansas City, the Athletics finished in the first division only twice. Finley jokingly remarked, "I wanted to get into baseball in the worst way and that's what I did."[22]

He soon learned that under his predecessor, Arnold Johnson, Kansas City actually functioned like a farm club for Dan Topping's Yankees. From 1955 to 1960, the Yankees and the Athletics traded 29 players and the Yankees almost always got the better of the trades. The Athletics sent stars such as Roger Maris, Hector Lopez, and Ralph Terry to the Yankees in exchange for questionable and generally over-the-hill players. The league-leading 1960 New York Yankees could thank their "farm club" for supplying the players who helped them win the pennant.[23]

Finley never forgave the Yankees for taking advantage of his team. Reminiscent of Clark Griffith, who also bitterly hated the New Yorkers,

Finley attempted to "punish" them.[24] First, he promised not to send any more of his players to the Yankees, and symbolically burned a bus behind the left field wall in the A's ballpark to show that the shuttle to New York had ended. "I gave the fans in Kansas City my word we would not trade with the Yankees," he said, "and my word is my bond." Six days later, Finley defaulted on that bond and traded pitcher Bud Daley to the Yankees for Deron Johnson and Art Ditmar.[25]

Finley also contended that the Yankees had won so many pennants because it was easy to hit home runs in Yankee Stadium. Playing half their games there, Finley maintained, gave the Yankees an unfair advantage. He proposed that the American League compel the Yankees to erect a screen in front of the lower right field stands asserting, "We owners in baseball should take steps to force the Yankees to bring their stadium up to par with the other parks.... Yankee domination is the worst thing that ever happened — and it can be ended overnight."[26]

American League President Joe Cronin turned down Finley's request to change Yankee Stadium, so Finley built what he called a Pennant Porch in Kansas City. The porch sat behind a fence that started at the right field foul pole, 325 feet from home plate, cut in across the outfield to match Yankee Stadium's 296-foot dimension, and then went off toward center field. Cronin and Commissioner Ford Frick ordered Finley to remove the bizarre fence or forfeit the A's home games. Finley bitterly replied, "So what? We lost most of our home games anyway." He did move his fences back and changed the name of the pavilion to "One-Half Pennant Porch."[27]

He also threatened to put up a monument in his park to honor Connie Mack, just as the Yankees had honored Babe Ruth, Lou Gehrig, and Miller Huggins. He never carried out that threat, claiming that the league would not allow it. Finley did install something far more galling to the officials: a 20-second electric clock to check the time it took a pitcher to deliver the ball to home plate with no runners on. Over the loudspeaker, Finley explained to the fans that the clock was a reminder that a major league rule allowed only 20 seconds for the pitcher to throw the ball, but that the rule was seldom enforced. The umpires complained bitterly and Finley responded, "I'm not trying to be popular. I'm trying to make it a fair game." The clock eventually came down.[28]

Charles Finley's A's were in Kansas City only seven seasons, from 1961 through 1967. During that time, the team finished higher than seventh only once and occupied the 10th-place cellar four times.[29] Understandably, few people came out to see the A's home games. To help attract fans to the ballpark, Finley, like Bill Veeck, began promoting the game by offering gimmicks designed to increase attendance. But he was more than a promoter;

many of his attractions also changed the game of baseball. He often commented, "The trouble with baseball is that it's got its head in the sand. What the game needs is progressive thinking and new ideas."[30]

Charlie refurbished Municipal Stadium, spending more than one-half million dollars on remodeling.[31] He made sure the rest rooms were clean, added pizza and other crowd favorites to the concession menu, and reserved a special area along the left-field line for disabled drivers. Finley put lights in the dugouts so fans could see what was happening there. The most noticeable change to the stadium was a new yellow, turquoise, and orange paint job that included fluorescent pink foul lines. "My feeling is that baseball should do everything possible to add color to the game," said Finley.[32] "I may not have the best team," he boasted, "but I sure have the sexiest ballpark."[33]

Finley's next colorful move led to radical changes in team uniforms throughout organized baseball. In 1963, Kansas City was the first team to wear colored uniforms, as Finley dressed his players in various mix-and-match shirts and pants in combinations of white, Kelly green and what he termed Finley gold. Opposing teams laughed and derisively stated that Finley's players looked like the neighborhood softball team. They were quick to add that most softball teams played better than the A's.[34] Commenting on his innovative use of colored uniforms, which all teams eventually copied to some extent, Finley said: "I knew the system of home whites and road grays couldn't continue. But I could sense a trend … they said we were making a farce of the game. Now I see other teams doing the same thing."[35] By 1969, even the umpires got on the color bandwagon, a change Finley urged for color TV. American League umpires sported blue coats and gray pants, and later went even further with royal-blue coats and then burgundy blazers, and red caps.[36]

Finley also attempted a number of Veeck-like promotions, although few of them were successful in attracting larger home crowds. Since much of the area around Kansas City was rural, many of Finley's early promotions concerned animals or agriculture. Charlie kept a children's zoo beyond the left field fence, a sheep pasture complete with a shepherd beyond the right field fence, and held greased pig chases and cow-milking contests before games. On Farmers Day in 1963, starting pitcher Diego Segui was delivered to the mound on a hay wagon.[37]

Finley's most long-standing animal attraction was the A's mascot, a mule who stayed with the team even after they moved to Oakland. In 1965, Missouri Governor Warren Hearnes personally selected and presented to Finley and the A's, a large, handsome Missouri mule named Charley O. "He's going to be the most famous mule in the country," said Finley. "We're going to take him to every park in the league."[38]

Charley O was not welcome at every park in the league. White Sox owners refused to allow Finley to lead the mule around the field at Comiskey Park. Undaunted, Finley rented a parking lot across from the stadium, hired a band and six models to attract a crowd, and then denounced White Sox management for being unfair to "Charlie O the man, the mule, baseball and the entire muledom."[39]

Finley never adopted the element of surprise to the extent Veeck did, but some of his promotions certainly unnerved opposing players. The most notorious was a mechanical rabbit named Harvey, which looked remarkably like the wisecracking cartoon character, Bugs Bunny. Harvey popped out of the ground near home plate and supplied new baseballs whenever the umpire pressed the button. Another gadget that emerged from underground was "Little Blowhard," a compressed-air device that dusted off home plate for the umpire. Fans lucky enough to catch foul balls or home runs also got a surprise. Finley insisted that his players autograph all balls so every ball hit into the stands would become a "personalized" souvenir.[40]

One notable contribution Finley made to women's liberation was in response to a dare. He employed ball girls and hired Betty Caywood to do color commentary on A's radio, making her the first woman to be part of a team's regular broadcasts.[41]

The only promotions that consistently enticed fans into the ballpark were cheap-ticket days, which Finley offered to every possible limited-interest group he could think of, including bald-headed persons, farmers, and Shriners.[42] Obviously, Finley needed to offer the fans a better team.

Finley tried to follow the advice of more experienced baseball people and hired as his GM in 1961, the veteran Frank Lane, signing him to a two-year contract. Lane did not even survive one year. Years later Finley explained his reasons. "Frank Lane ... was supposed to be the best general manager available.... Well, it doesn't take a genius to run a ball club. I fired Lane and became my own general manager.[43] Finley did eventually become his own general manager, but not until he hired and fired three more men — Pat Friday, an executive at his insurance company in Chicago; Ed Lopat, former Yankee pitcher; and Hank Peters.[44]

Not only did Finley act as his own GM for roughly 16 of the 20 years he owned the team, he tended to micromanage his field managers. Of his 13 different managers, only Alvin Dark and Dick Williams kept the job for more than a year — Dark managed in Kansas City in 1966 and 1967, and in Oakland in 1974 and 1975; Williams was the Oakland A's skipper in 1971, 1972, and 1973.[45] Finley would often sit in his private box and bark instructions to his manager over one of his many telephones.[46] According to Finley, "Most managers aren't worth a damn, they talk about how clever they are and how much strategy they use. In reality, you could get one of the park policemen to stand out there and wave pitchers in and out of the ball game."[47]

One area where Finley did initially value expert help was in scouting for the talent he needed to improve his team and his gate. The amateur draft adopted in 1965 favored second-division teams like the A's, and any team shrewd enough to draft well could benefit from baseball's finest new talent. Finley did have an innate ability to recognize talent and later did much of his own scouting, but in Kansas City, he hired top-quality scouts to identify and sign the best baseball players he could get. He also called other general managers to get their evaluation of certain players. Despite the fact that they often were competing with him for the same players, they accepted him as another GM and gave him quality advice at absolutely no cost.[48]

During the seven years that Finley's A's played in Kansas City, Finley was discovering young talent. In 1962 he paid $500 to sign shortstop Bert Campaneris, then a catcher for a Cuban team. Campaneris' major-league playing career would span 19 years, 13 of them for Finley.[49] In 1963 Finley signed 22-year-old second baseman Dick Green. Green and Campaneris formed an outstanding double-play combination from 1964 until 1974.[50]

Perhaps Finley's greatest find was in 1965 when he heard about a 19-year-old pitcher from Hertford, North Carolina, by the name of Jim Hunter. Finley drove to Hertford with a motorcycle escort, signed the young hurler to a $75,000 bonus contract, and then paid for an operation at the Mayo Clinic to repair a foot injury Hunter suffered earlier. Finley's penchant for color included nicknames. "Call yourself Catfish," he told the young pitcher. Catfish Hunter pitched for Finley from 1965 to 1974, and won a Cy Young Award and 244 ball games. He was voted into Baseball's Hall of Fame in 1987.[51]

Finley also drafted Rick Monday and Sal Bando from Arizona State University. He signed another 19-year-old pitcher, Blue Moon Odom, after his graduation from high school in Macon, Georgia. Future stars such as Reggie Jackson, Gene Tenace, Rollie Fingers, and Joe Rudi also signed contracts right out of high school; Finley was able to pay them a total of only $37,000 in bonuses.[52] Unfortunately for Kansas City, the talent Finley obtained didn't produce a winning club until a number of years after they relocated to Oakland.

When Finley purchased the Athletics, he promised the fans that he intended to keep the team in Kansas City. That promise had about as much value as his pledge to not trade with the Yankees. From virtually the beginning of his ownership, Finley was checking out possibilities and talking to officials in other cities about re-locating his baseball team. In 1962, the American League turned down his request to explore a move into the Dallas-Fort Worth area.

The A's, with a 71–90 record in 1962 and a 73–89 record in 1963, were still the laughing stock of the American League. Finley, never known for his patience, was unhappy. He stopped promoting the team in Kansas City and started working in earnest to move somewhere else.[53] Publicly, he claimed that problems over the lease of Municipal Stadium were behind his efforts to leave.

In 1963, Finley began to explore the possibility of Oakland. American League president Joe Cronin, a native of San Francisco, liked the idea of another American League team on the West Coast to make travel more efficient.[54] San Francisco Giant owner Horace Stoneham, however, vehemently opposed the plan, arguing that a major league team in Oakland was an infringement on his territory.[55]

The following year, Finley tried to relocate to Louisville, a city that had been without a major league team since 1900. The AL owners turned him down by a vote of nine to one. They were growing tired of Finley's constant attempts to move his team, and gave him a choice: sign a new pact with Municipal Stadium in Kansas City or be evicted from the league. Reluctantly, Finley agreed, and on February 27, 1964, he signed a new four-year lease on Municipal Stadium. In what seems a bizarre contradiction, then the league gave him permission to pursue a future move to Dallas or Oakland.[56]

Despite constant attempts to move the team, Finley and Kansas City suffered through the four seasons of the lease together. The team finished in the cellar in 1964. In 1965, the hapless A's won only five games during the entire month of April and ended with a 59–103 record, 43 games out of first. The A's struggled to seventh place in 1966.[57]

Following the 1967 season, the American League announced approval of Finley's move to Oakland, and promised Kansas City a replacement expansion team by 1971. They reckoned without Kansas City Mayor Ilus Davis or Missouri Senator Stuart Symington. The mayor threatened to get a court injunction to keep the team in Kansas City, while the senator threatened to open another investigation of baseball's antitrust exemption. Alarmed by the word "antitrust," president Joe Cronin called a meeting of the American League owners, and with only five present, rammed through a motion advancing the date of the new Kansas City franchise to 1969. The compromise was acceptable to both Davis and Symington.[58] Symington was not only pleased that Kansas City would get another major league team, he was elated that Charlie Finley was headed out of town. Offering his condolences to Oakland, he declared, "The loss of the A's is more than recompensed by the pleasure of getting rid of Mr. Finley. Oakland is the luckiest city since Hiroshima."[59]

The compromise that allowed Finley's move had a huge impact on the future of baseball. First, his relocation brought about expansion in both major leagues. In 1969, the American League added two teams: the Kansas City Royals, which replaced the Kansas City Athletics, and the Seattle Pilots. To mollify the National League, two expansion teams were also added to the senior circuit: the Montreal Expos and the San Diego Padres.[60] The National League accepted the realignment, but they were unhappy with a team in Oakland and with being preempted by the AL in Seattle.[61] Second, as a result of baseball's expansion to 12-team leagues, divisional play was introduced.

Charles Finley was also responsible for bringing about changes to the All Star Game and the World Series that enabled more fans to watch these events. Although he began advocating these changes shortly after he bought the A's, some were not fully implemented until his team had relocated to Oakland.[62]

Traditionally, the World Series never started on any particular day of the week and games were always played during the day. With working fans like his father in mind, Finley began to lobby for two modifications to World Series scheduling. First, he wanted the Series always to start on Saturday, with the second game to be played on Sunday. Monday would be a travel day and the following three games would be played Tuesday, Wednesday and Thursday evenings. If needed, Friday would be a travel day, and the Series would conclude the following Saturday and Sunday afternoons.[63] For the same reason, he also advocated playing the All-Star game at night. Eventually, the major leagues adopted all of Finley's All-Star and World Series game suggestions. In 1967, the first Major League All Star night game began at 8:15 P.M. Eastern time; it was 5:15 P.M. Pacific Time in Anaheim, California, where the game was played.[64] In 1970, the World Series opened on a Saturday afternoon.[65] The following year, weekday World Series games were played at night.[66]

Things were looking good for Charles Finley and the A's as they began play in the newly constructed Oakland-Alameda County Coliseum in 1968. Oakland, a blue-collar neighbor of the more cosmopolitan San Francisco, was overjoyed finally to have its own major league baseball team. Finley signed a $5 million radio and TV contract for five seasons, far richer than the $56,000 he got in Kansas City.[67] Most importantly, the A's roster was enhanced by several gifted young players, including Reggie Jackson, Catfish Hunter, Joe Rudi, and Bert Campaneris.

More than 50,000 people attended the A's opening game in Oakland. The following night, only about 5,000 showed up. To increase attendance, Finley ran many of the same promotions he used in Kansas City and added a few new ones, mostly with limited success. One new attraction was an informal fan club stationed behind Reggie Jackson in the Oakland Coliseum's right field bleachers. Finley recognized "Reggie's Regiment," with printed membership cards handed out to the faithful at every game.[68]

One of Charlie Finley's more successful Oakland promotions was a 1970s version of Ladies' Day known as "Hot Pants Day." All women wearing the fashionable short shorts known as hot pants were admitted free. In addition, the women were invited to parade on the field in their hot pants before the game and receive two tickets to a future game. The A's expected 500 participants; they got 5,000 and gave away 10,000 free passes.[69]

Finley brought his colorful uniforms to Oakland. Once considered garish, in 1968 they seemed right in step with the psychedelic colors of the era. A few years later, Finley's A's started wearing double-knit uniforms with pullover jerseys.[70] Instead of the traditional black baseball shoe, Charlie introduced shoes made from white-dyed kangaroo leather fastened with bright green laces. Opposing teams laughed, jeered, whistled, and shouted insults. Cleveland manager Joe Adcock went further, protesting to the league that the A's white shoes violated major league rules by too closely resembling the baseball. Adcock lost his protest.[71] When Finley's A's began having outstanding seasons in their white shoes, other teams could hardly wait to order their own colored footwear.[72]

During the Oakland years, Finley also changed the facial appearance of the game. In 1972, he promised a bonus to every player who grew a moustache for Moustache Day at the Coliseum. Every player went along; many also grew beards and most kept their "new look" even after the event. The unwritten rule that players had to be clean shaven, followed since the beginning of the 20th century, was ignored and soon became obsolete.[73]

The highlight of the 1968 season, the first year the A's played in Oakland, was May 8, when Catfish Hunter performed one of baseball's rarest feats—a perfect game. Finley gave Hunter a $5,000 bonus and gave his catcher, Jim Paglioroni, $1,000. Many observers noted that Finley was most generous when he could give spontaneously, but he resented being asked. (He called it being "held up.)[74] Only 6,300 fans were present to witness the event. Despite disappointing crowds at the A's home games and a sixth-place finish in 1968, they attracted 837,000 fans— about 100,000 more than they drew their last year in Kansas City.[75] The next two years the A's came in second in their six-team division, both times finishing nine games behind the division champions.[76]

Since Finley had so little respect for managers, he continued his hiring-firing practice the first three years in Oakland. In 1968, Bob Kennedy managed the A's; the following year Hank Bauer, who had managed briefly for Finley in Kansas City, began the season, but he was replaced with only two weeks remaining by John McNamara, who also managed the team in 1970. Although the A's finished the 1970 season with a record of 89–73, Finley did not rehire McNamara, replacing him with Dick Williams.[77]

Dick Williams was a managerial castoff. Although he had won a pennant for Tom Yawkey's Red Sox in 1967, he had several clashes with his players and his owner, and left Boston before the end of the 1969 season. In 1970, he served as a coach with the Montreal Expos and in 1971, Finley hired him for the managerial job in Oakland.[78]

From 1971 to 1975, the Oakland A's were the dominant team in the American League, finishing in first place all five years. They won three consecutive World Series in 1972, '73, and '74, a feat accomplished only by the New York Yankees.[79] In 1972, pitching was the story of the A's pennant. Ken Holtzman, who was acquired from the Cubs before the season started, was 19–11; Catfish Hunter was 21–7; Blue Moon Odom, 15–6; and Rollie Fingers won 11 games and saved 21 more. Hitting stars included Joe Rudi with a .305 average and Reggie Jackson who notched 25 home runs.[80] Oakland faced the Detroit Tigers in the American League Championship Series and won three games to two. In the World Series, Oakland opposed the Cincinnati Reds. Six of the seven games were decided by one run. With Reggie Jackson out of the Series with a pulled hamstring, the A's backup catcher, Gene Tenace, became the hero. He hit four of the team's five home runs, and drove in nine of their 16 runs. In the deciding seventh game, Tenace drove in two runs, and Oakland won the game 3–2. To cap the victory, Charlie Finley was named executive of the year.[81]

Although the 1972 A's were World Series champions, the clubhouse was rife with dissension and fighting. Some say the contentiousness echoed the feelings of revolt and dissatisfaction of the times. Infielder Ted Kubiak noted that "a lot had to do with the intensity of the ballclub and the fact that the players were there to win games." Kubiak also speculated about Charlie Finley's influence as team owner, "I think Charlie Finley had something to do with that because he was so outspoken. I don't know whether it was his design or whether it was just his method or just his personality, but he allowed the players to speak out also. There were guys that would be pissed off at him and they'd get angry and say things in the papers."[82]

Prior to the beginning of the 1973 season, the American League voted eight to four to institute for a trial period of three years one of Charlie Finley's most desired innovations— the designated hitter. Originally known as the Designated Pinch Hitter (DPH), the DH rule became permanent in the American League in 1976. The National League has yet to adopt it.[83]

The DH rule was part of Charlie Finley's effort to promote the kind of game he thought fans enjoyed most — high-scoring, with lots of hitting. The DH certainly added to the offense, but it also produced another result. Since the pitcher does not have to be removed for a pinch hitter, he stays in the game longer, especially in close situations, gets more decisions, and usually more wins. In 1973, when the DH was first used, the American League produced twelve 20-game winners, a new record.[84]

Finley almost outfoxed himself on the DH rule. The ideal candidate for the Oakland A's DH would have been Orlando Cepeda, who had signed with the team in June 1972. Cepeda had only three at-bats for Oakland in 1972 and was released at the end of the year.[85] One week after the DH rule became a reality, the Boston Red Sox signed Cepeda to a one-year contract, becoming the first American League team to sign a player specifically for the role of DH.[86] Fortunately for the A's, Finley's acquisition from the Philadelphia Phillies, Deron Johnson, served as the A's designated hitter. Johnson hit 19 homers and drove in 81 runs to help lead his team to their third consecutive pennant.[87]

The A's won the western division championship again in 1973, but despite their fine showing and a close race all year, they barely drew a million fans. Nearly every other team had better attendance figures. Furthermore, Oakland players were not offered extra money for personal appearances or commercial endorsements. Finley surmised that either Oakland was not a baseball town or the fans loved baseball, but refused to attend games because they hated Finley. It was evident that Charlie was not Oakland's favorite citizen. At one of the World Series games, disgruntled fans displayed a bed sheet banner, "Finley, Get Your Ass Out of Town."[88] Most people were pretty sure the sign didn't refer to the mule.

Not distracted by the fans' attitude toward their owner, the A's defeated the Baltimore Orioles three games to two in the 1973 League Champion Series. Catfish Hunter won two games and shut out the Orioles 3–0 on a five-hitter in the final game.[89]

The A's met the New York Mets in the 1973 World Series. For the second year in a row, the opposing team outscored, outpitched, and even outhit the A's, but Oakland prevailed in the seven-game series. Ken Holtzman won two of the A's four games, and Bert Campaneris and Reggie Jackson combined for 18 of the A's 51 hits.[90]

Behind-the-scene incidents during the 1973 Series were as interesting as the play on the field. Injuries had reduced the Oakland team to only 24 players. Finley made a last-minute request to allow Manny Trillo to be added to the A's roster for the Series, but the Mets said no. Angered, Finley informed Commissioner Bowie Kuhn before the first game started, that he intended to announce to the fans at Oakland Stadium exactly what the Mets had done. Kuhn replied that it was all right to talk to the press, but under no circumstances was Finley to make a public address announcement. He made the announcement anyway. The irate commissioner called Finley's action a "deliberate act to embarrass the Mets" and later fined him.[91]

Finley and Kuhn also clashed over two incidents in the second game. It started getting dark in Oakland while the game was still going on. Finley ignored a major league rule which clearly stated that lights could be turned on only at the beginning of an inning, waiting until the A's half of the inning to hit the switch. Kuhn, at the park for that game, ordered the lights off until the A's finished batting, and fined Charles Finley again.[92]

The game was still tied in the 12th inning when manager Dick Williams sent Mike Andrews in to play second base. Andrews committed two errors on two consecutive plays, allowing the Mets to win the game 10–7. The second baseman had no physical problems; he just allowed a ground ball to go through his legs for the first miscue, and made a wild throw on the following play. After the game Andrews contritely told reporters, "I accept blame for the loss and have no excuses for my misplay."[93]

Despite Andrews' statement, Finley was outraged, and ordered the team physician to pronounce Andrews unfit to continue for the remainder of the Series because of an old shoulder injury. Finley forced Andrews to sign a consent form and sent him home. Then Finley petitioned the commissioner to declare Andrews disabled and requested permission for Manny Trillo to replace him. Kuhn responded that only in the event of a new, serious injury could a player be replaced during the World Series. Not only did Kuhn deny Finley's request to use Trillo, he ordered Finley to reinstate Andrews. That suited the Oakland players just fine. They had overcome their usual divisiveness in an amazing display of solidarity behind Andrews, agreeing to wear his number 17 on their uniforms for the remainder of the Series.[94] Finley, of course, tried to get in the last word. "It is my ball club, my money and I don 't appreciate anyone telling me how to spend my money to run my business. I don't think the commissioner treated us fairly in turning down this request."[95]

Now in his third season as manager, Dick Williams had stoically watched the antics between Finley and his players. Finally, he broke his silence. Before the third game of the 1973 World Series, he met with his players and told them that he would deny what he was about to say if his words leaked out of the clubhouse, but, "Win, lose, or draw, I'm resigning at the end of this World Series." He did not explain his action, but many of the players thought that he simply couldn't take any more of the bitterness and turmoil Charlie Finley was causing. Veteran Sal Bando was not surprised. "We understood. Working for Charlie was not an everyday, normal occurrence."[96] Reggie Jackson probably summed it up most succinctly when he said, "Finley takes all the fun out of winning."[97]

Williams officially announced his resignation on October 21, moments after the 1973 Series had concluded. It was no secret that he wanted to manage the Yankees, replacing Ralph Houk, who been allowed to resign to manage Detroit. With a year remaining on Williams' Oakland contract, Finley told the Yankees that if they wanted Williams, they had to send Oakland some regular players in return. The Yankees refused. Williams sat idle until midway in the 1974 season, when Finley allowed him to take a job managing the Angels, replacing the fired Bobby Winkles. Williams remained with the Angels the following two seasons, then went on to manage the Expos and the Padres, and ended his career with the Seattle Mariners in 1988.[98]

Following the 1973 World Series, Finley suffered a heart attack and was told by his doctors to slow down. He followed their advice to some extent by selling his American Basketball Association team, the Tams, and his National Hockey League franchise, the California Golden Seals. Finley then indicated he would sell the World Champion Athletics to either Toronto or Denver, but he really had no intention of disposing of his baseball team. Whenever he received a serious offer, he simply increased the asking price.

Claiming that the team's poor attendance was affecting his finances, he resorted to the same tactics he had employed in Kansas City. He stopped promotions, and began cutting employees. Among the employees Finley felt were unessential were his scouts. By 1975, the A's were down to one full-time scout. A number had quit in disgust because they felt that Finley wanted to do it all himself. He questioned their expense accounts and they questioned his new policy of cutting back on bonus money. Except for outstanding prospects, the once-generous Finley's top offer now was $5,000.[99]

Finley also stopped pursuing TV deals. With a constant turnover of broadcasters, Finley was eventually unable to sell even radio rights to commercial stations. By the time he left Oakland, the A's games were being broadcast over a college station.[100]

Once the 1974 season began, Finley came up with another penny-pinching idea. On their off days, his starting pitchers were expected to provide color commentary on radio broadcasts, saving Finley the cost of hiring a full-time color commentator. Naturally, Finley did not pay his pitchers any extra money for their work.[101]

In 1974, the A's were still a winning ball team under "new" manager Alvin Dark. Dark and Hank Bauer were the only two men who managed for Finley in Kansas City and Oakland.[102] After Finley fired Dark from the Kansas City job at the conclusion of the 1967 season, he managed the Cleveland Indians. In Oakland, Dark kept his post for two years and left baseball in 1977 after a stint in San Diego.[103]

A religious man whose fundamentalist Christian views often alienated his players, Dark said that he simply wanted to carry out Finley's orders. When once asked who his DH would be, Dark told the reporter, "I don't know. Charlie's plane hasn't landed." Oakland pitcher, Vida Blue, observed that Dark, "...worships the wrong God — COF."[104]

Despite the usual chaos in the Oakland clubhouse, the A's finished five games ahead of the Rangers to win their division in 1974. They proceeded to defeat the Baltimore Orioles for the League Championship three games to one. In the World Series, they disposed of the Los Angeles Dodgers in five games, winning their third consecutive World Series title. The 1974 World Series was the first one held entirely on the West Coast.[105]

Three individual A's stood out in the 1974 season. Cy Young Award winner Catfish Hunter won 25 games, allowing fewer combined hits and walks than innings pitched. His 2.49 ERA also was the best in the American League.[106] Relief pitcher Rollie Fingers was named World Series MVP for winning one game and saving two others.[107] The third player was noted not so much for his contributions to the winning season but as the embodiment of one of Charles Finley's innovations: the designated pinch runner.

With the goal of producing a game with more scoring, Finley had for years pushed not only for a DH, but also for a designated runner. This player would retire to the dugout after each inning, but could re-enter the game as many times as a pinch runner was needed. Neither league ever implemented a "DR" rule, but in 1974, Charles Finley introduced his own version of a running specialist. Herb Washington was a world-class sprinter hired by Finley as a pinch runner for $40,000 and a signing bonus. Washington never swung a bat or put on a glove; his sole job was to run the bases. During the 1974 season, he stole 29 bases but was caught 18 times — a relatively poor success rate. In his only appearance in the 1974 World Series as a pinch runner, Washington was promptly picked off first base by Dodger hurler Mike Marshall. Before dropping out of major league ball at the end of the 1975 season, Washington appeared in 13 more games, stealing two bases and getting caught once.[108]

Another Finley innovation to improve offense that generated a lot of publicity was the orange baseball. Tennis balls had changed from white to "optic yellow for greater visibility"; Finley felt that changing the baseball from white to orange would result in more hitting. Reasoned Finley, "Batters can see an orange ball better, particularly at night. If we start using this ball, batting averages will increase. That means more action, and that's what the fans want to see."[109] The league refused to accept the orange ball.[110]

Finley also supported Bill Veeck's idea of allowing a walk on three balls, not only to speed up the game, but also to generate more excitement.[111] Finley went one step further and actually tried the system in an exhibition game between the Milwaukee Brewers and the Kansas City Athletics in Tempe, Arizona. The two teams combined for 19 free passes during the contest, and as expected, pitchers for both sides disliked the idea.[112]

Ewing Kauffman, who succeeded Finley as owner in Kansas City, commented on Finley's proposed series of innovations. "He had some wonderful ideas, but he rankled the owners so much that anything he proposed didn't have a chance of being approved."[113]

Although Finley had a championship team again, 1974 was a very bad year for the A's owner. Despite the A's incredible play, they drew twice as many on the road as they did in Oakland. Finley's players kept demanding higher salaries, Finley was having trouble with the IRS, and Mike Andrews was suing him for slander. In addition, Finley and his wife of 34 years had recently divorced.[114]

Nineteen seventy-four was also the first year that salary arbitration went into effect. A year earlier, Marvin Miller, head of the Players Association, formally proposed that baseball accept salary arbitration. Finley predicted "economic evil" to his fellow owners. "I contacted every owner personally or by telephone," Finley said, "and I told them, one and all, the evils of arbitration. They all listened attentively and thanked me.... If I had been a betting man, I would have bet all the tea in China at least 18 teams would vote against arbitration but ... only the St. Louis Cardinals and Oakland A's voted against it. They didn't like or trust me. At that time my club was doing too much winning."[115]

The owners also realized that Finley, with his low salaries, had more to lose than almost anyone. Nine of Finley's key players filed for arbitration, making up nearly one-third of the 29 total whose cases were heard in February 1974. One of those nine, former pitcher Ken Holtzman, who was with the A's from 1972–1975, observed that this situation resulted in a greatly increased number of player agents in baseball. "Finley forced so many of his players to seek arbitration that [they had] to find someone to represent them. I believe this is how the system really came about."[116] Surprisingly, Finley's combined arbitration losses in 1974 totaled only $87,000.[117]

Finley's star pitcher, Catfish Hunter, was not one of the A's who had gone to arbitration, since he had recently been given the $100,000 contract he requested. Players had become more financially savvy and often sought tax advantages as they negotiated their contracts. Hunter's contract called for $50,000 to be paid in salary and the other $50,000 to go into an annuity from which he would benefit later. Even before the 1974 World Series, Hunter began complaining that Finley had not made the required annuity payments. Whether Charlie had cash flow problems or simply wanted to claim Hunter's full $100,000 as tax-deductible salary, Hunter contended that his contract had been broken and announced he would file for free agency. "If I become a free agent I know I won't play for the A's." Catfish declared. "I don't think Finley appreciates what I've done for the A's."[118]

On October 17, 1974, the Players' Association filed two grievances for Hunter. One was against the baseball hierarchy for failing to recognize Hunter's free agency even though the Uniform Players' Contract specifically stated, "The player may terminate his contract ... if the club shall default in the payments."[119] The second grievance was against Charles Finley for breaking Hunter's contract by failing to make the $50,000 insurance payment.

The following month, Finley and the Players' Association pleaded their cases to the three-member arbitration panel. Peter Seitz, the neutral member of the panel, decided for Hunter. Seitz instructed Finley to pay Hunter's $50,000 annuity with interest and then dropped the bombshell. "Mr. Hunter's contract for service to be performed during the 1975 season no longer binds him and he is a free agent."[120] By refusing to pay Catfish Hunter his annuity, Charlie Finley created baseball's first free agent. Finley and the American League appealed, but California courts supported Seitz's decision. It was one of the rare times the American League stood with Finley.[121]

At first, Commissioner Kuhn would not allow the other 23 owners to negotiate with Hunter, but changed his mind a few days later, and the bidding began.[122] Hunter received offers from 12 teams, finally agreeing to sign with the Yankees for approximately $3.75 million for a five-year contract.[123] At that time, the average major league salary was $45,000.[124]

Other owners, the media, and especially the players were dumbstruck when they learned the terms of the deal. Players around both leagues started to wonder what they might be worth on the open market as Hunter's contract with the Yankees redrew the economic boundaries in baseball.[125] The Hunter decision did not directly address the reserve clause, but it did make it clear to the players how much they could gain if the reserve clause could be eliminated altogether.[126]

Many baseball observers claim that had Hunter pitched for the Athletics in 1975, the A's might have won a fourth straight World Series. Oakland did win its fifth consecutive divisional title, but it would be the last the A's would earn under Finley. The A's season ended when they lost three consecutive games to the Boston Red Sox in the American League Champion Series. Like the year before, remarkable individual performances characterized the season. Vida Blue won 22 games, Ken Holtzman had 18 victories, and Rollie Fingers won 10 games and saved 24 more. Reggie Jackson led the American League with 36 home runs.[127] And attendance increased. During the 1975 season, for only the second time, the Oakland A's drew over one million fans.

Not only did the A's not participate in the World Series in 1975, the team that Finley firmly believed was becoming a dynasty, completely fell apart after that year. The end of the reserve clause and the establishment of universal free agency affected every team, but none so much as Charlie Finley's A's.

All the baseball magnates were alarmed when, late in 1975, Seitz's arbitration panel nullified baseball's reserve clause. All players were free to negotiate with any team if they played out their contract or met certain other conditions. The owners' greatest worry was that large numbers of players would put themselves up for bid. Marvin Miller, the player union's executive director, had a background in economics; he knew that contrary to the fears of the owners, a large supply of free agents would depress, not increase, salaries. Miller also realized that Charles Finley, the pariah of major league baseball, was the only owner who truly understood the law of supply and demand: the more free agents, the lower the price.[128]

Charlie Finley also understood that when many of his players became eligible for free agency at the end of the 1976 season, he would end up with neither players nor compensation. He decided to do something about the situation, but Commissioner Bowie Kuhn had other ideas.

Kuhn and Finley did occasionally agree, but not often. They had cooperated on the designated hitter rule, and Kuhn supported Finley regarding colorful uniforms and the Catfish Hunter business.[129] But Kuhn disliked Finley. When the A's won the World Series in '72, '73, and '74, it galled him to present three championship trophies to a man he considered uncouth and undignified.[130] They battled over what Kuhn considered Finley's questionable conduct and public remarks. Kuhn prided himself on being the "guardian of tradition," while Finley was the "champion of change."[131]

One of the earliest skirmishes occurred in 1970. In 1969 Reggie Jackson led the league with 123 runs scored and a .608 slugging percentage, while hammering 47 home runs.[132] After a salary squabble, which Finley settled with a take-it-or-leave-it offer of $40,000, Jackson signed his 1971 contract only ten days before the season opener and started the new season very slowly. Finley announced that he was sending his star outfielder to the minors. Asserting that this was the sort of abuse that threatened to destroy fans' confidence in baseball, Kuhn reprimanded Finley for unfair action against a player strictly for personal reasons.[133]

The next confrontation occurred after the 1971 baseball season, and also centered on a salary dispute, this time with one of Finley's star pitchers, Vida Blue. Blue wanted $115,000; Finley would not budge from his offer of $50,000. The situation was receiving ugly publicity so "for baseball's sake," in April 1972, Kuhn drew up a compromise: pay Vida the $50,000 salary but add a bonus of a four-year college scholarship worth $8,000, plus an additional $5,000 signing bonus. Kuhn then gave Finley an ultimatum to sign Blue or make him a free agent. Finley went into a rage, questioning Kuhn's right to interfere in a salary dispute between owner and player, and denounced Kuhn repeatedly in the press using his usual obscene language. On June 27, 1972, Kuhn levied the maximum fine of $500 against Finley and issued a reprimand. Finley paid the $500, sending the check along with a seething letter stating that the commissioner, not Finley, was guilty of conduct not in the best interest of baseball.[134]

The next incident happened just a few months later, prior to the start of the 1972 World Series in Oakland. Finley snubbed Oakland's mayor and instead invited Mayor Joe Alioto of San Francisco to throw out the first ball. Despite Kuhn's remonstrances, Finley refused to cancel his invitation to Alioto, informing Kuhn, "Commissioner, I don't give a damn what you think."[135] Bowie Kuhn also fined Charles Finley for defying the major league rule of awarding financial bonuses to his team during a World Series.[136]

Kuhn and Finley were at loggerheads again a year later. Kuhn levied $7,000 in fines against the A's owner for his three infractions during the 1973 World Series—the public announcement of the Met's refusal to allow him to add a player, turning on the lights in the bottom half of an inning, and the Mike Andrews affair. Finley admitted that the fine for the lights incident was warranted, but felt the other two were "grossly unfair."[137]

Never one to take reprimands lightly, Finley led a "Dump-Bowie" movement in 1965 when Kuhn's seven-year term as commissioner was about to expire. To be re-elected, Kuhn needed nine of the 12 votes in each league. In the American League, Finley thought he had the four votes he needed to defeat Kuhn. In addition to his own, he had on his side Orioles owner Jerry Hoffberger, who resented Kuhn's interference when Hoffberger tried to sell his club earlier that year; Yankee boss George Steinbrenner, who had been suspended by Kuhn for making illegal political contributions; and Eddie Chiles, the owner of the Texas Rangers. Before a vote could be taken, Dodger owner Walter O'Malley, who was leading the pro–Kuhn forces, convinced Texas and New York to change their votes. Only Finley and Hoffberger voted against Kuhn.[138]

Next year, Kuhn retaliated. The arbitration board that nullified the reserve clause also laid out the conditions under which players would be eligible for free agency. A number of Finley's biggest stars were set to become free agents after the 1976 season. If they played out the season and then chose to leave the team, Finley would end up with nothing. Before that could happen, Finley decided to clean out the roster himself. First, he sent Ken Holtzman, Reggie Jackson, and a minor league prospect to the Orioles for designated hitter Don Baylor and pitchers Mike Torrez and Paul Mitchell. Within a period of 24 hours, he then proceeded to sell Vida Blue to the New York Yankees for $1.5 million and Joe Rudi and Rollie Fingers to the Boston Red Sox for $1 million each.[139]

Selling the team's best players was virtually a tradition for the A's. Connie Mack had done it when the club was still the Philadelphia Athletics. Nor was it a tactic unique to the A's. Mack's friend and contemporary, Clark Griffith, also used the strategy extensively in Washington. Finley reasoned that with the money he would receive for his stars, he could purchase new, young, unknown talent as he had done successfully in Kansas City. It was common knowledge that he had the ability to build a winning team.[140]

Bowie Kuhn could not fault Finley's trade with the Orioles. Kuhn was concerned, however, with the sale of Blue, Rudi, and Fingers because the A's had received only cash and no players in return. Kuhn cited Article 1, Section 4 of the major league agreement, which stated that the commissioner was to prevent developments such as "fire sales" of baseball players, "because they violated the best interests of baseball." Bowie Kuhn would repeat these words many times.[141]

Not only did Kuhn block the sale of Finley's three players, the commissioner imposed a $400,000 limit on all-cash player transactions between clubs. In an era when few players went for $400,000 or less, Kuhn's edict, in effect, ended these transactions.[142]

To many observers it appeared that Kuhn was deliberately punishing Finley for attempting to oust him as commissioner. Both Lee MacPhail, President of the American League, and Chub Feeney, National League President, advised Kuhn not to interfere with Finley's transactions. MacPhail was emphatic when he warned Kuhn, "If you get into this, Finley is surely going to start a fight. We're going to have the unpleasantness of court proceedings and I doubt that's very good for the game."[143] For once public opinion, too, sided with Finley.

Finley pleaded with Kuhn to allow him to sell his players. He told Kuhn that he was unable to sign Blue, Rudi, or Fingers, and if he were allowed to sell them at least he would be able to get something back. He described the sad state of his finances in Oakland and the stiff competition from the Giants. Kuhn was unmoved.[144]

Finley then proceeded to call the commissioner "the village idiot" and filed a $10 million lawsuit against him. Soon, he changed his description of Kuhn to "the nation's idiot," and ultimately to "his honor, the idiot in charge."[145] Fingers and Rudi had already been wearing Red Sox uniforms when they were forced to return to the A's, pending the outcome of the lawsuit. Oakland manager Chuck Tanner was told not to use any of the three in a game until the courts settled the issue, cutting Oakland's roster down to 22 players.[146]

Finley's $10 million lawsuit against the commissioner's office was futile. In March 1977, Federal District Judge Frank McGarr, after a 15-day trial, ruled in favor of Kuhn, citing a pre-existing agreement between the major league owners and the commissioner, stating that the owners would never challenge a ruling of the commissioner in a court of law. Concluded Judge McGarr, "It is the judgment of this court that plaintiff Charles O. Finley & Co. Inc, has failed to sustain the allegations of its complaint, and the relief sought therein is denied. Judgment is consequently entered for defendant Bowie K. Kuhn."[147] In 1978, the United States Court of Appeals affirmed McGarr's decision.[148] Finley threatened to take the case to the United States Supreme Court, but the nation's highest tribunal would not accept it. The two-year saga was over.[149]

Just as the Catfish Hunter case led the way to free agency, the Kuhn-Finley case resulted in a more powerful baseball commissioner. It is likely that neither Kuhn nor his supporters had that goal in mind initially; they just wanted to get Charlie Finley out of baseball.

While Finley's case was still in litigation, the only owner to publicly support him had been Jerrold Hoffberger of the Orioles, who defended Finley's right to sell his "assets."[150] Five days after the case concluded, Yankee owner George Steinbrenner made an interesting statement to the *New York Times*. "I like the commissioner," he said, "but no one should have the power the baseball constitution gives the Commissioner's office." Before long, Finley learned that other owners agreed with Steinbrenner, including some who had taken the witness stand to testify for Kuhn. "Sure, we lied," one admitted on the condition of anonymity. "We were co-defendants. What did you expect us to do?"[151]

What the owners had done was obvious. After Kenesaw Mountain Landis, the first and most powerful Commissioner of Baseball, the owners, concerned that they were losing control, hired weak successors. Upholding Kuhn's right to void Finley's sales of his own players told the public that the commissioner did, indeed, possess great powers.[152]

As Finley predicted, when the 1976 season ended, there was a mass exodus from the Athletics. Although the A's were close to capturing their division again, finishing only 2½ games behind the Kansas City Royals, Fingers, Rudi, Bando, Tenace, Baylor, and Campaneris all signed with other clubs as free agents. Vida Blue remained with the Athletics because he had signed a new contract only hours before Finley had tried to ship him to the Yankees. They had been part of what was arguably the most successful franchise of the decade, but the common feeling expressed by A's players when they left Oakland was relief. Sal Bando was asked if it was difficult to leave the A's after playing so many years for Finley. Bando replied, "It's about as hard as leaving the Titanic."[153] Reggie Jackson was a little more generous. "I have to admit it," he said. "Charlie can be a tyrant, but he can be a lot of fun, too…. He would be a great guy to have as a buddy as long as you didn't have to work for him."[154]

In addition to losing so many players, Finley also lost his manager. Tanner told his boss that one year of working for him was more than enough, and he went to Pittsburgh to manage the Pirates. In an unusual deal, the Pirates sent a catcher, Manny Sanguillen, and $100,000 to the A's in exchange for Tanner. For the next two years, Bobby Winkles and Jack McKeon would take turns managing the A's.[155]

With Tanner's departure after the 1976 season, the A's fared very poorly in 1977, finishing in the division's seventh-place cellar.[156] They drew only 500,000 fans and the Coliseum became known as the Mausoleum. Finley tried to improve attendance with half-price tickets for weekday games, but few fans were interested. The ballpark became run down, the scoreboard was not maintained, and the rest rooms and concession stands were the worst in the major leagues.[157]

During the 1977 season, Finley tried to trade Vida Blue to the Cincinnati Reds, but Kuhn, flexing his new muscle, annulled the deal, claiming that the Reds were strong enough, the A's were already weak, and the deal should be negated for "baseball's best interests."[158] In 1978, Finley finally was able to trade Blue, sending his southpaw to the San Francisco Giants and getting seven players in return. Finley sarcastically dared the commissioner to void that deal.[159]

Oakland finished sixth in 1978 but returned to the cellar the following year under manager Jim Marshall, finishing below the expansion Seattle Mariners.[160] Attendance in Oakland slumped to 300,000, roughly the same number the Philadelphia Athletics attracted 25 years previously at Shibe Park.[161]

In an attempt to improve the team and draw more fans to the park, Finley hired the fiery Billy Martin as Marshall's replacement in 1980. Martin was a proven winner in previous managerial stints with the Twins, Tigers, Rangers, and Yankees, and he accomplished both of Finley's goals. The A's five-man pitching rotation of Mike Norris, Marty Keough, Steve McCatty, Rick Langford, and Brian Kingman each produced more than 200 innings. The outfield of Rickey Henderson, Dwayne Murphy, and Tony Armas had three of the best defensive arms in baseball, and the team's offense was well balanced. Martin stressed a running game which the fans called "Billy Ball." It included Henderson's league-leading 100 stolen bases, one triple steal, 14 double steals, and seven steals of home. The A's finished in second place and the fans loved it. Attendance jumped to close to 850,000, half a million more than the previous season.[162] 1980 was to be Charlie Finley's last year in baseball.

In 1973, Charles Finley had threatened but then refused to sell the A's for both sentimental and economic reasons. Oakland City officials had given him a very favorable financial deal that included a 20-year lease of the Oakland-Alameda County Coliseum at a low rent and a generous share of TV, concessions, and parking revenues. No matter how much Charlie complained about attendance or competition, the A's were one of baseball's most profitable franchises.[163]

Near the end of 1977, Finley began a sincere effort to sell the team. Top choices under consideration were Memphis, New Orleans, and Denver.[164] Denver-based oilman Marvin Davis made the most serious offer, but after more than two years of negotiations, the deal never materialized, primarily because the city of Oakland would not release the team from its lease. By 1980, Finley's health was poor, and worn out by his battles with the league and the city, he lost his enthusiasm for remaining in baseball. On August 23, 1980, Finley agreed to sell the A's for $12.7 million to a local group, the Haas family, heirs to the long-established community business, Levi Strauss. The buyers included Walter Haas, his son Wally, and his son-in-law, Roy Eisenhardt.[165]

Finley easily got the approval of the American League owners for the sale. The new owners had to renegotiate the team's lease with the Coliseum, but that was no problem either. In his final press conference, Finley stated that he simply was unable to keep up with the other clubs. "When the game was a battle of wits," he said, "no one could compete with us. Today it's how much you've got on the hip. It's money."[166]

After he left baseball, Finley continued to run his insurance business and served as president of a Canadian firm, Century Energy Corporation.[167] He made one final attempt to re-enter baseball. In 1981, he tried to buy the Chicago Cubs. Finley called William Wrigley and told him that he and Marshall Field, then owner of the *Chicago Sun-Times*, would pay $25 million for the team. "I'm sorry, Charlie," Wrigley replied, "the club is sold." (The Tribune Company had just purchased the team for $20.5 million.)[168]

Charlie Finley made no more efforts to purchase a major league team, but he continued to have plenty to say about the game. He felt players' salaries were much too high and would cause teams to declare bankruptcy. According to Finley, "Bowie Kuhn was bad for baseball. The only reason some of the owners praise him today is they're trying to save face." Finley continued to oppose salary arbitration and stated that many players earning $250,000 would be lucky to have made his team. He still advocated a three-ball walk and a clock to speed up the game. Finley said that he and former White Sox owner Bill Veeck had a plan for a new International League with teams in minor league cities, Mexico, South America, and Japan. "Now, if Bill Veeck and I get around to starting this new league," he said, "we'll have three balls ... [and] the designated hitter for all teams. And we'll have the orange baseball."[169]

Charles Finley died of heart and vascular disease on February 19, 1996, at Northwestern Memorial Hospital in Chicago. He was 77 years old. Bowie Kuhn, the commissioner with whom Finley often sparred, said of the late A's owner, "I think Charlie will be remembered probably as a maverick. Charlie was Charlie.... He liked to do his thing, his own way."[170]

Some of Finley's former players learned over the years to appreciate what he had done for baseball. Catcher Dave Duncan, who played in Kansas City and Oakland from 1964 to 1972, said of Finley, "He was always trying to attract more interest in the game of baseball from the fan's standpoint." Outfielder Rick Monday lauded Finley's foresight, saying "A lot of things that he said about baseball way back in the seventies, if they had listened to him a little bit closer, maybe things would not have gotten out of hand..."[171]

Although Ken Holtzman pitched for only four seasons with Oakland, he served as the A's player representative and probably knew Charles Finley as well as anyone. Holtzman conceded that Finley certainly could have shown more respect toward his players and that he intensified the feeling of mistrust between player and owner, but also noted that Finley's negative behavior had one positive result: the formation of a grievance committee "which exists to help the multitude of disputes that arise today in baseball." He credited Finley with understanding how baseball worked better than most of the other owners and with "a wonderful work ethic." "He didn't have the best background in baseball, but he was one of the hardest workers I ever met."[172]

No matter what people thought of him personally, both friend and foe acknowledged that Charles Finley's innovations, such as brightly colored uniforms, World Series games played at night and the designated hitter, helped shape the game of baseball.[173]

8

August Busch
The CEO

August Anheuser Busch, Jr., was another latecomer to the game of baseball, but he became one of the game's strongest figures, influencing both the marketing and the ownership structure. When Busch took over the St. Louis Cardinals in 1953, he pioneered the era of corporate ownership of major league teams. Although it was Busch's company, Anheuser Busch, that actually bought the Cardinals, there was never any doubt that for nearly 35 years, "Gussie" Busch ran the team.

The Cardinals had had relatively stable ownership in the years since 1917, when Helene Britton sold the team to a consortium of St. Louis citizens. Local automobile salesman Sam Breadon was part of the group, originally owning only four shares, valued at $200. Breadon kept acquiring stock and became club president in 1920, a position he held for more than a quarter of a century. By the 1940s, he owned 78 percent of the team. In 1947, Breadon sold the Cardinals to Postmaster General Robert Hannegan and attorney Fred Saigh for more than $4 million.[1]

The following year, Saigh bought out Hannegan and became owner, president, and general manager.[2] Saigh's ownership lasted only a few years. On April 22, 1952, a grand jury indicted him for income tax evasion and, on January 28, 1953, he was sentenced to 15 months in prison and fined $15,000. Saigh was given roughly three months to wind up his business affairs, specifically to dispose of the Cardinals. A Wisconsin group intending to move the team to Milwaukee offered Saigh $4 million, just what he had paid for the team six years earlier. Saigh preferred keeping the Cardinals in St. Louis, but he desperately needed the money.[3]

A group of owners who had opposed Saigh in a disagreement with former Baseball Commissioner Happy Chandler a few years earlier, vetoed the sale of the Cardinals to the Milwaukee syndicate, insisting that the team stay in St. Louis.[4] Saigh agreed to sell the Cardinals to St. Louis-based Anheuser-Busch, Inc., one of America's leading breweries, for $3.75 million, about a quarter of a million less than the Milwaukee investors had offered him. On February 20, 1953, Anheuser-Busch purchased the St. Louis Cardinals and A-B's chief executive, August A. Busch, Jr., became club president.[5] Anheuser-Busch was the first corporation to own a major league baseball team in either league.[6] The sale of the Cardinals to the brewery helped spearhead what is now commonplace — a corporate executive's entry into big-time sports.[7]

August Anheuser Busch, Jr. (known to his friends as "Gus" but always "Gussie" to the press), was born in St. Louis on March 28, 1899, son of August Anheuser Busch, Sr., and Alice Ziseman Busch. At the time of his birth, the Busch family was already fabulously rich, thanks to Gussie's grandfather, Adolphus Busch, a young German immigrant who had married the daughter of Eberhard Anheuser, a St. Louis soapmaker and brewmaster. Adolphus assumed management of Anheuser's small brewery and, through his sales ability and energy, turned the business into a vigorous company. In 1880, he succeeded his father-in-law as president of the Anheuser-Busch Brewing Association.

On the death of Adolphus in 1913, Gussie's father, August Busch, Sr., assumed control of the brewery. Many breweries were unable to survive Prohibition, but August Sr. had the foresight to convert Anheuser-Busch's huge processing plants to factories for the production of diesel engines, truck bodies, soft drinks, near beer, malt syrup and other products. In 1922, August Jr. joined his father's firm as vat scrubber, determined to learn the brewing business. "I started from the bottom in every department. I learned the business from yeast to Budweiser, from the vat to the Michelob spigot."[8] In 1926 he became general manager. When Prohibition ended in 1933, the brewery resumed beer making. Years later, Gussie said that when the first trucks left the plant at the stroke of midnight to deliver cases of Budweiser, "It was the greatest moment of my life."[9]

August Busch, Sr., who had been suffering from a multitude of illnesses, committed suicide less than a year later, on February 13, 1934. Following family tradition, his oldest son, Adolphus III, became company president while his brother, Gussie, was named company vice-president, a post he held until he joined the Army in 1942. He directed tank production and rose to the rank of colonel.[10]

When the war ended, Gussie returned to the firm, taking over as company president when his brother died suddenly in 1946. Gussie was 47

AUGUST BUSCH, JR.— St. Louis Cardinals 1953–1989 — One of the country's most successful businessmen, "Gussie" Busch forcefully led his team and his brewery, proving that not only could baseball help sell beer, but that beer could help sell baseball (National Baseball Hall of Fame Library, Cooperstown, NY).

years old.[11] To Busch's dismay, Anheuser-Busch had slipped to second place among American breweries in 1946 and then to fourth place the following year. Gussie made it his mission to make A-B the number one brewery in the nation again. In temperament and determination, Busch resembled his hot-tempered, tough, and stubborn grandfather far more than his father and older brother, who Gussie felt had been too cautious in their approach to business.[12] Despite the objections of his own directors, Gussie totally renovated the St. Louis brewing plant and constructed additional breweries in other four cities to reduce shipping costs. By 1953, he had spent $134 million, but the brewery was first in national sales.[13]

Harry Caray, who would later broadcast St. Louis Cardinal games, described Busch as profane, shrewd, a vindictive bully, but also "a man who changed the history of brewing."[14] His employees described him as a tyrant–irascible and demanding that they always turn out a "quality" product. "Being first is everything and I believe in running the business in a way that would make my grandfather, my father and my brother proud of me." He had little patience with incompetence or opposition. In his usual hoarse voice, the 5' 10", 165-pound Busch would roar at board members when they questioned his decisions, "Dammit, because I said so."

One of Busch's closest personal counselors was Alfred Fleishman, founder of Fleishman-Hillard, which was to become one of the largest public relations firms in the world. He was credited with helping Busch become known as "the man with the soft heart and the hard nose," urging Busch to serve on civic boards and support local institutions such as the St. Louis Symphony. Fleishman, who also handled the brewery's publicity for many years, often joked that Gussie fired and then rehired him every Monday, Wednesday, and Friday.[15]

Gussie Busch lived life well, entertaining lavishly on his "Grant's Farm" estate in St. Louis County. Busch kept large numbers of big-game animals, including deer and buffalo, but his pride and joy were his horses. Anheuser-Busch's handsome Clydesdale horses were one of the brewery's best-known symbols, often pulling an old-fashioned Budweiser wagon in parades from coast to coast.[16]

After purchasing the team, Busch held a press conference to announce that Anheuser-Busch had bought the Cardinals strictly for the sport and to keep the team in St. Louis.[17] At the time, rival brewery, Griesedieck Bros., sponsored the broadcast of Cardinals' games, but Busch, driving home his message, stated, "I don't think that makes a great deal of difference. I am going at this from the sports angle and not as a sales weapon for Budweiser Beer." He did state, however, that A-B would begin sponsoring the broadcasts as soon as the current contract expired.[18]

Busch also told the press that he would take a very active role as club president, adding, "I am going to Florida very soon to watch the club in spring training." Knowing that Busch had never before shown much interest in baseball, a local reporter questioned this turnaround. "I've been a fan all my life," responded Busch, "but I've been too busy to get out to the park in recent years—unfortunately. However, the brewery has a box reserved for its use each season."[19]

Busch's admission that he previously had not participated much in baseball was certainly accurate. Other than seeing a few games at the ballpark, his only connection with the game had been occasional hunting trips with two Cardinal star players, Stan Musial and Red Schoendienst. Once, at Busch's hunting lodge, Musial suggested that Busch get into baseball, arguing that it would not only be fun but could be profitable. "Stan," Busch responded, "You go right on with baseball, and leave me to the beer." When Busch arrived in St. Petersburg after becoming president of the Cardinals, Musial reminded Busch of their previous conversation, and told his new boss, "Great that you made it."[20]

Much of the public also approved of the sale but didn't seem to believe that Busch would keep beer and baseball separate. *Business Week* called the purchase of the Cardinals good business for the brewery and a boost to one of organized baseball's financial weak spots. Busch did concede that the Cardinals and Anheuser-Busch were St. Louis institutions that "belong together."[21]

Opposition to the merger of the Cardinals and Anheuser-Busch came primarily from two sources. Mrs. D. Leigh Colvin, president of the

Women's Christian Temperance Union, stated vigorously that the purchase of the Cardinals by the brewery was simply an effort to persuade America's youth that alcohol was not harmful to athletes. "Up to now, the brewers haven't dared depict football and baseball players swigging beer, but this could be their next step." Gussie Busch strongly denied Mrs. Colvin's assertions, and reiterated that he had no plans to use the Cardinals to go around the country plugging his products. Mrs. Colvin answered Busch with one word, "Baloney."[22]

A more formidable adversary was Senator Edwin Johnson, a Colorado Democrat, who was also president of the Class A Western Baseball League. He opposed the sale because, "Busch's plans to broadcast Cardinal games over 120 radio stations under the sponsorship of Budweiser beer with total disregard for local ball clubs and breweries is appalling."[23] Johnson raised baseball's most feared word, "antitrust," in a bill aimed specifically at Busch, asking Congress to make teams owned by alcoholic beverage producers liable to antitrust laws.[24]

Baseball Commissioner Ford Frick took up Busch's cause, replying that he appreciated the minor leagues' problems, but he did not believe Johnson's bill was the answer. Senator Johnson replied that both Frick and Busch would have ample opportunity to express their opinions before the Judiciary Committee when hearings were held on the proposed legislation.[25]

At those hearings, Senator Johnson stated that sales of Busch beer had risen 17 percent in areas where A-B's beer was advertised on the Cardinals' radio network.[26] On May 25, 1954, in testimony before the Senate Judiciary subcommittee, Busch effectively refuted Johnson's statements and defended his actions with regard to the Cardinals. "Anheuser-Busch, Inc., was a leader in its field before any baseball broadcasts and even before organized baseball itself made an appearance on the American scene," said Busch. He pointed out that from 1945 through 1953, Cardinal radio broadcasts were sponsored by another St. Louis brewery and sales of Anheuser-Busch products still increased during that period of time. "It should be apparent, therefore, that there could be no connection between the broadcasts of the Cardinal game and the increase in Anheuser-Busch sales. Whatever sales results were accomplished by Anheuser-Busch prior to 1954, were achieved without one single Cardinal baseball radio broadcast. And that's the record, gentlemen!"

When Busch finished, Senator William Langer (R) North Dakota, reached down from his seat, shook hands with Gussie Busch and commended him for his frank and open statements.[27] The following day Johnson announced that there would be no further hearings on his bill to bar Anheuser-Busch from owning the St. Louis Cardinals.[28]

Actually, beer and baseball had long been associated. In 1892, St. Louisan Chris Von Der Ahe, who operated a tavern across the street from the Cardinals' home park, noted that he sold more beer outside the park when the Cardinals were at home, concluding that he could probably do even better selling his beer inside. Von der Ahe purchased the team in 1892 and owned them for five years. Brewer Jacob Ruppert owned the New York Yankees for a number of years, although the Yankees did not advertise his beer.[29] Many other breweries sponsored radio broadcasts and advertised their products at the ballparks; but, never before had a brewery itself owned a major league team.

Despite August A. Busch, Jr.'s public statements that the Cardinals would not be used to further the brewery interests, his message to his Board of Directors was quite different. Eager to justify the purchase of the team, Busch predicted to his directors, "Development of the Cardinals will have untold value for our company. This is one of the finest moves in the history of Anheuser-Busch."[30] These private predictions turned out to be far more accurate.

After just two years, Busch was enthusiastically acknowledging that the team helped sell more Budweiser.[31] In addition, the purchase of the Cardinals helped secure television outlets for marketing both his team and his beer.[32] Noted sportswriter Red Smith wrote of Busch, "Probably there never has been another owner in the major leagues with less personal interest in the game than Gussie Busch, or one who used his baseball connection more blatantly to shill for his product."[33] The Anheuser-Busch Brewery was now employing such stunts as having Gussie Busch drive an old beer wagon, pulled by the world-famous Clydesdale horses, around the ballpark on special occasions, such as opening day or the first game of a World Series. Gussie would wave to the crowd while the roaring fans applauded to the rhythm of the Budweiser song.[34] The Budweiser song also became a feature in the game itself. Although the brewery no longer owns the team, the park organist is still likely to play the song at least once between innings of almost every game.

When Anheuser-Busch acquired the Cardinals, they played their home games in Sportsman's Park, owned by Bill Veeck and the St. Louis Browns. The Cardinals paid a yearly rental of $35,000. Busch was appalled by the condition of the park and demanded that Veeck, the landlord, fix it up. Although Veeck had made clean stadiums part of his strategy in Milwaukee and Cleveland, he told Busch he simply did not have sufficient funds to maintain the St. Louis field. In need of cash, Veeck sold Sportsman's Park to Anheuser-Busch for $800,000 and leased it back for $175,000. Busch immediately placed a neon Budweiser eagle under the left field scoreboard. Whenever a Cardinal homered, the eagle flapped its wings and flew from one end to the other.[35]

Busch made other changes and upgraded the park. He installed a new drainage system and sod and constructed a warning track around the outfield. All seats were removed from the center field bleachers and replaced by a garden bordered by evergreens. All box seats were replaced with larger and more comfortable models. Busch also built loge boxes at the front of the lower deck. He remodeled all concession stands, installed apartment boxes under the roof of the upper deck for private parties, lengthened the dugouts, and remodeled the clubhouses.[36]

Buying the ballpark also gave Busch the opportunity to control the advertising inside. One of his first orders was to remove all ads from the walls of the stadium, or as Busch phrased it, "Get that crap off the walls."[37] Busch did not place a Budweiser sign on any of the outfield walls. Instead, he merely painted them a deep green.[38]

Busch then decided to rename the park. He concluded that since Anheuser-Busch, the maker of Budweiser, owned the Cardinals, the park should be renamed Budweiser Stadium. Fortunately, his publicist Al Fleishman and others helped change his mind by asking how he would feel if the Cubs renamed their park Juicy Fruit or Doublemint Stadium. Busch backed down and the following day announced that in memory of his grandfather, father and brother, Sportsman's Park would now be called Busch Memorial Stadium.[39]

The glory days of the St. Louis Cardinals had been between 1926 and 1946, when the team won nine pennants and six World Series.[40] During the 1950s, however, neither the refurbished stadium nor the frequent changes in team management seemed to improve the team's play. There were no pennants, and the Cardinals finished in the second division five times. Despite the time and money Busch was spending to develop another winning Cardinal team, he was accomplishing far more at his brewery, which kept increasing market share. Gussie, accustomed to getting immediate results from his subordinates, began to hire and fire managers. He employed five managers between 1953 and 1959 — Eddie Stanky, Harry Walker, Fred Hutchinson, Stan Hack and Solly Hemus.[41]

He also employed three general managers during this period: Dick Meyer, an Anheuser-Busch executive who supposedly got the job because he was the only one in brewery management with the slightest knowledge of the game; "Trader" Frank Lane; and Bing Devine. Lane, known for his wheeling and dealing as general manager of the Chicago White Sox, continued to earn his nickname with the Cardinals as he manufactured a dozen trades involving 40 players. Lane's deals got him into hot water with

Busch, who announced that if the Cardinals did not win the pennant in 1957, he would fire Lane. The Cardinals finished second that year and in 1958, Lane was working for the Cleveland Indians.[42]

Busch was soon to learn that success in baseball did not come cheaply. He offered the Giants $1 million for Willie Mays and was shocked when the Giants turned him down. He also learned quickly that he was more adept at raising thoroughbreds than at signing good ballplayers. Former general manager Bing Devine recalled that Gussie Busch once offered a $25,000 signing bonus to Fred Walker, a questionable pitching prospect, but the son of former major league star, Dixie Walker. Devine cautioned Busch about signing an unproven youngster, but Busch insisted, "Well, I know about horses and the bloodline is always important and he comes from a family of ballplayers, so let's go with the bloodline." Fred Walker flopped, never reaching the major leagues. Busch learned the hard way that ball players were not horses.[43]

St. Louis was geographically the most southern city in the major leagues in the 1950s and drew a lot of fan support from the Deep South. When Gussie Busch became president of the St. Louis Cardinals, there were few African-American ball players in the major leagues and none on the Cardinal roster. Veeck had brought Satchel Paige to the Browns, and Busch was determined to break the color barrier on the Cardinals. He proclaimed a "new policy with regard to Negro ballplayers," added an African-American to his scouting staff, and, in 1954, purchased the contract of first baseman Tom Alston, from San Diego in the Pacific Coast league for more than $100,000. The fancy-fielding, 22-year-old Alston had hit .297 with 23 homers and 101 RBIs for San Diego in 1953, but had little success in the majors. In not quite four complete seasons with the Cardinals, he hit just four home runs and played in only 91 games.[44] Busch was praised for integrating the team, but Gussie had signed the wrong man. Infielder Red Schoendienst said, "Mr. Busch knew the Cardinals needed to have black players, and some scout had recommended Alston, but he just didn't have the experience he needed to play at the major league level." Bob Broeg, who covered the Cardinals for the *St. Louis Post-Dispatch*, commented, "If [Alston] could have hit at all, he would have made it, but he just wasn't ready."[45]

Busch had more success with black pitcher Brooks Lawrence, who was also signed in 1954. Lawrence compiled a 15–6 record for the Redbirds his first year, although he dropped to 3–8 the next year and was traded to the Cincinnati Reds, where he won 51 games in the following five years.[46] The Cardinals finally had everyday black players when they acquired outfielder Curt Flood from the Cincinnati Reds in 1958 and first baseman

Bill White from San Francisco in 1959.[47] Both played for the Cardinals until 1969.

Despite Veeck's earlier experiences with the city's unequal treatment of black players, St. Louis accepted integration of the Cardinals rather well. Just as the Dodgers had, the Cardinals encountered racial problems in Florida. Both the New York Yankees and the Cardinals trained in St. Petersburg where African-American players lived separately from their team members. In 1961, a St. Petersburg civic organization unintentionally omitted inviting black players to their annual breakfast for Yankees and Cardinals. Bill White, who would go on to become president of the National League, angrily denounced the slight. His comments appeared in many newspapers, including the *St. Louis Post-Dispatch,* which called for a boycott of Anheuser-Bush products. (The identification of the team with the brewery had by now become a *fait accompli.*) Faced with the threat of a boycott, Busch immediately warned St. Petersburg officials that the Cardinals would no longer train there unless integrated accommodations were provided for his entire team. A St. Petersburg businessman purchased two of the city's choicest motels and made them available to the Cardinals. To show their solidarity, veteran players, such as Stan Musial and Ken Boyer, who normally rented private beachfront homes, moved their families into the motels with other members of the team. Gussie Busch instructed Cardinal management to create a small theatre on the premises where new movies were shown every night for the players and their families.[48]

It was in the 1960s that Busch finally had winning teams. During the early years of the decade, Busch continued to hire and fire managers. Hemus, who had been hired in 1959, was gone halfway through the 1961 season and replaced with Johnny Keane, who completed the 1961 season and managed the next three years. In 1960, the Cardinals finished in third place, and the following year they dropped to fifth. In 1962 they did even worse — finishing in sixth place.[49] They improved greatly in 1963, but still came in second, six games behind the Los Angeles Dodgers.[50]

Busch was becoming impatient and anxious for a winner. Frustrated, he fired general manager Bing Devine in July of 1964. Devine's replacement was Bob Howsam, a protégé of Branch Rickey, whom Busch had hired in late 1962 as the team's "special advisor," despite the fact that Rickey was in his eighties. Howsam was also put in charge of player development. Both of these moves infuriated Dick Meyer, Cardinal vice-president.[51] Busch defended his action by stating that Devine had been in charge for seven years and not won a pennant. "There's just one thing I want. I want a pennant for St. Louis at the end of the 1964 season."[52]

On June 15, 1964, before Devine was fired, he made a deal with the

Chicago Cubs that many Cardinal fans still consider one of the best trades in Cardinal history. The Cardinals sent outfielder Doug Clemens and pitchers Ernie Broglio and Bobby Shantz to the Cubs for pitchers Paul Toth and Jack Spring and outfielder Lou Brock. The Cardinals added two more key players to their roster in the next months—infielder Mike Shannon and veteran relief pitcher, Barney Schultz—but it was Brock who provided the ardor the team had been missing.[53]

Howsam would benefit from Devine's trades as the team began to rise in the standings. On the final day of the season, the Cardinals and the Reds were tied for first place, with the Phillies a game behind. The schedule seemed to favor the Cardinals, as the Phillies and Reds went head-to-head. The Cardinals were playing the Mets, who had already lost 108 games that season. After the Phillies shut out the Reds 10–0, all the Cardinals needed was a victory over the lowly Mets. The Mets took an early lead in the game. "When the Mets got ahead of us," Gussie recalled, "I left my box seat and went up to the Redbird Roost high up in the stands. It's my private club, and I walked around for a minute, and then I kicked a hole right in the wall. And then we won. It was wonderful."[54]

The Cardinals had a number of heroes in their 1964 pennant drive. Ken Boyer was voted the National League's MVP. Bob Gibson, Bill White, Curt Flood, Julian Javier, Dick Groat, and Tim McCarver all contributed greatly. Lou Brock, the ex–Cub, was probably most responsible for the Cardinals' first pennant in 18 years. He batted .348 for the Cardinals, scored 111 runs and ended the season with 43 stolen bases.[55]

Cardinal opponents in the 1964 World Series were the New York Yankees, who had won their 15th pennant in 18 years, and their 29th total. With the Series tied at three games apiece, Bob Gibson and his team built up a six-run lead after five innings. The Yankees cut the lead in half in the sixth inning. Manager Keane allowed Gibson to finish the game; and, although the Yankees scored two runs in the ninth, the Cardinals won 7–5 and became world champions.[56]

Despite their victory over the Yankees in the World Series, 1964 ended on a sardonic note. Bing Devine, who had been fired mid-season, was named Executive of the Year and Branch Rickey, Cardinal consultant and personal friend of Devine's successor, Bob Howsam, was let go. Most ironically, manager Johnny Keane, who had led the team to the World Championship, quit to become manager of the team he had just defeated. Busch and Keane had never gotten along, and Keane continually expected to be fired. As soon as the World Series ended, Keane announced that he was going to manage the New York Yankees in 1965. Keane was fired 20 games into the 1966 season and died less than a year later in Houston, Texas, at the age of 55.[57]

Gussie Busch selected Red Schoendienst to replace Keane as manager. Schoendienst, a longtime roommate of Stan Musial, was one of the most popular players ever to wear a Cardinal uniform. He had ended his playing career in 1963 as a Cardinal after playing briefly with the Giants and Milwaukee Braves during the 1956 and 1957 seasons. Schoendienst was player-coach with the Redbirds from 1962 to 1964 and managed the Cardinals for a franchise record 12 years.[58]

Schoendienst's first seasons as manager were less than auspicious. In 1965, the Cardinals won only 80 games and finished in seventh place, the first team in the 20th century to fall to seventh after winning a world championship.[59] In 1966, the Cardinals won 83 games and improved slightly to sixth place.[60]

Busch's chief satisfaction in 1966 was moving his Cardinals into new Busch Stadium. Gussie Busch had spent a lot of the brewery's money fixing up the former Sportsman's Park, but he recognized that it was still an old facility located in an inconvenient area. In 1959, Busch approached St. Louis city officials and civic leaders with a pioneering proposal. He wanted to construct a new stadium in downtown St. Louis to serve as the spur for a major redevelopment of the area. Busch announced that Anheuser-Busch would put up $5 million of the approximately $20 million needed to build the park. The stadium would be similar to others built in that era, a two-deck, nearly circular facility, covering more than 12 acres, but distinguished by 96 open arches around the top.[61] As a further incentive to raise private funds for the new Busch Memorial Stadium, Busch gave up all rights to concessions and parking incomes to a quasi-public group called Civic Center Redevelopment Corporation.[62] In 1964, ground was broken for the new park, and on May 12, 1966, a little more than six months after the St. Louis Gateway Arch was completed, downtown Busch Stadium officially opened as the new home of the St. Louis Cardinals.[63]

Bob Howsam, the only member of Cardinal management remaining from 1964, left at the end of 1966.[64] Like Devine, Howsam made two acquisitions that would greatly help the Cardinals after he left. First, he sent pitcher Ray Sadecki to the Giants for first baseman Orlando Cepeda. Next, he traded third baseman Charley Smith to the Yankees for outfielder Roger Maris, the man who had broken Babe Ruth's homerun record in 1961.[65]

Orlando Cepeda, who nicknamed the 1967 Redbirds "El Birdos," was the team leader in 1967. Once 12 games out of first place, the Cardinals finished the season with 101 wins and beat the second-place Giants by 10½ games.[66] Cepeda's .325 average, 25 home runs and 111 RBIs earned him the MVP award. Roger Maris, Lou Brock, and Curt Flood provided power at the plate and solid defense in the outfield. Although star pitcher,

Bob Gibson, who had 13 victories, broke his leg in July, the pitching slack was taken up by Nelson Briles, Steve Carlton, and 29-year-old Dick Hughes, whose 16–6 record earned him Rookie of the Year honors. These three hurlers combined for a total of 44 victories.[67]

The Cardinals breezed into the World Series in 1967, but their opponents, the Boston Red Sox, had to squeak by both the Minnesota Twins and the Detroit Tigers on the final day of the season, winning the pennant by one game. The Red Sox put up a good fight, taking the series to the seventh game, where the now-recovered Bob Gibson and the Cardinals defeated them 7–2. Gibson won three games for the Cardinals and had an overall earned-run average in the 1967 World Series of 1.00. Other outstanding performances came from Roger Maris, who had 10 hits and seven RBIs in the Series, and Lou Brock, who contributed 12 hits and seven steals.[68]

In 1967, Gussie Busch installed his old friend, Stan Musial, as general manager.[69] Musial held the post only one year and left following the 1967 season to tend to his many other business interests. When Musial stepped down as GM, Gussie Busch did something very unusual: he admitted he had made a mistake and rehired Bing Devine. This time Devine remained for 11 seasons. He remembered Busch as a tough boss and a tough businessman, but "he was also the kind of boss you liked having working for your side."[70]

Cardinal pitching helped the Red Birds win their second consecutive pennant in 1968 and the third for Gussie Busch. Bob Gibson led the major league with a 1.12 ERA and a 22–9 record. Nelson Briles won 19 games, Ray Washburn 14, and Steve Carlton 13. Even the bullpen contributed, with reliever Joe Hoerner winning eight games, saving 17, and finishing the season with an ERA of 1.47.[71] There were two similarities between the 1967 and 1968 World Series. Both went the full seven games and in both Series, a pitcher on the winning team won three of the four games. The only difference was that in 1968, the three-game winner was Tiger hurler Mickey Lolich, who led Detroit to the World Championship. The one bright spot for the Cardinals was Lou Brock, who had 13 hits and 7 stolen bases.[72]

The year 1969 was a turning point for both major league baseball and the St. Louis Cardinals. For baseball, it marked the beginning of divisional play. Although the divisions were called "eastern" and "western," there was little geographic relationship to the teams' divisional assignments. The Cardinals were placed in the eastern division while the teams in Atlanta and Cincinnati, both east of St. Louis, were placed in the west. Busch agreed to the realignment only after the league assured him that the

Chicago Cubs, the Cardinals' oldest rivals, would also be in the eastern division.[73]

For the Cardinals, 1969 began a stretch of mediocrity that lasted throughout the 1970s. By the time the Cardinals won their next pennant in 1982, Gussie Busch had changed his attitude towards his players and the game of baseball as a whole. Reflecting the unrest throughout the country, 1969 also marked the beginning of a period of player unrest. Busch, who successfully worked with labor unions at the brewery, approached his relationship with the players' union far differently.

In the late 1960s, Busch became concerned about the gulf that was developing between him and his players. He attributed his problems to labor lawyer Marvin Miller, who had become head of the Players' Association and had begun, in Gussie's opinion, to take advantage of the owners. In 1968, Miller had negotiated the first Basic Agreement between the players and the owners, giving players a say in how their contracts would be drawn, a minimum salary of $10,000, and the means of filing formal grievances against owners. Just before the 1969 spring training season began, the Association asked for increased health care, life insurance, and pension benefits. When the owners turned Miller down, the players threatened to strike. To prevent a problem with spring training, Commissioner Bowie Kuhn intervened, the owners backed down, and Miller and his players got their way.

The introduction of league playoffs raised another contentious issue: how to distribute revenues from televising these additional games. The owners wanted to separate the longtime link between the players pension fund and broadcast income, while the players accused management of hoarding all the money for themselves. Logic was probably on the side of the players, but public sentiment was on the side of management. A public outcry was raised that greedy baseball players were already making too much money. This disagreement became personal for Busch when Cardinal hurler Bob Gibson appeared on "The Tonight Show" to make a case for the players, straining his relations with Gussie Busch. Cardinal players in particular were insisting they be rewarded for bringing two consecutive pennants to St. Louis.[74]

Busch paid the highest salaries in the National League and had been the first owner with a $1 million payroll. He fully expected his team to play hard to earn their salaries, but instead of gratitude, all Busch heard were protests about player pensions. In an unusual move, on March 22, 1969, Gussie stormed into the Cardinals' spring training dressing room to address his players, bringing with him members of the press and directors of Anheuser-Busch. First, he tore into the players by lumping the rebellion of the Players' Association with the general spirit of protest that was taking place in America during the 1960s. He then outlined in detail all the benefits management had built into the players' pension system, and warned them that their demands for higher salaries and benefits could alienate the fans.[75] "We are beginning to lose sight of who really has to pay the ultimate bill for your salary and your pensions, namely the fans.... Too many fans are saying our players are getting fat. Fans are telling us that if we intend to raise prices to pay for the high salaries, they will stop coming to the games."[76] Busch may not have realized it, but his concluding remarks summed up his philosophy of life, when he said that he was "not a very good loser," and that he was not accustomed to losing in the beer business or in baseball.[77]

If Busch's speech was designed to inspire the Cardinals to improve their play in 1969, it did not work. Red Schoendiest's defending 1968 National League champions finished tied for fourth in 1969.[78] On October 7, 1969, the Cardinals completed one of their biggest deals ever and one which was to have a profound effect on all of baseball. The Cardinals agreed to send four players to the Philadelphia Phillies— Tim McCarver, Curt Flood, Joe Hoerner, and Byron Browne — in exchange for Dick Allen, Cookie Rojas, and Jerry Johnson. Almost immediately, trouble arose when Flood refused to go to Philadelphia and Busch refused to back down on the trade. Busch was anxious to dispose of Flood because he had demanded a raise after the 1969 season even though he was no longer playing that well. The Phillies wanted to get rid of Allen, even though he was one of their better players, because they considered him a troublemaker. Finally, a deal with the Phillies was completed when the Cardinals substituted minor leaguer Willie Montanez for Flood.

Flood felt he was justified in standing his ground. First, he was offended that after 12 years in the majors, his notice of the trade was an "impersonal phone call." He also objected to being sent to Philadelphia, a city supposedly hostile to African-Americans. More importantly, although Flood had not been personally involved in the black power struggle of the 1960s, he sympathized with its goals and was particularly upset about being "treated like property." Curt Flood decided that if he could not remain with the Cardinals, he would go to court and challenge the reserve clause that allowed him to be traded or sold at the whim of his team.[79]

Flood filed suit on January 16, 1970. He argued that the reserve clause dehumanized him, turning him into a consignment of goods to be bought and sold. Seven months later, the federal district court ruled against him. While an appeal was pending in the Supreme Court, the Phillies traded

Flood to the Washington Senators with the understanding that his playing for the Senators would not prejudice his case. But the years out of the
game had made him rusty. After batting only .200 in 13 games with the
Senators in 1971, Flood quit baseball.[80] By a 5 to 3 decision, the Supreme
Court upheld the reserve clause's restrictions on players' rights.[81] Even
though Flood had lost his case, his defiant action set the stage for arbitration, free agency, and the eventual repeal of the reserve clause by the
mid–1970s.[82]

For the 1970 season, the Cardinals remained active in the trade market, although their deal-making skills certainly didn't improve. They sent
Dave Giusti and Dave Ricketts to the Pirates for Carl Taylor and a minor
leaguer and traded Ray Washburn to the Reds for George Culver.[83] The
Cardinals ended up in fourth again in 1970.[84]

Flood was not the only Cardinal player to give Busch problems. Dick
Allen had been a key part of the Curt Flood deal between the Cards and
Phillies, but Allen refused to sign a contract for 1970. He had earned
$80,000 the year before and wanted $100,000. Busch bluntly stated that
the $90,000 deal the Cardinals had offered was final and added, "If he
doesn't take it, he won't ever play for the Cardinals."[85] Allen did agree to
terms and played for St. Louis in 1970, but the following year Gussie Busch
traded him to the Los Angeles Dodgers.[86] Schoendienst's team improved
to second place in the eastern division in 1971, but again missed post-season play.

According to Busch, it was not money but principle that was behind
two of his most publicized player disputes, both involving premium southpaw hurlers. Gussie Busch and Steve Carlton had a history of salary battles. In the 1969 season, Carlton posted an ERA of 2.17 and a won-lost
record of 17–11. For 1970, he wanted his salary doubled, and to make his
point, Carlton "held out" during most of the 1970 spring training season.
Furious, Busch refused to give in, growling, "I don't care if he ever pitches
another damn ball game for us." The two men finally reached agreement,
and the lefty had a satisfactory year in 1970. Carlton became a 20-game
winner for the Cardinals in 1971 and demanded $55,000 to sign his 1972
contract. Busch instructed his GM to give Carlton $50,000, which he
pointed out was "the biggest percentage increase of any regular player on
the team." If Carlton refused, Devine was to "get rid of him." Carlton kept
insisting on the extra $5,000; so, following instructions, Devine traded
him to the Philadelphia Phillies for pitcher Rick Wise. Busch claimed that
by making an example of Carlton, "My hope is [that] some of the other
owners will take the stand I'm going to take and get this thing back to normal."[87]

On principle, Busch might have been right in not giving Carlton the additional $5,000, but trading him to Philadelphia probably ranks as the one of the Cardinals' all-time worst deals. In 1972, Carlton won 27 games while losing only 10, compiled an ERA of 1.97 and won the first of his four Cy Young Awards. He would win 20 or more games for the Phillies four more times. When he retired from baseball in 1988, Steve Carlton had a lifetime total of 329 wins, second only to Warren Spahn among left-handed pitchers.[88]

Busch's disagreement with lefty Jerry Reuss was ostensibly over the cost of an airline ticket, but Busch saw it as a symbol of far more. Busch always felt that it helped team morale to allow the players' wives to travel to and from spring training on the team plane. At the end of the 1971 spring training season, the Cards chartered a flight to shuttle players and their wives back to St. Louis, but pitcher Jerry Reuss's wife took a commercial flight instead. The team paid for her ticket, but Busch deducted the amount from Reuss's paycheck. Reuss took the dispute to arbitration and won. Busch was infuriated, calling Reuss typical of a "new breed of player," unlike his duck-hunting pals, Stan Musial and Red Schoendienst. These were the types of players Busch respected — they signed their contracts and were happy to be major-leaguers.

Reuss pitched for the Cardinals the entire 1971 season, but after he, like Carlton, refused the salary compromise Busch offered, Reuss was traded to the Houston Astros for pitcher Scipio Spinks. Reuss would go on to win 198 games for other teams while Busch would continue to complain about "this player-rebellion stuff and all the damned protestors out there…. The player contracts are at their best, the pension plan is the finest, and the fringe benefits are better than ever, yet the players think that we [the owners] are a bunch of stupid asses," he remarked.[89] "I hope to God this is not a majority view," he added. "I can't understand what's happening here, or on the campuses, or in our great country."[90]

Busch's frustration reached an even higher level during the spring of 1972 when the players' union asked for a new pension plan that increased the players' share of TV revenue. The owners immediately turned down the request. The impasse continued throughout the spring, despite the union's threats to strike if agreement were not reached. A few owners argued that management would have to make substantial concessions, but hardliners, led by August Busch, believed that they could destroy the Players' Association by forcing a strike.[91]

At a meeting in late March, the owners agreed to hold firm and also decided to make no statements to the press camped outside the meeting. "No comment," replied each owner as he stepped out of the meeting room.

But Gussie Busch could not contain himself. In response to the barrage of questions, the irascible Busch snapped, "We voted unanimously to take a stand. We're not going to give them another goddam cent. If they want to strike — let 'em."[92]

The newspaper accounts of Busch's challenge were posted in numerous locker rooms as, on April 1, 1972, the players began the first baseball strike in the 20th century, threatening to wipe out the entire season. The owners had miscalculated; instead of removing Marvin Miller, the players stood united behind him. More moderate owners pleaded with those owners who were less flexible, such as Busch and O'Malley, to settle, pointing out the financial losses they were incurring. Busch was well aware of the toll, stating that the Cardinals might lose $1.5 million or more, but he refused to waver in his opposition to what he saw as unreasonable player demands and continued efforts to overturn the reserve clause.[93] Don't you believe in collective bargaining, Busch was asked. With a smile, he replied, "I wonder how the gentleman thinks we keep the world's largest brewery going. It's just that in baseball I believe we've reached the point where it's necessary to draw the line."[94]

Fans generally supported the owners, and Busch also received moral support from C. C. Johnson Spink, editor and publisher of the *Sporting News*. In two editorials, Spink agreed with Busch's position. He also mentioned the fans' resentment of higher ticket prices to pay the salaries of utility players who were making far more than most of their fans.[95] Spink urged the players to appreciate the strides they had made and to be realistic in their future demands. According to Spink, the ceiling had been reached in baseball under present conditions.[96] (It is interesting to note that many of the issues in baseball in 1972 continue to plague the game more than three decades later).

Ultimately, the moderates prevailed and the strike was settled. The season opened late and each team missed an average of eight games, which were never replayed.[97]

Busch considered the strike a personal insult and could not fathom why Cardinal players, whom he claimed he always treated well, had gone out. Many baseball observers agreed that Gussie Busch personified the paternalism of the "old" owners, a man who genuinely cared for his players and considered many of them an extension of his own family, with him as head of the clan.[98]

Even when the strike seemed imminent, Busch had met with his players in Florida. Although he tried to convince them to accept management's offer, he also told them that in the event of a strike, the team would provide airplane tickets for each player to return to his home.[99]

Disappointed in his players, Gussie chose to "get back" at them in small, but telling ways. According to *Newsweek,* instead of large chartered jets, Gussie ordered them to fly in smaller planes. The players no longer had individual rooms on the road, but were instructed to double up. As the ultimate retaliation, Gussie canceled the free cases of beer that had been delivered to their homes when they were playing in St. Louis.[100]

Negotiations between players and management continued even after the strike ended. Between 1973 and 1974, the players were able to win concessions from the owners, which Busch resented and fought. Disregarding warnings from Busch and Charlie Finley (whose support may have hurt more than it helped), the owners agreed that players with two years' experience could request salary arbitration after any signed contract had expired. No player could have his salary cut more than 20 percent in any given year. In addition, any player with a minimum of ten years in the major leagues and five years continuous service with his current club could block trades; those who had played in the majors for five years could refuse demotion to the minor leagues.[101] Ironically, many of these were privileges Curt Flood had been denied.

During these tumultuous years, the Cardinals came in fourth in 1972 and finished in second place in 1973 and 1974. In 1975, the team ended in a third-place tie.[102]

Elsewhere, 1975 proved to be a landmark year for Gussie Busch and baseball. Personally, Gussie's eldest son, Augustus Busch III, known as Auggie, convinced the company's Board of Directors to force his father's retirement as head of Anheuser-Busch, Inc. Auggie felt that Gussie was behind the times and not up to the financial challenge that A-B's competitors were mounting. According to a former district manager for A-B Brewery, Auggie was truly worried that under the leadership of 76-year-old Gussie, the company's commanding industry lead might slip away.

Gussie fought to stay in control but, finally, Auggie and the Board made him the ultimate offer. Sign over leadership of the brewery and he could stay in charge of the Cardinals. Otherwise, he would lose the team. Gussie did consider purchasing the St. Louis Cardinals from A-B, but, after an independent appraiser determined that they were worth $12 million, Gussie decided he would rather save money and just remain president of the club. Free of brewery responsibility, Gussie now began to devote his full attention to running the Cardinals.[103] He also began to take a much larger role in how the game as a whole was being run.

Everyone in baseball was affected by the truly defining event of 1975 — the repeal of baseball's reserve clause. Professional arbitrator Peter Seitz, upheld by two federal courts, nullified the perpetual renewal provision that bound a player to his team for life or until his team chose to get rid of him. Now, when a player signed a deal, he was obligated to the team for the duration of the deal and then was able to negotiate for himself as a free agent.[104] To most baseball observers, the Seitz decision was one of the events in the 20th century that changed the "face of baseball."[105]

In the 1976 season, Busch publicly announced that he would go out and sign free agents that would help his perpetually second- or third-place team win another pennant. "We are making a careful study of the situation and if we have to go out and spend to get the players we absolutely have to have, we are going to do it for our loyal fans," said Busch.[106] Then, Busch found out how much other teams were paying for free agents. Conceding that the Cardinals could probably afford to get into the free agent market, he nonetheless opted out, declaring that he would obtain the players he needed through trades or from the Cardinal farm system.[107]

Although owners knew before the 1976 season began that they could never restore the reserve clause, they still wanted some kind of restriction on free agency. As a negotiating ploy, late in February 1976, the owners refused to open spring training camps. On March 17, Commissioner Bowie Kuhn personally interceded to end the lockout and the 1976 season got under away as scheduled. He justified his action by saying, "It is now vital that spring training get under away without further delay. While nobody is more disappointed than I that we do not have solid progress to a final agreement, the fans are the most important people around and their interests now become paramount. Opening the camps and starting the season on time is what they want."[108] Kuhn's intervention in the training camp lockout was another mark against the commissioner in Busch's mind.[109]

On July 12, 1976, the owners and players hammered out their next Basic Agreement. Its first new provision allowed any player with at least six years of major league service to simply notify his club in writing at the end of season that he intended to become a free agent. The second provision worked out a schedule for players playing without contracts to become free agents.[110] Busch was outraged. He told his fellow owners they had been "jackasses" for agreeing to go on with the season without a signed contract with the players. "We have lost the war and the only question is can we live with the surrender terms?"[111]

Still irate over the agreement, at the National League owners meeting in August 1976, Gussie Busch called for the ouster of both John Gaherin as the NL labor representative and Chub Feeney as President of the National League. Busch compared the league's situation to one he was most familiar with as he asked his fellow owners, "Would anyone in this room, faced with a major labor fight concerning the welfare and possible continuation of his business, hire John Gaherin to represent him and feel he had the best man in the world?"[112] Busch also blasted Feeny's leadership abilities. "What kind of influence and guts does our league office have?" he asked. Busch accused Feeney of failing to visit National League cities and failing to exhibit any foresight or creativity.[113]

Chub Feeny remained president, but his contract was renewed for only two years instead of the customary five. In addition, Busch, who had criticized the National League for maintaining its offices in San Francisco, was successful in pressuring Feeney to move to New York.[114]

After the Cardinals fell to fifth place in 1976, Gussie replaced Red Schoendienst after 12 years as manager with Vernon Rapp. Rapp was known as a strict disciplinarian, and Busch felt he was exactly what the Cardinals needed. It soon became evident that Rapp was not the answer to the Cardinals' problems as the players, used to Schoendienst's more easy-going manner, had a great deal of trouble adjusting to Rapp. The Cardinal roster had a number of excellent players including pitcher John Denny, shortstop Garry Templeton, outfielder Jerry Mumphrey, catcher Ted Simmons, and first baseman Keith Hernandez. Rapp soon butted heads with most of them publicly, especially "the mad Hungarian," pitcher Al Hrabosky, who had been a Red Bird since 1970. When Rapp ordered Hrabosky to remove his trademark Fu Manchu mustache, Busch at first backed his manager. Later he relented, telling Hrabosky that in exchange, he expected his performance to improve. Busch dropped the hair code for the rest of the season, but Hrabosky was traded to Kansas City prior to the start of the 1978 season.[115] The Cardinals finished 1977 up two notches to third place, but they won only 13 more games than they had the year before.[116]

Rapp was fired after managing 19 games in 1978. It was a rebellious time, not just in baseball, but in society in general and Busch admitted that his manager was working under a handicap. According to Busch, the players had been in complete control ever since the 1976 Basic Agreement was approved.[117]

The Cardinals had three managers in 1978. After Busch dismissed Rapp, Jack Krol served as interim manager until Gussie Busch hired Ken Boyer. Boyer had been a star player for the Cardinals, and Busch hoped he would get the respect the players had not given Rapp. Despite the talent on the team and relative peace between players and management, Boyer got little out of his club. The Cardinals fell back to fifth place, with a dismal 69–93 record, only three games ahead of the last-place Mets.[118]

Gussie Busch was infuriated by Cardinal play in 1978 and let the team know it on a number of occasions. In June, he lambasted the players for "constant mental errors, for a loose and carefree attitude…. I am getting damn mad and I think it is time the players better start getting mad, too."[119] On another occasion he warned them, "There is no way, and I repeat no way, I am going to tolerate this type of performance for the most loyal fans in the world, and I mean this…. While I do not intend to make any drastic moves at the present time, I want this message carried loud and clear: The Big Eagle, the Boss, Gussie, whatever they want to call me, is not happy. I am tired of excuses."[120]

Despite Boyer's inability to improve the team, Busch rehired him to manage the Cardinals in 1979. Gussie took out his wrath on GM Bing Devine, firing him again, just as he had done more than decade earlier. In another ironic situation, Busch replaced Devine with John Claiborne, a man whom Devine had been helping find work in baseball. Devine was dumbfounded when he learned he was being replaced by Claiborne.[121]

Devine's legacy for the Cardinals this time was the acquisition of two 15-game winners in 1979, Pete Vuckovich and Silvio Martinez. Keith Hernandez won the National League batting title with a .344 average and shared MVP honors with Pittsburgh's Willie Stargell. Garry Templeton became the first switch-hitter to get 100 hits from each side of the plate and Lou Brock got his 3,000th hit. The Cardinals, however, still lacked solid pitching and finished in only third place.[122]

In 1980, Gussie Busch turned 81 years old and desperately wanted to see his team win another pennant. John Claiborne introduced Gussie to the man who would accomplish this for him when he suggested that Busch hire "Whitey" Herzog as manager. Herzog had managed the Kansas City Royals to three consecutive divisional titles in 1976, 1977 and 1978, but his team lost to the Yankees in the playoffs all three years. Herzog was fired at the end of the 1979 season, after a number of disagreements with Royals owner Ewing Kauffman.

On June 8, 1980, with the Cardinals posting a disappointing 18–33 record so far that season, Busch fired Boyer as Cardinal manager. He instructed his close friend and attorney, Lou Sussman, to offer Whitey Herzog the job.[123] Whitey was in his late forties, but despite the difference in age, Busch and Herzog took to each other immediately. They had similar temperaments, and, most importantly, saw eye to eye on almost every baseball issue.[124]

For the next few weeks, Herzog observed the team and then met Busch at Grant's Farm to report his findings. Pulling no punches, Herzog bluntly told Busch that the Cardinals had a drug problem, an almost universal concern in baseball during the 1980s. "You've got a bunch of mean people…. It's the first time I have ever been scared to walk through my own clubhouse ... we ain't going to win with this sorry bunch. We've got to do some housecleaning."[125]

On August 29, Busch fired Claiborne and offered Herzog the job of general manager. To take over Herzog's field duties, Busch talked Cardinal coach Red Schoendienst into coming back as manager for the remainder of the season. Herzog began his rebuilding almost immediately following the 1980 season. He signed catcher Darrell Porter, an old friend from Kansas City, as a free agent. Herzog then headed to the winter meetings in Dallas where he completed an 11-player swap with the San Diego Padres, getting Rollie Fingers, Bob Shirley, Gene Tenace, and minor-league catcher Bob Geren, in exchange for catchers Terry Kennedy and Steve Swisher, infielder Mike Phillips, and pitchers John Littlefield, John Urrea, Kim Seaman, and Al Olmstead.

Herzog then traded first baseman Leon Durham and infielders Ty Waller and Ken Reitz to the Chicago Cubs for ace relief pitcher Bruce Sutter. Ted Simmons, the regular Cardinal catcher, was unhappy about being displaced by Porter. He waived his no-trade clause, and agreed to go to Milwaukee. In addition to Ted Simmons, Herzog sent Rollie Fingers (who left before ever making a Cardinal appearance,) and Pete Vuckovich and got outfielders Sixto Lezcano and David Green and pitchers Lary Sorensen and Dave LaPoint from Milwaukee.[126]

In 1981, the Cardinals had the best overall record in the NL East, but came out of the strike-shortened season with nothing, thanks to the playoff scheme devised by Baseball Commissioner Kuhn. Since the beginning of the 1981 season, the owners and the players' union argued over free agent compensation. Marvin Miller, representing the union, announced that there would be a strike in 1981 if the issue could not be resolved. Despite this warning, the owners refused to negotiate and instead began establishing a strike fund. Gussie Busch, who headed the hard-liners as usual, stated flatly that he would not allow the union to dictate to him. With neither side willing to give in, professional baseball, for the first time, experienced a strike during the season. All games were canceled until further notice.

It was late July before both sides settled their differences and agreed to continue play, scheduling the "second half" of the season to begin after the delayed All Star break. More than 700 games had been canceled and determining which teams would compete in the 1981 post season was the most important question to be settled. The answer left at least two teams very dissatisfied.

Under Commissioner Bowie Kuhn's formula, the second-half champions in each division would play the first-half winners, assuming that different teams won each half. If a team won both halves, then it would face the number two team of the second half. Despite their total record, the Cardinals finished second during both halves of the season and, under Kuhn's formula, were eliminated from post-season play. The Cincinnati Reds, the team with the best overall stats in the NL West, suffered a similar fate. Gussie Busch would not forget that Kuhn had been responsible for his Cardinals missing the playoffs in 1981.[127]

Nineteen eighty-two marked two major events: the first World Series win for the Cardinals since 1967 and Busch's successful ouster of Commissioner Bowie Kuhn. Putting aside the debacle of the 1981 season, the Cardinals busied themselves for 1982. They obtained outfielder Willie McGee from the Yankees in exchange for pitcher Bob Sykes, acquired Lonnie Smith for pitchers Lary Sorensen and Silvio Martinez in a three-way trade with the Indians and Phillies, and then dumped shortstop Garry Templeton. Templeton had doomed himself with the Cardinals the previous August when he made an obscene gesture to the Ladies' Day crowd at Busch Stadium after being ejected from the game. The Cardinals definately got the better of the deal as they traded Templeton to the Padres for future Hall of Fame shortstop Ozzie Smith. With these players in place, the Cardinals captured their first division title and then went on to sweep the Atlanta Braves in the League Championship Series.[128]

The Cardinals met the Milwaukee Brewers in the 1982 World Series. The expected contest pitting Cardinal speed against Brewer power turned out to be a seven-game slugfest between the two teams. The Cardinals scored 39 runs to 33 for the Brewers. Down three games to two, the Cardinals won games six and seven to take the Series. Despite all the scoring, one of the heroes in the Series was Cardinal relief pitcher, Bruce Sutter, who saved two of the four Cardinal victories.[129]

The Cardinals had triumphed on the playing field in 1982. Gussie Busch won a personal victory that same year by removing Bowie Kuhn from his post as commissioner of baseball. The feud between Busch and Kuhn began in 1972, when Kuhn, much to Busch's chagrin, expressed his willingness to negotiate the reserve clause with the players. Four years later, the commissioner, in direct opposition to Busch, forced the owners to end their spring training lockout and, later that year, fined Busch $5,000 for some of his comments. "I suspect," said Kuhn, "that Busch has never been disciplined before in his long life."[130] On another occasion, when Kuhn again complained about profanity during a meeting of the baseball owners, Gussie leaped to his feet and growled, "Listen, Commissioner, I'm an American citizen who fought for the freedom of speech, and I'll be damned if you or anybody else is going to change me."[131] Kuhn dug himself in deeper with Busch with his "split-season" formula the previous year that, as Gussie saw it, deprived his Cardinals of their rightful play-off opportunity.

But the chief source of contention between Kuhn and Busch had as much to do with beer as with baseball, and proved, if anyone still had any doubts, just how closely the two were aligned.

Since 1975, the year Gussie was forced to leave the brewery, Miller Brewing had been cutting into Anheuser-Busch's market share, moving from a distant seventh to a strong second by 1976. Miller owed much of its success to aggressive marketing that sought to grab every potential TV spot at major sporting events. By 1980, Miller had become the almost exclusive beer sponsor for *Monday Night Football* and the sole sponsor of college football's *Game of the Week*, the 1980 Olympics, the Indy 500, and the World Series, just to name a few.

Anheuser-Busch was no slouch when it came to sports advertising, allocating 70 percent of its $400 million broadcast ad budget to various sport venues. By the early 1980s, A-B was sponsoring 23 of the 24 local major league team radio broadcasts, with Miller sponsoring only the Brewer games. To increase Anheuser-Busch's national presence in TV baseball, Gussie, son Auggie who now ran the brewery, and A-B attorney, Louis Susman, wanted to push Miller out of the sole beer sponsorship of NBC's and ABC's baseball telecasts. They expected Kuhn to help them, just as Football Commissioner Pete Rozelle had helped Anheuser-Busch obtain some *Monday Night Football* telecasts. Kuhn refused, telling the Busch family that it was solely a network matter and he would not intercede in a contract.[132]

Year earlier, Walter O'Malley had cautioned his protégé Kuhn to be wary of Anheuser-Busch. "Their potential is enormous," O'Malley had warned.[133] Kuhn was to find out how prophetic O'Malley had been. Spurned on the TV advertising request, Gussie, with the full backing of Anheuser-Busch, began a campaign to have baseball owners refuse to renew Kuhn's contract for a third seven-year term. Walter O'Malley had saved Kuhn's job seven years earlier, but O'Malley was no longer around to rally the troops.

Kuhn did have his supporters. In fact, a majority of the club owners favored retaining him and, on November 1, 1982, the pro–Kuhn forces, confident that they had the votes to give Kuhn another term, called a vote on the commissioner's fate. Kuhn got the votes of 11 of the 14 American League owners. In the National League, however, five teams—the Cardinals, Braves, Mets, Astros, and Reds—opposed him, while only seven clubs were behind him. Kuhn needed 20 of the 26 owners to vote in his favor;

only 18 did. Gussie Busch was delighted. Kuhn was allowed to remain in office until a search committee could come up with a suitable replacement candidate. Once the vote had been taken, Gussie Busch pounded the table with his cane, exulting, "He should clean out his desk tomorrow."[134] With a few exceptions, Gussie was now "King of Baseball" as well as "King of Beers."[135] (After Kuhn's defeat, the Los Angeles Dodgers, now run by Walter O'Malley's son Peter, removed Budweiser from Dodger Stadium, replacing it with Miller High Life.)[136]

Busch's ouster of Kuhn was his final activity as one of the true power brokers in major league baseball, as the years began to take their toll on Gussie's health. He remained an avid fan, however, and was to be rewarded with two more outstanding Cardinal seasons.

In 1985, the Cardinals won the National League pennant and met their cross-state rivals, the Kansas City Royals, in the World Series. The Cardinals won the first two games on the road, but were able to capture only one of the next three home games as Kansas City pitching completely stifled Cardinal offense. A controversial ninth-inning call in game six gave the Royals the win and tied the series at three-all. Completely demoralized, the Cardinals lost game seven to Kansas City 11–0.[137]

After finishing third in 1986, the Cardinals won their final pennant for Gussie Busch in 1987. Their opponents in this series were the Minnesota Twins, which became the first team in history to win a World Series by taking all four games at home and none on the road.[138] In the 1987 series, fans enthusiastically cheered the 88-year-old Gussie Busch as he ceremoniously drove the Budweiser wagon, Clydesdales and all, around Busch Stadium.[139]

On September 29, 1989, Gussie Busch died at his home, with his children at his bedside. He was 90 years old. Fred Kuhlmann, who had become chief operating officer of the Cardinals, said of Busch, "He was Mr. Anheuser-Busch, Mr. Budweiser, and he was Mr. St. Louis."[140] *The Sporting News* called him a driving force in his business, the key figure in the revitalization of downtown St. Louis, and "the man most responsible for the success of the Cardinals over the past 35 years."[141] But there was far more to his legacy.

August A. Busch, Jr., had entered baseball in 1953 with little knowledge of how the game operated. He learned quickly and soon took a leadership role in baseball's top hierarchy that was almost as powerful as the position he held in his beer business. In fact, he merged beer and baseball (and eventually beer and many other major sports) so closely that it is virtually impossible today to deny their mutual dependence. Busch established the concept of corporate ownership by arranging for his company to buy and officially own the team. His unyielding opposition to modifying the reserve clause eventually led to its repeal and the advent of free agency.

Experts and fans can debate whether the game is better or worse because of these changes, but no one can debate that Gussie Busch — along with Charles Ebbets, Barney Dreyfuss, Helene Britton, Clark Griffith, Walter O'Malley, Bill Veeck, and Charles Finley — helped shaped baseball.

Notes

Chapter 1

1. Frank Graham, *The Brooklyn Dodgers: An Informal History* (New York, 1948), 4.

2. *Ibid.*

3. *Ibid.*, 5.

4. Tommy Holmes, *Dodgers Daze and Knights* (New York, 1953), 20.

5. Graham, *The Brooklyn Dodgers*, 5; Jonathan Fraser Light, *The Cultural Encyclopedia of Baseball* (Jefferson, NC, 1997), 119.

6. Donald Dewey and Nicholas Acocella, *The Ball Clubs* (New York, 1996), 79.

7. Graham, *The Brooklyn Dodgers*, 6; Dewey and Acocella, *The Ball Clubs*, 79; Light, *The Cultural Encyclopedia of Baseball*, 120.

8. *The Reach Official American League Guide*, undated, 245; *The Sporting News*, January 8, 1898; Burt Solomon, *Where They Ain't* (New York, 1999), 141.

9. Steven A. Reiss, *Touching Base* (Westport, CT, 1980), 71.

10. Graham, The *Brooklyn Dodgers*, 7.

11. *Ibid.*, 8.

12. Dewey and Acocella, *The Ball Clubs*, 80.

13. Light, *Cultural Encyclopedia of Baseball*, 120.

14. Dewey and Acocella, *The Ball Clubs*, 80.

15. Solomon, *Where They Ain't*, 141.

16. Graham, *The Brooklyn Dodgers*, 9.

17. Solomon, *Where They Ain't*, 141.

18. Dewey and Acocella, *The Ball Clubs*, 80; Graham, *The Brooklyn Dodgers*, 10; Light, *Cultural Encyclopedia*, 434; Solomon, *Where They Ain't*, 142; *The Sporting News*, January 8, 1898.

19. Light, *Cultural Encyclopedia of Baseball*, 193.

20. Dewey and Acocella, *The Ball Clubs*, 80.

21. Richard Goldstein, *Superstars and Screwballs: 100 Years of Brooklyn Baseball* (New York, 1991), 72.

22. Dewey and Acocella, *The Ball Clubs*, 80.

23. Goldstein, *Superstars and Screwballs*, 72.

24. David Quentin Voigt, *The League That Failed* (Lanham, MD, 1998), 88.

25. Dewey and Acocella, *The Ball Clubs*, 81; Graham, *The Brooklyn Dodgers*, 12.

26. Goldstein, *Superstars and Screwballs*, 75.

27. Light, *The Cultural Encyclopedia of Baseball*, 22. For a more complete story of the founding of the American League see Eugene C. Murdock's *Ban Johnson, Czar of Baseball* (Westport, CT, 1982).

28. Graham, *The Brooklyn Dodgers*, 12–16; Peter C. Bjarkman (ed.), *Encyclopedia of Baseball's Team Histories: National League* (Westport, CT, 1991), 77.

29. *The Sporting News*, July 12, 1902.

30. *Ibid.*

31. Eugene G. Murdock, *Ban Johnson: Czar of Baseball* (Westport, CT, 1982), 62.

32. *Ibid.*; Light, *The Cultural History of Baseball*, 23.

33. Graham, *The Brooklyn Dodgers*, 12–16; Bjarkman, *Encyclopedia of Baseball's Team Histories: National League*, 77.

34. Dewey and Acocella, *The Ball Clubs*, 81.

35. Graham, *The Brooklyn Dodgers*, 16–17.

36. *Ibid.*, 12.

37. *Ibid.*, 13.

38. Larry D. Mansch, *Rube Marquard: The Life and Times of a Baseball Hall of Famer* (Jefferson, NC, 1998), 162; Light, *The Cultural Encyclopedia of Baseball*, 120.

39. Daniel Okrent and Steve Wulf, *Baseball Anecdotes* (New York, 1989), 41; Light, 120; Donald Dewey and Nicholas Acocella, *The Biographical History of Baseball* (New York, 1995), 129–130; *The Sporting News*, February 25, 1905.

40. John Thorn, Pete Palmer and Michael Gershman (eds.), *Total Baseball* (Kingsport, NY, 2001), 2424.

41. *New York Times*, January 25, 1912.

42. Graham, *The Brooklyn Dodgers*, 17; Holmes, *Dodger Daze and Knights*, 23; Dewey and Acocella, *The Ball Clubs*, 81–82; Thorn et al., *Total Baseball*, 2420, 2428.

43. Graham, *The Brooklyn Dodgers*, 32.

44. Dewey and Acocella, *The Ball Clubs*, 80.

45. *The Sporting News*, March 14, 1903.

46. *Ibid.*, May 2, 1909.

47. Harold Seymour, *Baseball: The Golden Age* (New York, 1971), 62.

48. Light, *Cultural Encyclopedia of Baseball*, 86; Seymour, *Baseball, the Golden Age*, 128.

49. *Ibid.*, 59; *The Sporting News*, January 20, 1907.

50. *Ibid.*, January 12, 1911.

51. Dean A Sullivan, *Early Innings: A Documentary History of Baseball 1825–1908* (Lincoln, 1995), 219.

52. Seymour, *Baseball, the Golden Age*, 13; Voigt, *The League That Failed*, 37.

53. *The Sporting News*, December 18, 1913.

54. *Ibid.*

55. Jack Kavanaugh and Norman Macht, *Uncle Robbie* (Cleveland, 1999), 145.

56. Stanley Cohen, *Dodgers: The First 100 Years* (New York, 1990), 13; Graham, *The Brooklyn Dodgers*, 25.

57. *Ibid.*

58. John A. Garraty (ed.), *American National Biography* (New York, 1999), 1; Thorn et al., *Total Baseball*, 1274; Goldstein, *Superstars and Screwballs*, 83.

59. *Ibid.*, 713.

60. Cohen, *Dodgers: First 100 Years*, 13; Holmes, *Dodger Daze and Knights*, 27.

61. Cohen, *Dodgers: First 100 Years*, 13.

62. Charles H. Ebbets, "Why I Am Building a Baseball Stadium," *Leslie's Weekly* (April 4, 1912) (unpaginated article, Ebbets file, Hall of Fame, Cooperstown, New York.)

63. G. Edward White, *Creating the National Pastime: Baseball Transforms Itself, 1903–1905* (Princeton, NJ, 1996), 1.

64. Reiss, *Touching Base: Politics, Ball-Parks and the Neighborhood*, 102–103.

65. *Ibid.*, 104.

66. Peter Golenbeck, *Bums: An Oral History of the Brooklyn Dodgers* (New York, 1984), 19.

67. Seymour, *Baseball: The Golden Age*, 52; Graham, *The Brooklyn Dodgers*, 35.

68. Curt Smith, *Storied Stadiums: Baseball's History Through Its Ballparks* (New York, 2001), 102; Golenbeck, *Bums*, 19; *New York Times*, March 14, 1912.

69. Quoted in Richard Goldstein, *Superstars and Screwballs*, 102.

70. Cohen, *Dodgers: The First 100 Years*, 15; Light, *The Cultural Encyclopedia of Baseball*, 225.

71. Cohen, *Dodgers: The First 100 Years*, 15.

72. Dewey and Acocella, *The Ball Clubs*, 82.

73. Michael Gershman, *Diamonds: The Evolution of the Ballpark* (Boston, 1993), 110.

74. Bjarkman, *Encyclopedia of Baseball Team Histories: National League*, 79; David Porter (ed.), *Biographical Directory of American Sports* (Westport, CT, 2000), 432.

75. Light, *The Cultural Encyclopedia of Baseball*, 253; Goldstein, *Screwballs and Superstars*, 105.

76. Thorn et al., *Total Baseball*, 1234.

77. Goldstein, *Superstars and Screwballs*, 105; Graham, *The Brooklyn Dodgers*, 41.

78. *Ibid.*, 49; Robert W. Creamer, *Stengel: His Life and Times* (New York, 1984), 76.

79. *Ibid.*, 76–77.

80. *Ibid.*, 81.

81. *The Sporting News,* December 13, 1915.

82. Graham, *The Brooklyn Dodgers,* 39; Thorn et al., *Total Baseball,* 2420.

83. Bjarkman, *Encyclopedia of Baseball Team Histories: National League,* 79.

84. Graham, *The Brooklyn Dodgers,* 40; Bjarkman, *Encyclopedia of Baseball Team Histories: National League,* 79–80.

85. Holmes, *Dodger Daze and Knights,* 31.

86. Thorn, et al., *Total Baseball,* 2110, 2113.

87. Bjarkman, *Encyclopedia of Baseball Team Histories: National League,* 80.

88. Kavanaugh and Macht, *Uncle Robbie,* 92; Dewey and Acocella, *The Ball Clubs,* 84.

89. Holmes, *Dodger Daze and Knights,* 34; Thorn et al., *Total Baseball,* 1491.

90. Goldstein, *Superstars and Screwballs,* 124.

91. *Ibid.,* 125.

92. Seymour, *Baseball, The Golden Age,* 352; Graham, *The Brooklyn Dodgers,* 64.

93. Seymour, *Baseball, The Golden Age,* 355.

94. Edward Bayer Moss, "The Dollars Behind the Diamond," *Harper's Weekly* (August 31, 1912), 13–14.

95. Seymour, *Baseball, The Golden Age,* 19.

96. Dewey and Acocella, *The Ball Clubs,* 84.

97. Kavanaugh and Macht, *Uncle Robbie,* 85; Graham, *The Brooklyn Dodgers,* 32.

98. Holmes, *Dodger Daze and Knights,* 35.

99. Garraty, *American National Biography,* 2.

100. Dewey and Acocella, *The Biographical History of Baseball,* 130.

101. Light, *The Cultural Encyclopedia of Baseball,* 709.

102. Riess, *Touching Base,* 125–126.

103. Benton Stark, *The Year They Called Off the World Series, A True Story* (Garden Park, NY, 1991), 108.

104. *New York Times,* February 16, 1904.

105. Light, *The Cultural Encyclopedia of Baseball,* 709; Stark, *The Year They Called Off the World Series,* 109; Dewey and Acocella, *The Ball Clubs,* 82.

106. Dewey and Acocella, *The Ball Clubs,* 82; Riess, *Touching Base,* 129.

107. *Ibid.*

108. Stark, *The Year They Called Off the World Series,* 136.

109. Riess, *Touching Base,* 126–127.

110. *The Sporting News,* November 19, 1904.

111. Riess, *Touching Base,* 130.

112. *Ibid.,* 132.

113. Dewey and Acocella, *The Ball Clubs,* 82.

114. Riess, *Touching Base,* 132.

115. *Ibid.,* 133.

116. *The Sporting News,* June 22, 1916.

117. *New York Times,* November 1, 1917; Matthew and Hannah Josephson, *Al Smith: Hero of the Cities* (Boston: 1969), 184.

118. *New York Times,* November 30, 1917.

119. Riess, *Touching Base,* 134.

120. *Ibid.,* 135–136.

121. *Ibid.;* Dewey and Acocella, *The Ball Clubs,* 84.

122. Light, *The Cultural Encyclopedia of Baseball,* 710.

123. Holmes, *Dodger Daze and Knights,* 34; Thorn et al., *Total Baseball,* 1491; Goldstein, *Superstars and Screwballs,* 128.

124. Bjarkman, *Encyclopedia of Baseball Team Histories: National League,* 80–81; Holmes, *Dodger Daze and Knights,* 35.

125. Goldstein, *Superstars and Screwballs,* 134.

126. *Ibid.,* 134–35; Kavanaugh and Macht, *Uncle Robbie,* 121–122; Dewey and Acocella, *The Ball Clubs,* 85.

127. Goldstein, *Superstars and Screwballs,* 138–139.

128. *Ibid.; New York Times,* October 13, 1920.

129. Kavanaugh and Macht, *Uncle Robbie,* 130.

130. Goldstein, *Superstars and Screwballs,* 139.

131. Holmes, *Dodger Daze and Knights,* 37; Solomon, *Where They Ain't,* 277.

132. Thorn et al., *Total Baseball,* 1802.

133. Holmes, *Dodger Daze and Knights,* 36–37.

134. *Ibid.,* 37.

135. *New York Times,* October 20, 1920.

136. *Ibid.,* January 17, 1923.

137. Goldstein, *Superstars and Screwballs,* 145.

138. *Ibid.*

139. Seymour, *Baseball, the Golden Age,* 456.

140. *Ibid.;* Graham, *The Brooklyn Dodgers,* 95.

141. Holmes, *Dodger Daze and Knights,* 38.

142. Goldstein, *Superstars and Screwballs,* 147.

143. Kavanaugh and Macht, *Uncle Robbie,* 46.

144. Goldstein, *Superstars and Screwballs,* 148.

145. *The Sporting News,* April 23, 1925.

146. Quoted from the Reach Official American League Guide in *Brooklyn Spectator,* April 15, 1981.

147. Ford C. Frick, *Games, Asterisks, and People: Memoirs of a Lucky Fan* (New York, 1973), 69.

148. Graham, *The Brooklyn Dodgers,* 27.

149. Frick, *Games, Asterisks, and People,* 69.

Chapter 2

1. Daniel M. Daniel, "Dreyfuss, Last of the Baseball Squires" (September 1931), 439, Dreyfuss Files, Baseball Hall of Fame, Cooperstown, New York.

2. *The Sporting News,* July 6, 1944.

3. Robert Slater, *Great Jews In Sports* (New York, 1983), 63.

4. Fred S. Wertenbech, *Barney Dreyfuss Was a Dreamer Who Made Visions Come True* (unnamed, undated article, Barney Dreyfuss file, *The Sporting News,* St. Louis, Missouri).

5. Porter (ed.), *Biographical Directory of American Sports,* 413.

6. Wertenbach, *Barney Dreyfuss Was a Dreamer Who Made Visions Come True.*

7. Dewey and Acocella, *The Ball Clubs,* 301–303.

8. Thorn et al., *Total Baseball,* 2075.

9. Light, *Cultural Encyclopedia of Baseball,* 425; Dennis de Valeria and Jeanne Burke de Valeria, *Honus Wagner, A Biography* (New York, 1995), p. 61.

10. Early history of Pirates found on the Internet in story by Robert Dvorchak of *Pittsburgh Post-Gazette,* on www.postgazette.com; Thorn et al., *Total Baseball,* 52.

11. John McCollister, *The Bucs, Story of the Pittsburgh Pirates* (Lenexa, KS, 1998), 41–42; Dewey and Acocella, *The Ball Clubs,* 304; Arthur D. Hittner, *Honus Wagner: The Life of Baseball's Flying Dutchman* (Jefferson, NC, 1996), 72.

12. Dewey and Acocella, *The Ball Clubs,* 456.

13. Frederick G. Lieb, *The Pittsburgh Pirates* (New York, 1948), 48.

14. Slater, *Great Jews in Sports,* 63–64; Bernard Postal, Jesse Silver, Roy Silver, *Encyclopedia of Jews in Sports* (New York, 1965), 28.

15. Undated clipping, Barney Dreyfuss Files, Hall of Fame, Cooperstown, New York.

16. Bob Smizik, *The Pittsburgh Pirates: An Illustrated Story* (New York, 1990), 13.

17. *Ibid.*

18. McCollister, *The Story of the Pittsburgh Pirates,* 42.

19. Hittner, *Honus Wagner,* 85–86; Dewey and Acocella, *The Ball Clubs,* 457; McCollister, *The Bucs,* 44; Allen, *The National League Story,* 89–90; Glenn Dickey, *The History of National League Baseball Since 1876* (Lanhan, MD, 1979), 49; an interesting first-hand account of the sale of the club to Dreyfuss appeared in the *Pittsburgh-Press,* April 22, 1931.

20. McCollister, *The Bucs,* 44.

21. Light, *The Cultural Encyclopedia of Baseball,* 193.

22. Solomon, *Where They Ain't,* 217–218.

23. *Ibid.,* 219.

24. Dewey and Acocella, *The Ball Clubs,* 457.

25. Hittner, *Honus Wagner,* 100; Dewey and Acocella, *The Ball Clubs,* 457.

26. *The Sporting News,* November 3, 1900.

27. *Ibid.,* September 21, 1901.

28. *Ibid.,* November 8, 1902.

29. Thorn et al., *Total Baseball,* 1390–1391, 1783.

30. Murdock, *Ban Johnson, Czar of Baseball,* 60.

31. Hittner, *Honus Wagner,* 94; *Pittsburgh-Post Gazette,* April 13, 1931.

32. Light, *The Cultural Encyclopedia of Baseball,* 480; McCollister, *The Bucs,* 53; Lieb, *The Pittsburgh Pirates,* 4; Charles Alexander, *Our Game: An American Baseball History* (New York, 1991), 82.

33. Smizik, *The Pittsburgh Pirates,* 16.

34. *Ibid.;* Thorn et al., *Total Baseball,* 594.

35. Smizik, *The Pittsburgh Pirates,* 17; McCollister, *The Bucs,* 53

36. Joseph L. Reichler, (ed.), *The World Series: A 75th Anniversary* (New York, 1978), 11.

37. De Valeria and De Valeria, *Honus Wagner,* 121.

38. Leonard Koppett, *Leonard Koppett's Major League Baseball* (Philadelphia: 1998), 98.

39. *World Telegram and Sun Magazine,* September 16, 1953, 12.

40. Sullivan, *Early Innings,* 114.

41. Seymour, *Baseball: The Golden Age,* 14.

42. Smizik, *The Pittsburgh Pirates,* 17; McCollister, *The Bucs,* 53.

43. Reichler, *The World Series: A 75th Anniversary,* 12.

44. Lieb, *The Story of the World Series* (New York, 1949), 26–27.

45. Koppett, *Koppett's Concise History of Major League Baseball,* 98.

46. De Valeria and De Valeria, *Honus Wagner,* 137.

47. *The Sporting News,* October 24, 1903.

48. *Ibid.,* February 26, 1914.

49. McCollister, *The Bucs,* 55.

50. Lieb, *The Story of the World Series,* 33.

51. Glenn Dickey, *The History of the World Series Since 1903* (New York, 1984), 21.

52. *Ibid.*

53. *Ibid.*

54. Information derived from internet www.subwayseriesnow.com/history.html.

55. *Ibid.*

56. Lieb, *The Pittsburgh Pirates,* 112–113.

57. Thorn et al., *Total Baseball,* 1256, 931.

58. Lieb, *The Pittsburgh Pirates,* 113.

59. *The Sporting News,* December 29, 1909.

60. *Ibid.,* October 19, 1911.

61. *Ibid.,* January 20, 1927.

62. *Press Sports,* April 27, 1961.

63. DeValeria and DeValeria, *Honus Wagner,* 97.

64. *The Sporting News,* April 17, 1930.

65. Seymour, *Baseball: The Golden Age,* 65.

66. *Ibid.*

67. *The Sporting News,* June 22, 1916.

68. *Ibid.,* February 18, 1912.

69. Seymour, *Baseball: The Golden Age,* 104.

70. *The Sporting News,* November 16, 1911; December 14, 1911.

71. Seymour, *Baseball: The Golden Age,* 389.

72. Material found on internet, detroit.freenet.org/tigers/history/1905.

73. *The Sporting News,* February 14, 1918.

74. Unnamed, undated article, Dreyfuss Files, Archives Baseball Hall of Fame, Cooperstown, New York.

75. Hittner, *Honus Wagner,* 75.

76. *The Sporting News,* June 18, 1901.

77. Lieb, *The Pittsburgh Pirates,* 73.

78. Charles Fountain, *Sportswriter: The Life and Times of Grantland Rice* (New York, 1995), 122.

79. Charles C. Alexander, *John McGraw* (New York, 1988), 113–114.

80. Hittner, *Honus Wagner,* 140.

81. *Ibid.;* Seymour, *Baseball: The Golden Age,* 26; *Sporting Life,* June 3, 1905, June 10, 1905.

82. Seymour, *Baseball: The Golden Age,* 17.

83. Lieb, *The Pittsburgh Pirates,* 121; Thorn et al., *Total Baseball,* 1829.

84. *Ibid.,* 1256.

85. McCollister, *The Bucs,* 57.

86. Thorn et al., *Total Baseball,* 2096.

87. *Ibid.,* 1256.

88. *Ibid.;* Smizik, *The Pittsburgh Pirates,* 19.

89. Dewey and Acocella, *The Ball Clubs,* 304.

90. De Valeria and De Valeria, *Honus Wagner,* 201–202.

91. Hittner, *Honus Wagner,* 178.

92. Smith, *Storied Stadiums*, 71–72.

93. *The Sporting News*, December 31, 1908.

94. Smith, *Storied Stadiums*, 72; De Valeria and De Valeria, *Honus Wagner*, 209; Gershman, *Diamonds*, 88.

95. *The Pittsburgh Press*, April 22, 1931.

96. *The Sporting News*, July 1, 1909; Gershman, *Diamonds*, 88.

97. John P. Rossi, *The National Game* (Chicago, 2000), 78; De Valeria and De Valeria, *Honus Wagner*, 210; Seymour, *Baseball: The Golden Age*, 51.

98. Gershman, *Diamonds*, 88.

99. *Ibid.*, 90.

100. Seymour, *Baseball, The Golden Age*, 51.

101. Gershman, *Diamonds*, 88; unnamed, undated article, Dreyfuss files, Baseball Hall of Fame, Cooperstown, New York; Postal, Silver and Silver, *Encyclopedia of Jews in Sports*, 28.

102. Lieb, *The Pittsburgh Pirates*, 132.

103. *Ibid.*, 134; Dewey and Acocella, *The Ball Clubs*, 459; McCollister, *The Bucs*, 64.

104. Thorn et al., *Total Baseball*, 1256.

105. Lieb, *The Pittsburgh Pirates*, 139–140; Bjarkman, *Encyclopedia of Major League Baseball Team Histories: The National League*, 447.

106. Lieb, *The Pittsburgh Pirates*, 157.

107. *Ibid.*; Smizik, *The Pittsburgh Pirates*, 22.

108. *Ibid.*

109. Lieb, *The Pittsburgh Pirates*, 161–172; Bjarkman, *Encyclopedia of Major League Baseball Team Histories: The National League*, 447.

110. Lieb, *The Pittsburgh Pirates*, 173.

111. De Valeria and De Valeria, *Honus Wagner*, 260.

112. *Ibid.*, 259.

113. *Ibid.*

114. *Ibid.*, 264.

115. Alexander, *Our Game*, 104; Light, *The Cultural Encyclopedia of Baseball*, 153.

116. *Ibid.*, 254.

117. *The Sporting News*, February 13, 1916.

118. *Ibid.*, January 18, 1917.

119. Seymour, *Baseball: The Golden Age*, 259.

120. *Ibid.*, 17.

121. Murdock, *Ban Johnson, Czar of Baseball*, 159.

122. Michael Santa Maria and James Costello, *In the Shadows of the Diamonds: Hard Times in the National Pastime* (Carmel, IN, 1992), 209.

123. Murdock, *Ban Johnson, Czar of Baseball*, 160.

124. Seymour, *Baseball: The Golden Age*, 260.

125. *Ibid.*, 261

126. Maria and Costello, *In the Shadows of the Diamonds*, 209.

127. *Ibid.*

128. Murdock, *Ban Johnson, Czar of Baseball*, 163.

129. Maria and Costello, *In the Shadows of the Diamond*, 209.

130. Seymour, *Baseball: The Golden Age*, 261.

131. *New York Times*, November 26, 1918.

132. *The Sporting News*, December 5, 1918.

133. J.G. Taylor Spink, *Judge Landis and Twenty-Five Years of Baseball* (New York, 1947), 43.

134. *Ibid.*, 45–46; 75th Anniversary of the Commissioner's Office, www.roadsidephotos.com/baseball/75thCOMM.htm—Internet.

135. *Ibid.*

136. Seymour, *Baseball: The Golden Age*, 312.

137. Alexander, *Our Game*, 125.

138. *The Sporting News*, November 9, 1916.

139. Spink, *Judge Landis and Twenty-Five Years of Baseball*, 67.

140. Murdock, *Ban Johnson, Czar of Baseball*, 180–181.

141. Alexander, *Our Game*, 125–126.

142. Seymour, *Baseball: The Golden Age*, 322.

143. *The Sporting News*, November 25, 1920.

144. Thorn et al., *Total Baseball*, 2118.

145. Smizik, *The Pittsburgh Pirates*, 24; Dewey and Acocella, *The Ball Clubs*, 460.

146. McCollister, *The Bucs*, 77.

147. *Ibid.*

148. Bjarkman, *Encyclopedia of Major League Baseball Team Histories: The National League*, 448.

149. McCollister, *The Bucs*, 80.

150. *Ibid.*, 83.

151. Bjarkman, *Encyclopedia of Major League Team Histories: The National League*, 449.

152. *Ibid.*

153. Dewey and Acocella, *The Ball Clubs*, 461.

154. *New York Times*, February 6, 1932.

155. Thorn et al., *Total Baseball*, 1262–1263.

156. Dewey and Acocella, *The Ball Clubs*, 462.

157. McCollister, *The Bucs*, 91.

158. Smizik, *The Pittsburgh Pirates*, 47.

159. *Ibid.*

160. *Ibid.*, 49; McCollister, *The Bucs*, 99; Lieb, *The Pittsburgh Pirates*, 242.

161. Thorn et al., *Total Baseball*, 53.

162. Lieb, *The Pittsburgh Pirates*, 243–244.

163. Smizik, *The Pittsburgh Pirates*, 49.

164. *The Sporting News*, February 11, 1932.

165. *Pittsburgh Post-Gazette*, May 29, 1932.

166. *Ibid.*

Chapter 3

1. Rob Rains, *The St. Louis Cardinals: The 100th Anniversary History* (New York, 1992), 7.

2. Charles Alexander, *Rogers Hornsby* (New York, 1995), 24.

3. Mike Eisenbath, *Cardinals Encyclopedia* (Philadelphia, 1999), 388; Rains, *The St. Louis Cardinals*, 9.

4. Rains, *The St. Louis Cardinals*, 10.

5. *Ibid.*; Bob Broeg, *Bob Broeg's Redbirds: A Century of Cardinals Baseball* (St. Louis, 1981), 17.

6. *Ibid.*, 17.

7. Donald Honig, *The St. Louis Cardinals, An Illustrated History* (New York, 1991), 6.

8. *Ibid.*

9. Broeg, *Bob Broeg's Redbirds*, 18.

10. Honig, *St. Louis Cardinals*, 12.

11. *Ibid.*, 8–9.

12. *Ibid.*, 9; Rains, *The St. Louis Cardinals*, 12.

13. *Ibid.*, 13; Eisenbath, *Cardinals Encyclopedia*, 388; Broeg, *Bob Broeg's Redbirds*, 18; Honig, *The St. Louis Cardinals*, 13.

14. Honing, *The St. Louis Cardinals*, 13; Rains, *The St. Louis Cardinals*, 13.

15. Rains, *The St. Louis Cardinals*, 14; Eisenbath, *Cardinals Encyclopedia*, 388.

16. *Ibid.*

17. Rains, *The St. Louis Cardinals*, 15–16.

18. *The Sporting News*, March 30, 1911; *St. Louis Post-Dispatch*, March 24, 1911.

19. Rains, *The St. Louis Cardinals*, 16.

20. "My Experience As a Big League Owner," *Baseball Magazine*, (February 1917), 14.

21. Gai Berlage, *Women in Baseball* (Westport, CT, 1994), 65.

22. "My Experience As a Big League Owner," 18.

23. *St. Louis Star Times*, April 6, 1911.

24. Berlage, *Women in Baseball*, 65.

25. "My Experience as a Big League Owner," 14.

26. Bill Borst, *Baseball Through a Knothole* (St. Louis, 1980), 33–34; Bob Broeg, *The St. Louis Cardinals Encyclopedia* (Chicago, 1998), 11; Bjarkman, *Encyclopedia of Major League Baseball Team Histories: National League*, 517; Rains, *The St. Louis Cardinals*, 16.

27. *St. Louis Star Times*, September 21, 1911; Rains, *The St. Louis Cardinals*, 18.

28. *St. Louis Globe-Democrat*, December 12, 1911.

29. *The Sporting News*, December 21, 1911.

30. *Ibid.*

31. Frederic G. Lieb, *St. Louis Cardinals: Story of a Great Baseball Club* (New York, 1944), 46.

32. *The Sporting News*, December 21, 1911.

33. Lieb, *St. Louis Cardinals*, 47.

34. *Ibid.*; Rains, *The St. Louis Cardinals*, 16; Martin Appel and Burt Goldblatt,

Baseball's Best: The Hall of Fame Gallery (New York, 1917), 46.

35. Eisenbath, *Cardinals Encyclopedia*, 399.

36. Lieb, *St. Louis Cardinals*, 48.

37. Appel and Goldblatt, *Baseball's Best*, 46; Rains, *The St. Louis Cardinals*, 17; Lieb, *The St. Louis Cardinals*, 48; Mario Vricella, *St. Louis Cardinals: First Century — A Short History of the National League's Greatest Team* (New York, 1992), 39; Broeg, *Bob Broeg's Redbirds*, 21.

38. Rains, *The St. Louis Cardinals*, 15.

39. Honig, *The St. Louis Cardinals*, 21.

40. Rains, *The St. Louis Cardinals*, 17.

41. Lieb, *St. Louis Cardinals*, 49.

42. *Ibid.*

43. Broeg, *Bob Broeg's Redbirds*, 21.

44. Berlage, *Women in Baseball*, 68.

45. *The Sporting News*, February 13, 1913.

46. *Reedy's Mirror*, December 18, 1914.

47. *The Sporting News*, April 17, 1913.

48. "My Experience As a Big League Owner," 18.

49. Borst, *Baseball Through a Knothole*, 37; Joel Zoss and John Bowman, *Diamonds in the Rough* (New York, 1989), 220.

50. Borst, *Baseball Through a Knothole*, 36–37; Zoss and Bowman, *Diamonds in the Rough*, 220.

51. Undated, untitled editorial, Britton File, Baseball Hall of Fame, Cooperstown, New York.

52. Rains, *The St. Louis Cardinals*, 17; Honig, *The St, Louis Cardinals*, 21.

53. Alexander, *Our Game*, 102; Vricella, *St. Louis Cardinals*, 40.

54. Alexander, *Our Game*, 102–103.

55. Lieb, *St. Louis Cardinals*, 51.

56. Honig, *The St. Louis Cardinals*, 24–25.

57. Berlage, *Women in Baseball*, 68.

58. *The Sporting News*, January 6, 1916.

59. *Ibid.*, November 26, 1914.

60. *Ibid.*

61. *Ibid.*; Borst, *Baseball Through a Knothole*, 5–6; undated, unnamed article, Britton File, Baseball Hall of Fame, Cooperstown, New York.

62. Berlage, *Women in Baseball*, 68.

63. Vricella, *St. Louis Cardinals*, 41; Bjarkman, *Encyclopedia of Major League Baseball Team Histories: National League*, 517.

64. Lieb, *St. Louis Cardinals*, 55.

65. Alexander, *Our Game*, 104–105; Vricella, *St. Louis Cardinals*, 41.

66. Vricella, *St. Louis Cardinals*, 49; Bjarkman, *Encyclopedia of Major League Baseball Team Histories: National League*, 518.

67. *New York Times*, November 18, 1916.

68. *St. Louis Globe-Democrat*, November 18, 1916.

69. *Ibid.*

70. Berlage, *Women in Baseball*, 68.

71. *St. Louis Star Times*, November 18, 1916; *St. Louis Post-Dispatch*, November 18, 1916; *The Sporting News*, November 23, 1916.

72. Alexander, *Rogers Hornsby*, 24.

73. *The Sporting News*, December 7, 1916.

74. *Ibid.*, December 14, 1916.

75. *Ibid.*, December 28, 1916.

76. *Ibid.*, January 11, 1917.

77. *Ibid.*, January 25, 1917.

78. Lieb, *St. Louis Cardinals*, 59.

79. *Ibid.*, 60; Eisenbath, *The St. Louis Cardinals*, 389.

80. Lieb, *The St. Louis Cardinals*, 60.

81. Vricella, *St. Louis Cardinals*, 49; Bjarkman, *Encyclopedia of Major League Baseball Team Histories: National League*, 518.

82. *Ibid.*, 60; Bjarkman, *Encyclopedia of Major League Baseball Team Histories: National League*, 517; Broeg, *The St. Louis Cardinals Encyclopedia*, 13.

83. *The Sporting News*, March 8, 1917.

84. Lieb, *St. Louis Cardinals*, 61; *St. Louis Post-Dispatch*, July 19, 1981; Broeg, *The St. Louis Cardinals*, 13; Robert E. Hood, *The Gashouse Gang* (New York, 1976), 32; Borst, *Baseball Through a Knothole*, 39; Seymour, *Baseball: The Golden Age* (New York, 1989), 61.

85. *Ibid.*; Bjarkman, *Encyclopedia of Major League Baseball's Team Histories: National League*, 518; Honig, *The St. Louis Cardinals*, 28; Broeg, *The St. Louis Cardinals Encyclopedia*, 13; Lieb, *The St. Louis Cardinals*, 61.

86. *The Sporting News*, March 29, 1917.

87. *Ibid.*, April 5, 1917.

88. *New York Times*, August 19, 1918; Borst, *Baseball Through a Knothole*, 39.

89. *Cleveland Plain Dealer,* September 16, 1999; obituary notices found in *St. Louis Globe-Democrat, St. Louis Post-Dispatch, New York Times* and *Philadelphia Inquirer,* January 10, 1950.

Chapter 4

1. Tom Deveaux, *The Washington Senators, 1901–1971* (Jefferson, NC, 2001), 30.

2. *Ibid.*

3. Anna Rothe (ed.), *Current Biography 1950* (New York, 1950), 198.

4. Garraty, *American National Biography,* 597; Henry W. Thomas, *Walter Johnson: Baseball's Big Train* (Washington DC, 1995), 88–89; David Porter (ed.), *Biographical Directory of American Sports* (Westport, CT, 2000), 589.

5. Thorn et al., *Total Baseball,* 1490.

6. Rothe, *Current Biography,* 1950 199.

7. Thomas, *Walter Johnson,* 89.

8. Jules Tygiel, *Past Time* (New York, 2000), 42.

9. Unnamed, undated biographical article on Clark Griffith, 186, Griffith Files, Baseball Hall of Fame, Cooperstown, New York.

10. Tygiel, *Past Time,* 41.

11. Deveaux, *The Washington Senators,* 31.

12. Al Stump, *Cobb A Biography* (Chapel Hill, 1994), 363.

13. Tygiel, *Past Time,* 44; Alexander, *Our Game,* 53.

14. Tygiel, *Past Time,* 47; Stark, *The Year They Called the World Series Off,* 213; Lee Lowenfish and Tony Lupien, *The Imperfect Diamond, The Story of Baseball's Reserve System and the Men Who Fought to Change It* (New York, 1980), 61.

15. *Washington Post,* January 23, 1938.

16. *Ibid.*

17. *Ibid.*

18. Lowenfish and Lupien, *The Imperfect Diamond,* 61.

19. Tygiel, *Past Time,* 50.

20. *Washington Post,* January 25, 1938.

21. Tygiel, *Past Time,* 47–48.

22. Thomas, *Walter Johnson,* 89.

23. Lee Allen, *The American League Story* (New York, 1965), 18; Richard Carl Lindberg, *Stealing First in a Two-Team Town* (Champaign, IL, 1994), 50.

24. Allen, *The American League Story,* 18.

25. Tygiel, *Past Time,* 51.

26. Thorn et al., *Total Baseball,* 1490.

27. Garraty, *American National Biography,* 597.

28. Tygiel, *Past Time,* 51.

29. Garraty, *American National Biography,* 597.

30. Tygiel, *Past Time,* 47–48; unnamed, undated article on Clark Griffith, 186, Griffith Files, Baseball Hall of Fame, Cooperstown, New York.

31. Shirley Povich, "This Morning" undated newspaper clipping, Griffith Files, Baseball Hall of Fame, Cooperstown, New York.

32. Alexander, *John McGraw,* 104–105.

33. "Clark Griffith For Hall of Fame," undated article, Griffith Files, Baseball Hall of Fame, Cooperstown, New York.

34. Thorn et al., *Total Baseball,* 1490; Rothe, *Current Biography 1950,* 199; Unnamed, undated article on Griffith, 186, Griffith Files, Baseball Hall of Fame, Cooperstown, New York.

35. Porter, *Biographical Directory of American Sports,* 589.

36. Unnamed, undated article on Clark Griffith, 187, Griffith Files, Baseball Hall of Fame, Cooperstown, New York; Dewey and Acocella, *The Biographical History of Baseball,* 185.

37. *The Sporting News,* November 16, 1939; Talmage Boston, *1939, Baseball's Pivotal Year: From the Golden Age to the Modern Era* (Fort Worth, 1994), 128–129; Alexander, *Our Game,* 173.

38. *The Sporting News,* July 27, 1939.

39. Garraty, *American National Biography,* 597.

40. Deveaux, *The Washington Senators,* 33.

41. Shirley Povich, *The Washington Senators* (New York, 1954), 62.

42. Rothe, *Current Biography 1950,* 199; Thomas, *Walter Johnson,* 89–90; Jon Kerr, *Calvin: Baseball's Last Dinosaur* (Dubuque, 1990), 14; Deveaux, *The Washington Senators,* 34.

43. Peter C. Bjarkman, *Encyclopedia*

of Baseball Team Histories: The American League (Westport, CT, 1991), 488.

44. Thorn et al., *Total Baseball*, 1490, 2423.

45. Thomas, *Walter Johnson*, 91–92; Dewey and Acocella, *The Ball Clubs*, 579; Rothe, *Current Biography 1950*, 199.

46. Thorn et al., *Total Baseball*, 1549.

47. Paul M. Gregory, *The Baseball Player: An Economic Study* (Washington, DC, 1956), 188–189.

48. "Unionism in Baseball," *U S News and World Report* (May 10, 1946), 42–43.

49. Seymour, *Baseball: The Golden Age*, 203.

50. Tygiel, *Past Time*, 59.

51. Thorn et al., *Total Baseball*, 1549.

52. *Ibid.*, 1120; Dewey and Acocella, *The Ball Clubs*, 580.

53. Thorn et al., *Total Baseball*, 2117, 2119, 2121, 2123.

54. William Mead and Paul Dickson, *Baseball — The President's Game* (Washington, DC, 1993), 17–20.

55. Shirley Povich, "Clark Griffiths 50 Years in Baseball," undated article, Griffith Files, *The Sporting News*, St. Louis, Missouri.

56. *The Sporting News*, April 6, 1974; Mead and Dickson, *Baseball — The President's Game*, 28.

57. Thomas, *Walter Johnson*, 109.

58. *Ibid.*, 35.

59. Jack Kavanaugh, *Walter Johnson, A Life* (South Bend, 1995), 64, 113.

60. Mead and Dickson, *Baseball — The President's Game*, 34.

61. Glenn Dickey, *The History of American League Baseball Since 1901* (New York, 1980), 50; Light, *The Cultural Encyclopedia of Baseball*, 800.

62. Thomas, *Walter Johnson*, 155.

63. Deveaux, *The Washington Senators*, 47; Seymour, *Baseball: The Golden Age*, 249.

64. Deveaux, *The Washington Senators*, 47.

65. *The Sporting News*, November 11, 1917.

66. *Ibid.*, October 25, 1917.

67. Seymour, *Baseball: The Golden Age*, 246.

68. *The Sporting News*, April 10, 1919.

69. *Ibid.*

70. William Marshall, *Baseball's Pivotal Era 1945–1951* (Lexington, 1999), 188.

71. *Ibid.*

72. *New York Times*, October 28, 1955.

73. Unnamed, undated newspaper clipping, Griffith files, Baseball Hall of Fame, Cooperstown, New York.

74. Kerr, *Calvin: Baseball's Last Dinosaur*, 14; Dewey and Acocella, *The Biographical History of Baseball*, 186; Deveaux, *The Washington Senators*, 49–50; Rothe, *Current Biography 1950*, 199; Garraty, *American National Biography*, 598.

75. Bjarkman, *Encyclopedia of Baseball Team Histories: The American League*, 495; Dewey and Acocella, *The Ball Clubs*, 580.

76. Garraty, *American National Biography*, 598; Michael Lenehan, "The Last of the Pure Baseball Men," *The Atlantic Monthly* (August 1981), 36.

77. *Ibid.*, 37.

78. Thorn et al., *Total Baseball*, 810.

79. Dewey and Acocella, *The Ball Clubs*, 581.

80. *Ibid.*

81. Thorn et al., *Total Baseball*, 2133; Kerr, *Calvin: Baseball's Last Dinosaur*, 15.

82. *Ibid.*, 14.

83. Povich, *The Washington Senators*, 119.

84. Article on the internet, "Clark Griffith," cbs.sportsline.com, The Baseball Online Library, CBS Sports Inc; Light , *The Cultural Encyclopedia of Baseball*, 306; Baseball historian Henry Thomas dubbed Griffith "a relief pitching pioneer," while sportswriter Shirley Povich frankly stated, "The relief pitcher was invented by Harris under the tutelage of Griffith." (Both quotes are found on the internet www. efqreview.com.)

85. Povich, *The Washington Senators*, 129.

86. Dewey and Acocella, *The Ball Clubs*, 581.

87. *Ibid.*, 582.

88. Thorn et al., *Total Baseball*, 702, 2420.

89. Dewey and Acocella, *The Ball Clubs*, 582.

90. Bjarkman, *Encyclopedia of Baseball Team Histories: The American League*,

498; Dewey and Acocella, *The Ball Clubs,* 583.

91. Bjarkman, *Encyclopedia of Baseball Team Histories: The American League,* 498–499.

92. Dewey and Acocella, *The Biographical History of Baseball,* 186.

93. Bjarkman, *Encyclopedia of Baseball Team Histories: The American League,* 499.

94. Thorn et al., *Total Baseball,* 1446.

95. *Ibid.,* 662, 1252.

96. Povich, *The Washington Senators,* 206–208; Samuel O. Regalado, *Viva Baseball* (Urbana, 1998), 26.

97. Peter C. Bjarkman, *Baseball with a Latin Beat: A History of the Latin American Game* (Jefferson, NC, 1994), 119.

98. *Newsweek,* May 29, 1944, 90.

99. Thorn et al., *Total Baseball,* 755.

100. *Ibid.,* 1679; Dewey and Acocella, *The Ball Clubs,* 584.

101. Dewey and Acocella, *The Biographical History of Baseball,* 186; Rossi, *The National Game,* 143.

102. Robert F. Burk, *Much More Than A Game: Players, Owners & American Baseball Since 1921* (Chapel Hill, 2001), 72.

103. Donald Honig, *A Donald Honig Reader* (New York, 1988), 294.

104. Mead and Dickson, *Baseball— The President's Game,* 76.

105. G. Richard McKelvey, *The McPhails: Baseball's First Family of the Front Office* (Jefferson, NC, 2000), 54.

106. Marshall, *Baseball's Pivotal Era 1945–1951,* 6.

107. Mead and Dickson, *Baseball— The President's Game,* 77–78; Light, *The Cultural Encyclopedia of Baseball,* 801.

108. Richard Goldstein, *Spartan Seasons: How Baseball Survived the Second World War* (New York, 1980), 20.

109. *Ibid.,* 21–22.

110. Burk, *Much More Than a Game,* 69–70; Dewey and Acocella, *The Biographical History of Baseball,* 186.

111. Garraty, *American National Biography,* 598.

112. David Pietrusza, *Lights On!: The Wild Century-Long Saga of Night Baseball* (Lanham, MD, 1997), 77–78.

113. Tygiel, *Past Times,* 96–97.

114. Peter Levine (ed.), *Baseball and the Great Depression* (Westport, CT, 1989), 57.

115. F. C. Lane, "Will the Major Leagues Adopt Night Baseball?" *Baseball Magazine,* (October, 1935) 487–492.

116. *The Sporting News,* November 7, 1935.

117. Lee Allen, *The American League Story* (New York, 1965), 158.

118. Pietrusza, *Lights On!,* 139–141; Allen, *The American League Story,* 159.

119. Pietrusza, *Lights On!,* 157; Light, *The Cultural Encyclopedia of Baseball,* 543.

120. Mead and Dickson, *Baseball— The President's Game,* 78; William B. Mead, *Even the Browns* (Chicago, 1978), 38.

121. Povich, Shirley, "Shading Night Baseball," *Baseball Digest* (February 1945), 57–58.

122. Povich, *The Washington Senators,* 219–220.

123. Thorn et al., *Total Baseball,* 2171.

124. *Ibid.,* 80.

125. *The Sporting News,* November 13, 1913.

126. *Ibid.,* August 9, 1945.

127. Unnamed clipping, March 14, 1946, Griffith Files, *The Sporting News,* St. Louis, Missouri.

128. John Lardner, "The Great Baseball Bamboozle," *Liberty* (June 29, 1946), 18.

129. Garraty, *American National Biography,* 597; Porter, *Biographical Directory of American Sports,* 590.

130. Dickey, *The History of American League Baseball Since 1901,* 145; Donald Honig, *Baseball America: The Heroes of the Game and the Times of Their Glory* (New York, 1985), 215.

131. Light, *The Cultural Encyclopedia of Baseball,* 678.

132. Thorn et. al., *Total Baseball,* 225–226, 228, 230.

133. Bjarkman, *Baseball With a Latin Beat,* 204.

134. Robert Peterson, *Only the Ball Was White* (Englewood, NJ, 1970), 176; Jules Tygiel, *Baseball's Great Experiment: Jackie Robinson and His Legacy* (New York, 1997), 32.

135. White, *Creating the National Pastime,* 151.

136. Mark Ribowsky, *The Power and the Darkness: The Life of Josh Gibson in the Shadow of the Game* (New York, 1996), 183–184.

137. *Ibid.*, 191.

138. Steven Gietschier, Senior Managing Editor, News Research, *The Sporting News,* to authors, April 5, 2002; Thorne et al., *Total Baseball,* 1080.

139. Dewey and Acocella, *The Ball Clubs,* 586; Thorn et al., *Total Baseball,* 1128.

140. Bjarkman, *Encyclopedia of Baseball Team Histories: American League,* 500; Dewey and Acocella, *The Ball Clubs,* 585; Thorn et al., *Total Baseball,* 2181, 2183.

141. Bjarkman, *Encyclopedia of Baseball Team Histories: American League,* 505.

142. *The Sporting News,* August 30, 1950.

143. St. Louis *Globe-Democrat,* October 28, 1955.

144. "Baseball Man," *Sports Illustrated* (November 7, 1955), 13.

Chapter 5

1. *The Sporting News,* October 28, 1955.

2. *Los Angeles Times,* August 10, 1979.

3. *Ibid.*

4. Milton Gross, "The Artful O'Malley and the Dodgers," *True* (May 1954), 112.

5. Don Kowet, *The Rich Who Own Sports* (New York, 1977), 60; Melvin Durslag, "A Visit With Walter O'Malley," *Saturday Evening Post* (May 14, 1960), 106.

6. *The Sporting News,* September 28, 1955.

7. Kowet, *The Rich Who Own Sports,* 60–61.

8. Gross, "The Artful O'Malley and the Dodgers," 112–113.

9. Durslag, "A Visit With Walter O'Malley," 106.

10. Solomon, *Where They Ain't,* 277.

11. *Ibid.*

12. Garraty, *American National Biography,* 70.

13. *The Sporting News,* September 28, 1955.

14. *Los Angeles Times,* August 10, 1979.

15. Roger Kahn, *The Era 1947–1957: When the Yankees, the Giants and the Dodgers Ruled the World* (New York, 1993), 263.

16. *Vero Beach Press Journal,* October 18, 1997.

17. John Heylar, *Lords of the Realm: The Real History of Baseball* (New York, 1994), 40–41.

18. Thorn et al., *Total Baseball,* 2166.

19. Golenbock, *Bums,* 84; *Vero Beach Press Journal,* October 18, 1997.

20. *The Brooklyn Eagle* quoted in Burt Solomon, *Where They Ain't,* 278.

21. Kowet, *The Rich Who Own Sports,* 61.

22. *Ibid.*, 43.

23. John C. Chalberg, *Rickey and Robinson: The Preacher, the Player, and America's Game* (Wheeling, IL, 2000), 148.

24. Helyar, *Lords of the Realm,* 46.

25. *Ibid.*

26. Marshall, *Baseball's Pivotal Era,* 208.

27. Chalberg, *Rickey and Robinson,* 151.

28. Goldstein, *Superstars and Screwballs,* 285.

29. Harvey Frommer, *Rickey and Robinson: The Men Who Broke Baseball's Color Barrier* (New York, 1982), 173.

30. Marshall, *Baseball's Pivotal Era,* 208.

31. Helyar, *Lords of the Realm,* 48; Kahn, *The Era,* 267.

32. Thorn et al., *Total Baseball,* 1130.

33. *Vero Beach Press Journal,* October 18, 1997.

34. Light, *The Cultural Encyclopedia of Baseball,* 616.

35. *Ibid.*

36. Dewey and Acocella, *The Ball Clubs,* 97.

37. Kowet, *The Rich Who Own Sports,* 62.

38. Porter, *Biographical Directory of American Sports,* 1143; *Los Angeles Times,* August 10, 1979.

39. Dewey and Acocella, *The Ball Clubs,* 98.

40. *Ibid.*, 98–99.

41. *Ibid.*, 99.

42. Thorn et al., *Total Baseball,* 2416.

43. Dewey and Acocella, *The Ball Clubs*, 99.

44. Thorn et al., *Total Baseball*, 331.

45. Kahn, *The Era*, 299.

46. Unnamed newspaper clipping, November 5, 1952, O'Malley Files, Baseball Hall of Fame, Cooperstown, New York.

47. *Wall Street Journal*, October 5, 1978.

48. *Ibid.*

49. Gross, "The Artful O'Malley and the Dodgers," 50.

50. *Ibid.*, 110.

51. Neil J. Sullivan, *The Dodgers Move West* (New York, 1987), 35.

52. Alexander, *Our Game*, 231.

53. Miller, *The Baseball Business*, 52; Burk, *Much More Than a Game*, 109.

54. *Ibid.*, 111.

55. Kahn, *The Era*, 311; Tom Meany, "Baseball's Answer to TV," *Collier's* (September 27, 1952), 61–62.

56. Kowet, *The Rich Who Own Sports*, 62.

57. *Ibid.*; Sullivan, *The Dodgers Move West*, 39.

58. Kahn, *The Era*, 311; Meany, "Baseball's Answer to TV," 61–62.

59. Sullivan, *The Dodgers Move West*, 37.

60. *Ibid.*, 44; "Walter In Wonderland," *Newsweek* (April 28, 1958), 59.

61. *Ibid.*

62. Kowet, *The Rich Who Own Sports*, 67–68.

63. Kahn, *The Era*, 335.

64. Kowet, *The Rich Who Own Sports*, 67; "Walter In Wonderland," 59.

65. Kahn, *The Era*, 336; Kowet, *The Rich Who Own Sports*, 67.

66. Rader, *Baseball, A History of America's Game*, 172.

67. *New York Times*, May 23, 1955.

68. *Ibid.*; December 2, 1955.

69. Sullivan, *The Dodgers Move West*, 70.

70. Goldstein, *100 Years of Brooklyn Baseball*, 325.

71. Kowet, *The Rich Who Own Sports*, 68.

72. Dewey and Acocella, *The Ball Clubs*, 100; Thorn et al., *Total Baseball*, 1603.

73. *Ibid.*, 332.

74. Dewey and Acocella, *The Ball Clubs*, 100.

75. *Vero Beach Press Journal*, October 18, 1997.

76. *Ibid.*; Honig, *Baseball America*, 297; Kowet, *The Rich Who Own Sports*, 71.

77. Dewey and Acocella, *The Ball Clubs*, 101; Solomon, *Where They Ain't*, 280.

78. Dewey and Acocella, *The Ball Clubs*, 101.

79. Carl E. Prince, *Brooklyn's Dodgers: The Bums, the Borough, and the Best of Baseball 1947–1957* (New York, 1996), 144.

80. Golenbock, *Bums*, 446–448.

81. *Ibid.*

82. Kowet, *The Rich Who Own Sports*, 71.

83. Sullivan, *The Dodgers Move West*, 115.

84. Garraty, *American National Biography*, 716.

85. J. Ronald Oakley, *Baseball's Last Golden Age 1946–1960: The National Pastime in a Time of Glory and Change* (Jefferson, NC, 1994), 267.

86. Dickey, *The History of National League Baseball Since 1876*, 188.

87. Heylar, *Lords of the Realm*, 59.

88. Alexander, *Our Game*, 239.

89. Honig, *Baseball America*, 297; Helyar, *Lords of the Realm*, 59.

90. Neil J. Sullivan, *The Diamond Revolution: The Prospects For Baseball After the Collapse of Its Ruling Class* (New York, 1992), 64.

91. *Ibid.*

92. Voigt, *American Baseball*, 129.

93. *The Sporting News*, October 30, 1957.

94. Dewey and Acecello, *The Ball Clubs*, 288.

95. *Ibid.*; Bjarkman, *Encyclopedia of Baseball Team Histories: The National League*, 103.

96. Dewey and Acocella, *The Ball Clubs*, 288.

97. *Ibid.*, 288–289; Thorn et al., *Total Baseball*, 2202.

98. Bjarkman, *Enclyclopedia of Baseball Team Histories: National League*, 104.

99. *Ibid.*, Thorn et al., *Total Baseball*,

335; Dewey and Acocella, *The Ball Clubs*, 289.

100. *Ibid.*; Bjarkman, *Encyclopedia of Baseball Team Histories: National League*, 106.

101. Sullivan, *The Dodgers Move West*, 138.

102. Alexander, *Our Game*, 242–243.

103. Helyar, *Lords of the Realm*, 60.

104. Alexander, *Our Game*, 251.

105. Dickey, *The History of National League Baseball Since 1876*, 192.

106. Rader, *Baseball: A History of America's Game*, 180.

107. Kahn, *The Era*, 343; Helyar, *Lords of the Realm*, 59.

108. Dewey and Acocella, *The Ball Clubs*, 290.

109. Voigt, *American Baseball*, 131.

110. *The Wall Street Journal*, October 5, 1978.

111. Dickey, *The History of National League Baseball Since 1876*, 192.

112. Voigt, *American Baseball*, 130–131.

113. Helyar, *Lords of the Realm*, 60.

114. Melvin Durslag, "How To Become a Baseball Millionaire," *TV Guide* (April 6, 1975), 17.

115. Helyar, *Lords of the Realm*, 60.

116. Thorn et al., *Total Baseball*, 339.

117. *Ibid.*, 341.

118. *Ibid.*, 342.

119. *Ibid.*, 1571.

120. Dewey and Acocella, *The Ball Clubs*, 290.

121. *Ibid.*, 290–291.

122. Bjarkman, *Encyclopedia of Baseball Team Histories: National League*, 112.

123. Porter, *Biographical Directory of American Sports*, 1144.

124. Gershman, *Diamonds*, 178.

125. *Ibid.*

126. *Ibid.*, 178–179.

127. Voigt, *American Baseball*, xxvi; Rader, *Baseball: History of America's Game*, 181.

128. Gershman, *Diamonds*, 179; Porter, *Biographical Directory of American Sports*, 1143.

129. Walter Bingham, "Ticker Tape, Dyed Grass, Blue Cowboy Hats," *Sports Illustrated* (April 23, 1962), 18–19; Helyar, *Lords of the Realm*, 60.

130. Kowet, *The Rich Who Own Sports*, 72–73; Dewey and Acocella, *The Ball Clubs*, 290; Voigt, *American Baseball* , 132.

131. Miller, *The Baseball Business*, 83; Voigt, *American Baseball*, 112.

132. Gershman, *Diamonds*, 179.

133. Voigt, *American Baseball*, 114.

134. *Detroit Free Press*, December 8, 1968.

135. *The Sporting News*, March 9, 1968.

136. Sullivan, *The Dodgers Move West*, 228.

137. Thorn et al., *Total Baseball*, 362.

138. *Ibid.*, 371.

139. Dewey and Acocella, *The Ball Clubs*, 292.

140. Thorn et al., *Total Baseball*, 374.

141. Garraty, *American National Biography*, 717.

142. Voigt, *American Baseball*, 131–132.

143. *The Sporting News*, February 19, 1977.

144. *Los Angeles Times*, March 4, 1970.

145. Heylar, *Lords of the Realm*, 61.

146. *Ibid.*, 177.

147. Education Resources Information Clearinghouse on Teaching and Teacher Education, Washington, DC; Biographical Sheet on Walter O'Malley sent to author by Los Angeles Dodgers Baseball Team.

148. Light, *The Cultural Encyclopedia of Baseball*, 546; *The Sporting News*, February 1, 1969.

149. Dewey and Acocella, *The Ball Clubs*, 345.

150. Andrew Zimbalist, *Baseball and Billions: A Probing Look Inside the Big Business of Our National Pastime* (New York, 1992), 44; The French term *eminence grise* was a term originally applied to Pere Joseph (1577–1638), confidential agent of Cardinal Richelieu; the term is now extended to describe one who wields real, though not titular control. *The Oxford English Dictionary*, Vol. V (Oxford, England, 1989), 179.

151. Voigt, *American Baseball*, 131–132.

152. *Ibid.*, 309.

153. *Ibid.*, 310.

154. Heylar, *The Lords of the Realm*, 93; Alexander, *Our Game*, 272; Marvin Miller, *A Whole Different Ball Game: The Sport and Business of Baseball* (New York, 1991), 102.

155. Jerome Holtzman, *The Commissioners: Baseball's Midlife Crisis* (New York, 1998), 182.

156. *The Sporting News,* February 19, 1977.

157. *Ibid.,* December 31, 1984.

158. Koppett, *Koppett's Concise History of Major League Baseball,* 372–373.

159. Voigt, *American Baseball,* 311.

160. Bowie Kuhn, *Hardball: The Education of a Baseball Commissioner* (1987, New York), 23.

161. *The Sporting News,* February 19, 1977.

162. Dewey and Acocella, *The Ball Clubs,* 290–291.

163. Kuhn, *Hardball,* 239; *New York Times,* August 10, 1979.

164. Jerry Kirshenbaum, (ed.), "The Man Who Won the West," *Sports Illustrated* (August 20, 1979), 5–6.

165. *Los Angeles Times,* August 10, 1979.

166. Kuhn, *Hardball,* 240.

Chapter 6

1. William Barry Furlong, "Master of the Joyful Illusion," *Sports Illustrated* (July 4, 1960), 58.

2. Garraty, *American National Biography,* 313.

3. Many of the odd jobs given Veeck were reminiscent of the tasks given to Charlie Ebbets by the Brooklyn Dodgers.

4. Light, *The Cultural Encyclopedia of Baseball,* 652.

5. Anna Rothe (ed.), *Current Biography 1948* (New York, 1949), 645.

6. Porter, *Biographical Directory of American Sports,* 1595–1596.

7. *St. Louis Post-Dispatch,* July 1, 1951.

8. Lindberg, *Stealing First In a Two-Team Town,* 210; Garraty, *American National Biography,* 313–314.

9. Undated, untitled biographical sketch of Bill Veeck, Veeck Files, Baseball Hall of Fame, Cooperstown, New York.

10. Garraty, *American National Biography,* 314.

11. "Borchert Was Brewers First Home," found on internet on milwaukee.com, feature article by Mike Nelson.

12. Undated, unnamed biographical sketch of Bill Veeck, Veeck Files, Baseball Hall of Fame, Cooperstown, New York.

13. *Ibid.;* John C. Hoffman, "Squirrel Night at the Brewers," *Esquire* (September 1943), 53–54.

14. Garraty, *American National Biography,* 314.

15. Rothe, *Current Biography 1948,* 646.

16. Ed Linn, "Veeck As In White Sox," *Sport* (April 1976), 33.

17. *St. Louis Post Dispatch,* July 1, 1951.

18. Rothe, *Current Biography 1948,* 646.

19. Porter, *Biographical Directory of American Sports,* 1596; Garraty, *American National Biography,* 314.

20. *St. Louis Post-Dispatch,* July 1, 1951.

21. Steve Raphael and Terry Brewster, "Bill Veeck: Send in the Clowns," *Friends* (May 8, 1950), 15.

22. "Baseball's Dynamo," *Sportfolio* (April 1949), 11.

23. Dick Condon, "How Bill Veeck Got That Way," *Chicago Sunday Tribune Magazine* (May 10, 1959), 32.

24. Koppett, *Koppett's Concise History of Major League Baseball,* 233–234; Dewey and Acocella, *The Biographical History of Baseball,* 480.

25. Rothe, *Current Biography 1948,* 646.

26. Ted Shane, "Veeck — The Barnum of Baseball," *Baseball Magazine* (April 1952), 11–12.

27. *Ibid.,* 9.

28. Marshall, *Baseball's Pivotal Era,* 1171.

29. *Ibid.*

30. Porter, *Biographical Directory of American Sports,* 1596.

31. Glenn Dickey, *Champs and Chumps: An Insider's Look at America's Sports Heroes* (San Francisco, 1955), 117–118.

32. Untitled, undated profile of Bill Veeck, Veeck Files, Baseball Hall of Fame, Cooperstown, New York.

33. Dickey, *Champs and Chumps,* 117–118; Honig, *A Donald Honig Reader,* 284.

34. Garraty, *American National Biography,* 314.

35. Shane, "Veeck — The Barnum of Baseball," 30.

36. *Newark Star Ledger,* July 19, 1991.

37. Marshall, *Baseball's Pivotal Era,* 173.

38. *Ibid.,* 175.

39. Oakley, *Baseball's Last Golden Age,* 74.

40. Thorn et al., *Total Baseball,* 2177.

41. *Ibid.,* 2179.

42. Warren Brown, "Bill Veeck," *Sportfolio* (April 1949), 4.

43. Dewey and Acocella, *The Ball Clubs,* 220; "Selling a Ball Club to the Fans," *Business Week* (October 2, 1948), 53.

44. Dewey and Acocella, *The Ball Clubs,* 220; Gordon Cobbledick, "Bill Veeck, Baseball's Greatest Showman," *Sport* (September 1948), 61; "Baseball Dynamo," *Sportfolio,* 18.

45. Marshall, *Baseball's Pivotal Era,* 175.

46. David M. Jordan, Larry R. Gerlach, and John P. Rossi, "A Baseball Myth Exploded," *The National Pastime* (1998), 3–13.

47. Rossi, *The National Game,* 156.

48. *Ibid.,* 212.

49. Tygiel, *Baseball's Great Experiment,* 215; George Will, *Bunts, Curt Flood, Camden Yards, Pete Rose and Other Reflections on Baseball* (New York, 1998), 89.

50. Thorn et al., *Total Baseball,* 731.

51. A. S. (Doc) Young, "A Black Man in the Wigwam," *Ebony* (February 1969), 71; Tygiel, *Baseball's Great Experiment,* 218–219.

52. *Ibid.*

53. Hank Greenberg, "Unforgettable Bill Veeck," *Reader's Digest* (July 1986), 70.

54. Allen, *The American League Story,* 180–181.

55. *New York Newsday,* February 28, 1991.

56. Bjarkman, *Encyclopedia of Baseball Team Histories: American League,* 104–106.

57. Thorn et al., *Total Baseball,* 324.

58. Bjarkman, *Encyclopedia of Baseball Team Histories: American League,* 106.

59. Garraty, *American National Biography,* 314.

60. Marshall, *Baseball's Pivotal Era,* 183.

61. Condon, "How Bill Veeck Got That Way," 34.

62. Wayne Stewart, "Just a Regular Joe: Honored With a Night to End All Nights," *Beckett Baseball Cards* (August 1991), 105–109.

63. Oakley, *Baseball's Last Golden Age,* 92; Shane, "Veeck — The Barnum of Baseball," 30.

64. Bill Veeck, "What's Wrong With Baseball? What Can Be Done About It?" *Look* (April 12, 1949), 94–99.

65. Garraty, *American National Biography,* 314.

66. Furlong, "Master of the Joyful Illusion," 59.

67. *St. Louis Globe-Democrat,* June 22, 1951.

68. Marshall, *Baseball's Pivotal Era,* 404.

69. Light, *The Cultural Encyclopedia of Baseball,* 596; Bjarkman, *Encyclopedia of Baseball Team Histories: American League,* 366; Furlong, "Master of the Joyful Illusion," 59.

70. Oakley, *Baseball's Last Golden Age,* 133–134.

71. Furlong, "Master of the Joyful Illusion," 59.

72. Tygiel, *Baseball's Great Experiment,* 311–312.

73. Marshall, *Baseball's Pivotal Era,* 402.

74. Oakley, *Baseballs Last Golden Age,* 134.

75. Al Hirshberg, "Bill Veeck — Ladies Man of Baseball," *Today's Woman* (September 1952), 25–26.

76. Oakley, *Baseballs Last Golden Age,* 134; Dewey and Acocella, *The Ball Clubs,* 522.

77. Oakley, *Baseball's Last Golden Age,* 134; Dewey and Acocella, *The Ball Clubs,* 522; Okrent and Wulf, *Baseball Anecdotes,* 211.

78. Bjarkman, *Encyclopedia of Baseball Team Histories: American League,* 366.

79. Thorn et al., *Total Baseball,* 2189.

80. *Ibid.,* 1791.

81. *Ibid.,* 1052; Dewey and Acocella, *The Ball Clubs,* 522.

82. Hirshberg, "Bill Veeck — Ladies Man of Baseball," 26; Dewey and Acocella, *The Biographical History of Baseball,* 480–481.

83. Thorn et al., *Total Baseball,* 2425,

2429; Alexander, *Rogers Hornsby,* 257; Alexander, *Our Game,* 227.

84. Thorn et al., *Total Baseball,* 2189.

85. *Ibid.,* 1675.

86. Dewey and Acocella, *The Ball Clubs,* 522.

87. Koppett, *Koppett's Concise History of Major League Baseball,* 234.

88. Steve Gietschier, "Bill Veeck, Indian Chief," 35; Koppett, *Koppett's Concise History of Major League Baseball,* 234; Dewey and Acocella, *The Ball Clubs,*522; Greenberg, "Unforgettable Bill Veeck," 70–71.

89. *The Sporting News,* October 14, 1953.

90. Gietschier, "Bill Veeck, Indian Chief," *Time Line,* April-May 1990, 35; Koppett, *Koppett's Concise History of Major League Baseball,* 234; Dewey and Acocella, *The Ball Clubs,* 522; Greenberg, "Unforgettable Bill Veeck," 70–71.

91. *The Sporting News,* October 14, 1953.

92. *Ibid.*

93. Koppett, *Koppett's Concise History of Major League Baseball,* 234.

94. Unnamed article, September 1954, Veeck Files, *The Sporting News,* St. Louis, Missouri.

95. Alexander, *Our Game,* 227.

96. Miller, *The Baseball Business,* 30.

97. Koppett, *Koppett's Concise History of Major League Baseball,* 234.

98. Peter Golenbock, *The Spirit of St. Louis: A History of the St. Louis Cardinals and Browns* (New York, 2000), 356.

99. Thorn et al., *Total Baseball,* 2191.

100. Dewey and Acocella, *The Ball Clubs,* 523, 527; Bjarkman, *Encyclopedia of Baseball Team Histories: American League,* 366–367.

101. Miller, *The Baseball Business,* 31.

102. *Ibid.*; Thorn et al., *Total Baseball,* 2473; Koppett, *Koppett's Concise History of Major League Baseball,* 234.

103. Oakley, *Baseball's Last Golden Age,* 178.

104. Sullivan, *The Diamond Revolution,* 52.

105. Oakley, *Baseball's Last Golden Age,* 194.

106. Unnamed article, September 1954, Veeck Files, *The Sporting News,* St. Louis, Missouri.

107. Unnamed article, February 9, 1955, Veeck Files, *The Sporting News,* St. Louis, Missouri.

108. Bill Furlong, "The Veeck-Yankee Feud is for Real," *Sport* (April 1960), 69.

109. Dewey and Acocella, *The Biographical History of Baseball,* 481.

110. Furlong, "Master of the Joyful Illusion," 60.

111. Thorn et al., *Total Baseball,* 777.

112. Dewey and Acocella, *The Ball Clubs,* 160.

113. William Cook, *The 1919 World Series, What Really Happened?* (Jefferson, NC, 2001), 170.

114. Dewey and Acocella, *The Ball Clubs,* 160.

115. Thorn et al., *Total Baseball,* 335.

116. Unnamed article, June 1959, Veeck Files, *The Sporting News,* St. Louis, Missouri.

117. *The Sporting News,* June 15, 1960.

118. Bob Broeg and William Miller, *Baseball from a Different Angle* (South Bend, 1988), 35.

119. *The Sporting News,* June 21, 1961.

120. Allen, *The American League Story,* 227–228.

121. *The Sporting News,* June 1, 1960.

122. *Ibid.,* August 3, 1960.

123. Bill Veeck, "Are Umpires Ruining Baseball?" *Sport* (April 1961), 16–18.

124. Light, *The Cultural Encyclopedia of Baseball,* 452.

125. Golenbock, *The Spirit of St. Louis,* 332.

126. *Ibid.*; Oakley, *Baseball's Last Golden Age,* 135–136; Marshall, *Baseball's Pivotal Era,* 402–403; Allen, *The American League Story,* 189; *The Sporting News,* August 15, 1951; *The Sporting News,* August 29, 1951; Bill Veeck and Ed Linn, "The Midget at the Bat," *Reader's Digest* (October 1962) 73–77; Okrent and Wulf, *Baseball Anecdotes,* 209.

127. Dewey and Acocella, *The Biographical History of Baseball,* 481.

128. *The Plain Dealer,* February 23, 1965.

129. Bill Veeck, "Bill Veeck's Free Advice to the New Commissioner," *True* (April 1966), 59, 106–108.

130. Lawrence Doherty, "Baseball Braces for Promotion Binge as Veeck Returns to White Sox Helm," *Advertising Age* (December 22, 1975), 3.

131. Bjarkman, *Encyclopedia of Baseball Team Histories: American League*, 81; Dewey and Acocella, *The Ball Clubs*, 164; Lindberg, *Stealing First In a Two-Team Town*, 163.

132. *Ibid.*, 167; Bjarkman, *Encyclopedia of Baseball Team Histories: American League*, 81.

133. "Hustler's Return," *Newsweek* (December 22, 1975), 50–51; *The Sporting News*, December 11, 1975.

134. Dewey and Acocella, *The Ball Clubs*, 164.

135. *Washington Post*, December 3, 1975.

136. Porter, *The Biographical History of Baseball*, 481.

137. William Brashler, *Josh Gibson* (New York, 1978), 157.

138. Alexander, *Our Game*, 296–297; Lindberg, *Stealing First in a Two-Team Town*, 169.

139. *Ibid.*; Dewey and Acocella, *The Ball Clubs*, 164.

140. *Kansas City Star*, January 5, 1986; Lindbergh, *Stealing First in a Two-Team Town*, 172.

141. *Ibid.*, 170.

142. *New York Times*, June 11, 1970.

143. Thorn et al., *Total Baseball*, 2433, 2237–2245.

144. The Indians hired Frank Robinson in 1975 as the first African-American manager. Tygiel, *Baseball's Great Experiment*, 339; Thorn et al., *Total Baseball*, 2237–2245.

145. Dewey and Acocella, *The Ball Clubs*, 165; Thorn et al., *Total Baseball*, 2427.

146. *Ibid.*, 2237–2245.

147. *Ibid.*, 787, 1305.

148. Dewey and Acocella, *The Ball Clubs*, 164; William A. Cook, *The 1919 World Series: What Really Happened* (Jefferson, NC, 2001), 171; Helyar, *Lords of the Realm*, 240.

149. *Ibid.*, 240–241.

150. *The Sporting News*, July 28, 1979.

151. Helyar, *Lords of the Realm*, 241.

152. *Ibid.*, 242; Lindberg, *Stealing First in a Two-Team Town*, 178; Dewey and Acocella, *The Ball Clubs*, 165; Bjarkman, *Encyclopedia of Baseball Team Histories: American League*, 83.

153. Lindbergh, *Stealing First in a Two-Team Town*, 179; Bjarkman, *Encyclopedia of Baseball Team Histories: American League*, 83.

154. *Chicago Tribune*, February 4, 1981.

155. *The Arizona Daily Star*, February 3, 1981

156. Helyar, *Lords of the Realm*, 244.

157. *Ibid.*

158. *Newsweek*, January 13, 1986.

159. *Newark Star Ledger*, February 3, 1981.

160. *Washington Post*, January 3, 1986.

161. *Newsweek*, January 13, 1986.

162. Zimbalist, *Baseball and Billions*, 41.

163. Holtzman's interview with authors, July 30, 2002.

164. "A Conversation With Bill Veeck, *Baseball Quarterly* (Fall 1978), 17.

165. *National Sports Daily*, February 27, 1991.

166. *Washington Post*, February 27, 1991.

167. *Kansas City Star*, January 5, 1986; *Time*, January 12, 1986.

168. Dewey and Acocella, *The Ball Clubs*, 160.

Chapter 7

1. Unnamed newspaper clipping December 1960, Finley Files, *The Sporting News*, St. Louis, Missouri.

2. Helyar, *Lords of the Realm*, 73.

3. Kowet, *The Rich Who Own Sports*, 122.

4. Helyar, *The Lords of the Realm*, 73.

5. *Ibid.*, 122–23; William Barry Furlong, "Charlie Finley: Triumph and Turmoil," *Saturday Evening Post* (October 1975), 31.

6. Helyar, *Lords of the Realm*, 73.

7. Kowet, *The Rich Who Own Sports*, 123; Porter, *Biographical Directory of American Sports*, 472.

8. Charles Moritz (ed.), *Current Biography 1974* (New York, 1974, 1975), 113.

9. Furlong, "Charlie Finley: Triumph and Turmoil," 31; Kowet, *The Rich Who Own Sports*, 124.

10. Dickey, *Champs and Chumps*, 148; Kowet, *The Rich Who Own Sports*, 124–125;

"Charlie Finley: Baseball's Barnum," *Time* (August 18, 1975), 43; Moritz, *Current Biography 1974*, 114.

11. Tom Clark, *Champagne and Baloney: The Rise and Fall of Finley's A's* (New York, 1976), 9; Helyar, *Lords of the Realm*, 73; Dickey, *Champs and Chumps*, 149.

12. Helyar, *Lords of the Realm*, 73; Porter, *Biographical Directory of American Sports*, 472; Dickey, *Champs and Chumps*, 149.

13. Moritz, *Current Biography 1974*, 114.

14. Bjarkman, *Encyclopedia of Major League Baseball Team Histories: The American League*, 329–330.

15. Clark, *Champagne and Baloney*, 12.

16. Kowet, *The Rich Who Own Sports*, 126; *New York Times*, December 20, 1960.

17. Bjarkman, *Encyclopedia of Major League Baseball Team Histories: The American League*, 330.

18. Helyar, *Lords of the Realm*, 73.

19. Kowet, *The Rich Who Own Sports*, 126.

20. Moritz, *Current Biography 1974*, 115; Murray quoted in Bjarkman, *Encyclopedia of Major League Baseball Team Histories: The American League*, 230.

21. Dewey and Acocella, *The Ball Clubs*, 276.

22. Clark, *Champagne and Baloney*, 12.

23. Helyar, *Lords of the Realm*, 73; Clark, *Champagne and Baloney*, 13; Thorn et al., *Total Baseball*, 2205.

24. Edwin Shrake, "A Man and a Mule in Missouri," *Sports Illustrated* (July 19, 1965), 36.

25. Furlong, "*Charlie Finley: Triumph and Turmoil*," 32; Kowet, *The Rich Who Own Sports*, 127.

26. *Sporting News*, April 4, 1964.

27. Sharke, "A Man and a Mule In Missouri," 37; Broeg and Miller, Jr., *Baseball From a Different Angle*, 82; Smith, *Storied Stadiums*, 245.

28. Shrake, "A Man and a Mule in Missouri," 38.

29. Thorn et al., *Total Baseball*, 2207–2219; Bjarkman, *Encyclopedia of Major League Baseball Team Histories; The American League*, 329.

30. Kowet, *The Rich Who Own Sports*, 131.

31. Furlong, "Charlie Finley: Triumph and Turmoil," 32.

32. *The Sporting News*, February 9, 1963.

33. "What Every Team Needs," *Time* (January 24, 1964), 30; Smith, *Storied Stadiums*, 245; Bjarkman, *Encyclopedia of Major League Baseball Team Histories: The American League*, 331.

34. Clark, *Champagne and Baloney*, 16.

35. Kowet, *The Rich Who Own Sports*, 131.

36. Broeg and Miller, Jr., *Baseball From a Different Angle*, 109.

37. Clark, *Champagne and Baloney*, 15–16; Helyar, *Lords of the Realm*, 74.

38. *Kansas City Times*, February 17, 1965; Shrake, "A Man and a Mule in Missouri," 43.

39. Dewey and Acocella, *The Ball Clubs*, 277.

40. Dewey and Acocella, *The Biographical History of Baseball*, 142.

41. Dewey and Acocella, *The Ball Clubs*, 277.

42. Clark, *Champagne and Baloney*, 15–16; Helyar, *Lords of the Realm*, 74.

43. Kowet, *The Rich Who Own Sports*, 121; Moritz, *Current Biography 1974*, 114.

44. Dewey and Acocella, *The Ball Clubs*, 277.

45. Thorn et al., *Total Baseball*, 420, 2438.

46. Moritz, *Current Biography 1974*, 114.

47. Kowet, *The Rich Who Own Sports*, 121.

48. Kuhn, *Hardball*, 129.

49. Thorn et al., *Total Baseball*, 654.

50. Bjarkman, *Encyclopedia of Major League Baseball Team Histories: The American League*, 332.

51. *Ibid.*; Dewey and Acocella, *The Ball Clubs*, 278.

52. "Charlie Finley: Baseball's Barnum," 43.

53. Clark, *Champagne and Baloney*, 16.

54. Koppett, *Koppett's Concise History of Major League Baseball*, 297.

55. Dewey and Acocella, *The Ball Clubs*, 277.

56. Clark, *Champagne and Baloney*, 18.

57. *Ibid.*; Thorn et al., 2213, 2217.

58. Unnamed newspaper clipping,

February 29, 1964, Finley Files, *The Sporting News*, St. Louis, Missouri.

59. *San Francisco Chronicle*, August 26, 1980; Will, *Bunts*, 299.

60. Dewey and Acocella, *The Ball Clubs*, 278–279; Dewey and Acecella, *The Biographical History of Baseball*, 142.

61. McKelvey, *The MacPhails*, 164.

62. Bjarkman, *Encyclopedia of Major League Baseball Team Histories: The American League*, 321.

63. Unnamed clipping, December 1963, Finley Files, *The Sporting News*, St. Louis, Missouri.

64. Donald Honig, *The All Star Game: A Pictorial History: 1933–the Present* (St. Louis, 1987), 166, 171.

65. *The Sporting News*, October 18, 1969.

66. "One For Charlie O," *Sports Illustrated* (January 18, 1971), 8; Helyar, *Lords of the Realm*, 75.

67. Bjarkman, *Encyclopedia of Major League Baseball Teams Histories: The American League*, 334.

68. Helyar, *Lords of the Realm*, 50.

69. Light, *The Cultural Encyclopedia of Baseball*, 593.

70. *Ibid.*, 768.

71. *Ibid.*, 667.

72. Clark, *Champagne and Baloney*, 31–32.

73. *Ibid.*, 31–32, 86–87.

74. Furlong, "Charlie Finley: Triumph and Turmoil," 72.

75. Thorn et al., *Total Baseball*, 2221; Sullivan, *The Diamond Revolution*, 56.

76. Dickey, *Champs and Chumps*, 150; Thorn et al., *Total Baseball*, 2223, 2224; Porter, *Biographical Directory of American Sports*, 473.

77. Dewey and Acocella, *The Ball Clubs*, 407.

78. Dickey, *Champs and Chumps*, 154.

79. Alexander, *Our Game*, 283.

80. Bjarkman, *Encyclopedia of Major League Baseball Team Histories: The American League*, 336.

81. *Ibid.*, 336–337; Thorn et al., *Total Baseball*, 355–356.

82. Bruce Markusen, *Baseball's Last Dynasty: Charlie Finley's A's* (Indianapolis, 1998), 139.

83. Light, *The Cultural Encyclopedia of Baseball*, 204.

84. Dickey, *Champs and Chumps*, 152.

85. Thorn et al., *Total Baseball*, 667.

86. Markusen, *Baseball's Last Dynasty*, 184.

87. Thorn et al., *Total Baseball*, 891; Dewey and Acocella, *The Ball Clubs*, 408.

88. Bjarkman, *Encyclopedia of Major League Baseball Team Histories: The American League*, 339.

89. Thorn et al., *Total Baseball*, 358.

90. *Ibid.*, 359.

91. Bjarkman, *Encyclopedia of Major League Baseball Team Histories: The American League*, 338; Dewey and Acocella, *The Ball Clubs*, 408.

92. *Ibid.*

93. Markusen, *Baseball's Last Dynasty*, 244.

94. Dewey and Acocella, *The Ball Clubs*, 409.

95. Markusen, *Baseball's Last Dynasty*, 248.

96. *Ibid.*, 249.

97. Bjarkman, *Encyclopedia of Major League Baseball Team Histories: The American League*, 339; Dewey and Acocella, *The Ball Clubs*, 409.

98. *Ibid.*; Thorn et al., *Total Baseball*, 2438; Dickey, *Champs and Chumps*, 154–155.

99. *Ibid.*, 158.

100. Bjarkman, *Encyclopedia of Major League Baseball Team Histories: The American League*, 339; Dewey and Acocella, *The Ball Clubs*, 409.

101. Markusen, *Baseball's Last Dynasty*, 297.

102. Dickey, *Champs and Chumps*, 155.

103. Thorn et al., *Total Baseball*, 2420.

104. Dickey, *Champs and Chumps*, 156.

105. Thorn et al., *Total Baseball*, 362.

106. *Ibid.*, 1537.

107. *Ibid.*, 362.

108. *Ibid.*, 1266; Dickey, *Champs and Chumps*, 153.

109. "Charlie Finley: Baseball's Barnum," 50.

110. Koppett, *Koppett's Concise History of Major League Baseball*, 345; Dickey, *Champs and Chumps*, 152.

111. *The Sporting News*, November 23, 1968.

112. *Ibid.*, March 20, 1971.

113. Helyar, *Lords of the Realm*, 75.

114. Bjarkman, *Encyclopedia of Major League Baseball Team Histories: The American League*, 340; Dewey and Acocella, *The Ball Clubs*, 410.

115. Holtzman, *The Commissioners*, 166–167.

116. Ken Holtzman interview with authors, July 30, 2002.

117. Burk, *Much More Than a Game*, 185–187; Helyar, *Lords of the Realm*, 152.

118. Markusen, *Baseball's Last Dynasty*, 345; Burk, *Much More Than a Game*, 188.

119. Helyar, *Lords of the Realm*, 137.

120. *Ibid.*, 140.

121. McKelvey, *The MacPhails*, 189–190.

122. Dewey and Acocella, *The Ball Clubs*, 410.

123. *Ibid.;* Markusen, *Baseball's Last Dynasty*, 348; Miller, *The Baseball Business*, 215; Light, *The Cultural Encyclopedia of Baseball*, 284.

124. McKelvey, *The MacPhails*, 190.

125. *Ibid.*

126. Dewey and Acocella, *The Ball Clubs*, 410; Alexander, *Our Game*, 296.

127. Dewey and Acocella, *The Ball Clubs*, 410.

128. Holtzman, *The Commissioners*, 162; Ken Holtzman interview with authors, July 30, 2002.

129. Kuhn, *Hardball*, 128.

130. Helyar, *Lords of the Realm*, 189.

131. *Ibid.*

132. Thorn, et al., *Total Baseball*, 883.

133. Kuhn, *Hardball*, 127.

134. *Ibid.*, 131–135; Moritz, *Current Biography 1974*, 115; Koppett, *Koppett's Concise History of Major League Baseball*, 372; Helyar, *Lords of the Realm*, 189.

135. Kuhn, *Hardball*, 130.

136. Moritz, *Current Biography 1974*, 115; Holtzman, *The Commissioners*, 172.

137. *New York Times*, October 29, 1973; Helyar, *Lords of the Realm*, 189.

138. Koppett, *Koppett's Concise History of Major League Baseball*, 372–373; Miller, *The Baseball Business*, 214; Helyar, *Lords of the Realm*, 190–191.

139. Dewey and Acocella, *The Ball Clubs*, 410; Will, *Bunts*, 29.

140. Koppett, *Koppett's Concise History of Major League Baseball*, 373.

141. Markusen, *Baseball's Last Dynasty*, 393; Will, *Bunts*, 125.

142. Rader, *Baseball: A History of America's Game*, 204.

143. Helyar, *Lords of the Realm*, 193.

144. *Ibid.*, 192; *New York Times*, June 26, 1976.

145. Helyar, *Lords of the Realm*, 194.

146. Dewey and Acocella, *The Ball Clubs*, 410–411; *New York Times*, June 19, 1976.

147. Holtzman, *The Commissioners*, 189–190; *New York Times*, March 17, 1977.

148. Kuhn, *Hardball*, 182.

149. Markusen, *Baseball's Last Dynasty*, 395; *The Sporting News*, April 22, 1978; *The Sporting News*, October 14, 1978.

150. Miller, *The Baseball Business*, 224.

151. Holtzman, *The Commissioners*, 190.

152. Koppett, *Koppett's Concise History of Major League Baseball*, 374.

153. Dewey and Acocella, *The Ball Clubs*, 411.

154. Kowet, *The Rich Who Own Sports*, 136.

155. Dewey and Acocella, *The Ball Clubs*, 411.

156. Thorn et al., *Total Baseball*, 2239.

157. Dewey and Acocella, *The Ball Clubs*, 411.

158. Broeg and Miller, *Baseball From a Different Angle*, 231.

159. Dewey and Acocella, *The Ball Clubs*, 411–412.

160. Thorn et al., *Total Baseball*, 2239.

161. Bjarkman, *Encyclopedia of Major League Baseball Team Histories: The American League*, 342.

162. *Ibid.;* Dewey and Acocella, *The Ball Clubs*, 412.

163. Kowet, *The Rich Who Own Sports*, 134–135; Moritz, *Current Biography 1974*, 115.

164. Porter, *Biographical Directory of American Sports*, 473.

165. Bjarkman, *Encyclopedia of Major League Baseball Team Histories: The American League*, 342.

166. *Wall Street Journal*, August 25, 1980; Helyar, *Lords of the Realm*, 233.

167. Porter, *Biographical Directory of American Sports*, 474.

168. *The Sporting News*, May 28, 1981.

169. *Ibid.*

170. *New York Times,* February 20, 1996.

171. Markusen, *Baseball's Last Dynasty,* 87.

172. Holtzman interview with authors, July 30, 2002.

173. *New York Times,* February 20, 1996.

Chapter 8

1. *The Sporting News,* March 4, 1953.

2. Dewey and Acocella, *The Ball Clubs,* 505.

3. Rains, *The St. Louis Cardinals,* 127; Dewey and Acocella, *The Ball Clubs,* 505.

4. *Ibid.*

5. Bjarkman, *Encyclopedia of Baseball Team Histories: The National League,* 531.

6. *St. Louis Business Journal,* June 10–16, 1991; Porter, *Biographical Directory of American Sports,* 189.

7. *Ibid.*

8. Garraty, *American National Biography,* 70; *The Sporting News,* May 20, 1953.

9. Marjorie Dent Candee (ed.), *Current Biography 1973* (New York, 1954), 70; Harold H. Martin, "The Cardinals Strike It Rich," *Saturday Evening Post* (June 27, 1953), 75.

10. *Ibid.*

11. *St. Louis Globe-Democrat,* December 24, 1961.

12. Golenbock, *The Spirit of St. Louis,* 399.

13. Garraty, *American National Biography,* 71.

14. Golenbock, *The Spirit of St. Louis,* 399.

15. *Ibid.*

16. *St. Louis Post-Dispatch,* February 20, 1953.

17. *The Sporting News,* March 4, 1953; *New York Times,* February 21, 1953; "Sporting Venture," *Time* (March 2, 1953), 46.

18. Martin, "The Cardinals Strike It Rich," 74; *St. Louis Post-Dispatch,* February 20, 1953.

19. *Ibid.*

20. *The Sporting News,* May 20, 1953.

21. "Beer Teams Up With Baseball," *Business Week* (February 28, 1953), 32; "Sporting Venture," 46.

22. Martin, "The Cardinals Strike It Rich," 74.

23. *New York Times,* February 24, 1954.

24. Peter Hernon and Terry Ganey, *Under the Influence* (New York, 1991), 213; *New York Times,* February 24, 1954.

25. *Ibid.,* February 25, 1954.

26. Hernon and Ganey, *Under the Influence,* 213; *New York Times,* March 19, 1954.

27. *St. Louis Business Journal,* August 12–18, 1991.

28. *St. Louis Post-Dispatch,* May 26, 1954.

29. Hernon and Ganey, *Under the Influence,* 213; *New York Times,* March 19, 1954.

30. Golenbock, *The Spirit of St. Louis,* 40.

31. "The Baron of Beers," *Time* (July 11, 1955), 84.

32. Miller, *The Baseball Business,* 28.

33. *New York Herald-Tribune,* June 15, 1955.

34. Dewey and Acocella, *The Ball Clubs,* 505.

35. Smith, *Storied Stadiums,* 161.

36. *Ibid.;* Bill Bennett, "Sportalk," *Sport* (March 1954), 6–7; "Time Of His Life," *Time* (March 22, 1954), 81.

37. Golenbock, *The Spirit of St. Louis,* 40.

38. "Time of His Life," 81.

39. Hernon and Ganey, *Under the Influence,* 214; Golenbock, *The Spirit of St. Louis,* 40; *St. Louis Business Journal,* July 15–21, 1991; *New York Times,* April 11, 1953.

40. Thorn et al., *Total Baseball,* 302, 322, 2136–2176.

41. Rains, *St. Louis Cardinals,* 268–269; Dewey and Acocella, 506; Bjarkman, *Encyclopedia of Baseball Team Histories: The National League,* 531.

42. Rains, *The St. Louis Cardinals,* 138.

43. Thorn et al., *Total Baseball,* 1258; Hernon and Ganey, *Under the Influence,* 216–217.

44. Thorn et al., *Total Baseball,* 567; Tygiel, *Baseball's Great Experiment,* 293.

45. Golenbock, *The Spirit of St. Louis,* 408.

46. Thorn et al., *Total Baseball,* 1582; Rains, *The St. Louis Cardinals,* 140.

47. *Ibid.*, 145–146.

48. *St. Louis Business Journal*, August 19–25, 1991; James N. Giglio, *Musial: From Stash to Stan the Man* (Columbia, MO: 2000), 253; Dewey and Acocella, *The Ball Clubs*, 506–507; Burk, *Much More Than a Game*, 133; Rains, *The St. Louis Cardinals*, 151; Dewey and Acocella, *The Biographical History of Baseball*, 55.

49. Thorn et al., *Total Baseball*, 2204–2210.

50. *Ibid.*

51. Dewey and Acocella, *The Ball Clubs*, 507.

52. Rains, *The St. Louis Cardinals*, 153.

53. *Ibid.*, 152.

54. Hernon and Ganey, *Under the Influence*, 219.

55. Thorn et al., *Total Baseball*, 632.

56. *Ibid.*, 340; Rains, *The St. Louis Cardinals*, 158.

57. *Ibid.*, 158–161; Dewey and Acocella, *The Ball Clubs*, 507; Hernon and Ganey, *Under the Influence*, 219.

58. Thorn et al., *Total Baseball*, 1156–1157; Borst, *Baseball Through a Knothole*, 84; Dewey and Acocella, *The Ball Clubs*, 508.

59. *Ibid.*

60. Bjarkman, *Encyclopedia of Baseball Team Histories: The National League*, 532.

61. Information found on internet — St. Louis Cardinals Ballpark, mlb.com; *St. Louis Post-Dispatch*, March 23, 1963.

62. *The Sporting News*, April 15, 1972.

63. Rains, *The St. Louis Cardinals*, 162.

64. *Ibid.*, 158–161; Dewey and Acocella, *The Ball Clubs*, 507; Hernon and Ganey, *Under the Influence*, 219.

65. Dewey and Acocella, *The Ball Clubs*, 508.

66. Thorn et al., *Total Baseball*, 2218.

67. Rains, *The St. Louis Cardinals*, 164–168; Dewey and Acocella, *The Ball Clubs*, 508.

68. Rains, *The St. Louis Cardinals*, 164–168; Dewey and Acocella, *The Ball Clubs*, 508; Thorn et al., *Total Baseball*, 343.

69. Dewey and Acocella, *The Ball Clubs*, 508.

70. Rains, *The St. Louis Cardinals*, 176.

71. Dewey and Acocella, *The Ball Clubs*, 508.

72. Thorn et al., *Total Baseball*, 344.

73. Dewey and Acocella, *The Ball Clubs*, 508; Thorn et al., *Total Baseball*, 2222.

74. Golenbock, *The Spirit of St. Louis*, 503.

75. Helyar, *Lords of the Realm*, 100.

76. *New York Times*, March 23, 1969; Statement by August Busch, Jr., at Players Meeting, Busch Files, *The Sporting News*, St. Louis, Missouri; Helyar, *Lords of the Realm*, 100.

77. *Ibid.*, 99.

78. Bjarkman, *The Encyclopedia of Baseball Team Histories: The National League*, 533.

79. Lowenfish and Lupien, *The Imperfect Diamond*, 208.

80. Thorn et al., *Total Baseball*, 771; Vricella, *St. Louis Cardinals First Century*, 236.

81. *The Sporting News*, April 15, 1978.

82. Dewey and Acocella, *The Ball Clubs*, 509; Rains, *The St. Louis Cardinals*, 185.

83. Vricella, *St. Louis Cardinals First Century*, 236.

84. Bjarkman, *The Encyclopedia of Baseball Team Histories: The National League*, 533.

85. *The Sporting News*, March 13, 1970.

86. Thorn et al., *Total Baseball*, 564.

87. Unidentified newspaper clipping March 13, 1970, Busch Files, *The Sporting News*, St. Louis, Missouri.

88. Helyar, *Lords of the Realm*, 111; Thorn et al., *Total Baseball*, 1382.

89. Helyar, *Lords of the Realm*, 111–112; Thorn et al., *Total Baseball*, 1711; Rains, *The St. Louis Cardinals*, 191.

90. William Leggett, "A Bird In Hand And A Burning Busch," *Sports Illustrated* (March 23, 1970), 21; *The Sporting News*, March 28, 1970.

91. Miller, *The Baseball Business*, 185.

92. Heylar, *Lords of the Realm*, 113.

93. *New York Times*, March 16, 1972.

94. *St. Louis Post-Dispatch*, April 1, 1972.

95. *The Sporting News*, April 1, 1972.

96. *Ibid.*, April 15, 1972.

97. Vricella, *St. Louis Cardinals First Century*, 240.

98. Sullivan, *The Diamond Revolution*, 175.

99. Statement by August Busch at Players Meeting Al Lang Field, March 24, 1972; Busch Files, *The Sporting News,* St. Louis, Missouri.

100. Hernon and Ganey, *Under the Influence,* 248; Rains, *The St. Louis Cardinals,* 192; "Gussie vs. the Cards," *Newsweek* (June 19, 1972), 61.

101. Burk, *Much More Than Just a Game,* 186.

102. Bjarkman, *The Encyclopedia of Baseball Team Histories: The National League,* 533.

103. *Ibid.,* 295; Hernon and Ganey, *Under the Influence,* 288.

104. Alexander, *Our Game,* 197; Vricella, *St. Louis Cardinals First Century,* 253–255.

105. *Ibid.,* 255.

106. *St. Louis Post-Dispatch,* July 31, 1976.

107. Vricella, *St. Louis Cardinals First Century,* 256.

108. Holtzman, *The Commissioners,* 164.

109. Hernon and Ganey, *Under the Influence,* 295.

110. Holtzman, *The Commissioners,* 164; Alexander, *Our Game,* 297.

111. Hernon and Ganey, *Under the Influence,* 195; Statement of August Busch Jr. As Read by Louis Susman at Joint Major League Meeting in Philadelphia, July 14, 1976, Busch Files, *The Sporting News,* St. Louis, Missouri.

112. *St. Louis Post-Dispatch,* August 14, 1976.

113. *The Sporting News,* August 28, 1976.

114. *Ibid.,* July 23, 1977.

115. *St. Louis Post-Dispatch,* August 6, 1977; Borst, *Baseball Through a Knothole,* 87.

116. Vricella, *St. Louis Cardinals First Century,* 257.

117. Rains, *The St. Louis Cardinals,* 207.

118. Thorn et al., *Total Baseball,* 2240.

119. *St. Louis Post-Dispatch,* June 24, 1978.

120. *Ibid.,* July 8, 1978.

121. Golenbock, *The Spirit of St. Louis,* 527.

122. Dewey and Acocella, *The Ball Clubs,* 509; Rains, *The St. Louis Cardinals,* 208.

123. Thorn et al., *Total Baseball,* 2418.

124. Golenbock, *The Spirit of St. Louis,* 528.

125. Many years later, Keith Hernandez would admit that he was a heavy cocaine user in 1980. Vricella, *St. Louis Cardinals First Century,* 270.

126. Rains, *The St. Louis Cardinals,* 214–215; Dewey and Acocella, *The Ball Clubs,* 510.

127. Vricella, *St. Louis Cardinals First Century,* 275; Dewey and Acocella, *The Ball Clubs,* 510; Bjarkman, *Encyclopedia of Baseball Team Histories: The National League,* 535; Rains, *The St. Louis Cardinals,* 215–216; Thorn et al., *Total Baseball,* 2246.

128. Rains, *St. Louis Cardinals,* 217–222; Dewey and Acocella, *The Ball Clubs,* 510–511.

129. Thorn et al., *Total Baseball,* 390.

130. Hernon and Ganey, *Under the Influence,* 296.

131. *Ibid.*

132. Helyar, *Lords of the Realm,* 368.

133. Hernon and Ganey, *Under the Influence,* 296.

134. *Ibid.,* 297; Vricella, *St. Louis Cardinals First Century,* 287.

135. *Ibid.*

136. *Ibid.*; Hernon and Ganey, *Under the Influence,* 297.

137. Dewey and Acocella, *The Ball Clubs,* 511; Bjarkman, *Encyclopedia of Baseball Team Histories: The National League,* 537; Thorn et al., *Total Baseball,* 399.

138. *Ibid.,* 405; Rains, *The St. Louis Cardinals,* 246.

139. Sullivan, *The Diamond Revolution,* 176.

140. *Albany Times Union,* September 30, 1989.

141. *The Sporting News,* October 9, 1989.

Bibliography

Archives

Baseball Hall of Fame, Cooperstown, New York.
Missouri Historical Society, St. Louis, Missouri.
The Sporting News, St. Louis, Missouri.

Books

Alexander, Charles. *John McGraw*. New York: Viking, 1988.
______. *Our Game: An American Baseball History*. New York: Henry Holt, 1991.
______. *Rogers Hornsby*. New York: Henry Holt, 1995.
Allen, Lee. *The American League Story*. New York: Hill & Wang, 1965.
______. *The National League Story: The Official History*. New York: Hill & Wang, 1961.
Appel, Martin, and Burt Goldblatt. *Baseball's Best: The Hall of Fame Gallery*. New York: McGraw-Hill, 1977.
Berlage, Gai. *Women in Baseball*. Westport, CT: Praeger Publishers, 1994.
Bjarkman, Peter C. *Baseball with a Latin Beat: A History of the Latin American Game*. Jefferson, NC: McFarland, 1994.
______, ed. *Encyclopedia of Baseball's Team Histories: American League*. Westport, CT: Meckler, 1991.
______, ed. *Encyclopedia of Major League Baseball Team Histories: National League*. Westport, CT: Meckler, 1991.
Borst, Bill. *Baseball Through a Knothole*. St. Louis: Krank Enterprises, 1980.
Boston, Talmage. *1939 Baseball's Pivotal Year: From the Golden Age to the Modern Era*. Fort Worth: The Summit Group, 1994.
Brashler, William. *Josh Gibson: A Life in the Negro Leagues*. Chicago: Ivan R. Dee, 2000.
Broeg, Bob. *Bob Broeg's Redbirds — A Century of Cardinals Baseball*. St. Louis: River City, 1981.
______. *The St. Louis Cardinals Encyclopedia*. Chicago: NTC Contemporary Publishing Group, 1998.
______, and William Miller, Jr. *Baseball from a Different Angle*. South Bend: Diamond Communication, 1988.
Burk, Robert F. *Much More Than a Game: Players, Owners & American Baseball Since 1921*. Chapel Hill: The University of North Carolina Press, 2001.

Candee, Marjorie Dent, ed. *Current Biography 1954*. New York: H.W. Wilson, 1954.

Chalberg, John C. *Rickey and Robinson: The Preacher, the Player, and America's Game*. Wheeling, IL: Harlan Davidson, 2000.

Clark, Tom. *Champagne and Baloney*. New York: Harper & Row, 1976.

Cohen, Stanley. *Dodgers: The First 100 Years*. New York: Carol Publishing Group, 1990.

Cook, William A. *The 1919 World Series: What Really Happened*. Jefferson, NC: McFarland, 2001.

Creamer, Robert W. *Stengel: His Life and Times*. New York: Simon and Schuster, 1984.

De Valeira, Dennis, and Jeanne Burke De Valeria. *Honus Wagner: A Biography*. New York: Henry Holt, 1998.

Deveaux, Tom. *The Washington Senators, 1901–1971*. Jefferson, NC: McFarland, 2001.

Dewey, Donald, and Nicholas Acocella. *The Ball Clubs*. San Francisco: Harper Collins, 1996.

_____, _____, and Jerome Holtzman. *The Biographical History of Baseball*. New York: Carroll & Graf, 1995.

Dickey, Glenn. *Champs and Chumps: An Insider's Look at America's Sports Heroes*. San Francisco: Chronicle Books, 1976.

_____. *The History of American League Baseball Since 1901*. New York: Stein and Day, 1980.

_____. *The History of National League Baseball Since 1876*. Lanham, MD: Rowman & Littlefield, 1979.

_____. *The History of the World Series Since 1903*. New York: Stein and Day, 1984.

Durso, Joseph. *Baseball and the American Dream*. St. Louis: Sporting News, 1986.

Eisenbath, Mike. *Cardinals Encyclopedia*. Philadelphia: Temple University Press, 1999.

Eskenazi, Gerald. *The Lip: A Biography of Leo Durocher*. New York: William Morrow, 1993.

Fountain, Charles. *Sportswriter: The Life and Times of Grantland Rice*. New York: Oxford University Press, 1993.

Frick, Ford C. *Games, Asterisks, and People: Memoirs of a Lucky Fan*. New York: Crown, 1973.

Frommer, Harvey. *Rickey and Robinson: The Men Who Broke the Baseball's Color Line*. New York: Macmillan, 1982.

Garraty, John A., ed. *American National Biography*. New York: Mark C. Carnes, 1999.

Gershman, Michael. *Diamonds: The Evolution of the Ballpark*. Boston: Houghton Mifflin, 1993.

Giglio, James N. *Musial: From Stash to Stan the Man*. Columbia: University of Missouri Press, 2000.

Gilbert, Tom. *Baseball and the Color Line*. New York: Franklin Watts, 1995.

Goldstein, Richard. *Spartan Seasons: How Baseball Survived the Second World War*. New York: Macmillan, 1980.

_____. *Superstars and Screwballs: 100 Years of Brooklyn Baseball*. New York: Dutton, 1991.

Golenbock, Peter. *Bums: An Oral History of the Brooklyn Dodgers*. New York: G. B. Putnam's Sons, 1984.

_____. *The Spirit of St. Louis: A History of the St. Louis Cardinals and Browns*. New York: Avon Books, 2000.

Graham, Frank. *The Brooklyn Dodgers.* New York: G. P. Putnam's Sons, 1948.

Gregory, Paul M. *The Baseball Player: An Economic Study.* Washington, DC: Public Affairs Press, 1956.

Helyar, John. *Lords of the Realm: The Real History of Baseball.* New York: Villard Books, 1994.

Hernon, Peter, and Terry Ganey. *Under the Influence.* New York: Simon & Schuster, 1991.

Hittner, Arthur D. *Honus Wagner: The Life of Baseball's "Flying Dutchman."* Jefferson, NC: McFarland, 1996.

Holmes, Tommy. *Dodger Daze and Knights.* New York: David McKay, 1953.

Holtzman, Jerome. *The Commissioners: Baseball's Midlife Crisis.* New York: Total Sports, 1998.

Holway, John B. *Blackball Stars: Negro League Players.* Westport, CT: Meckler, 1988.

Honig, Donald. *The All Star Game: A Pictorial History 1933–Present.* St. Louis: The Sporting News, 1987.

_____. *Baseball America: The Heroes of the Game and the Times of Their Glory.* New York: Macmillan, 1985.

_____. *A Donald Honig Reader.* New York: Simon & Schuster, 1988.

_____. *The St. Louis Cardinals: An Illustrated History.* New York: Prentice-Hall, 1991.

Hood, Robert E. *The Gashouse Gang.* New York: Wm. Morrow, 1976.

Kahn, Roger. *The Era 1947–1957: When the Yankees, the Giants and the Dodgers Ruled the World.* New York: Ticknor & Fields, 1993.

Kavanaugh, Jack. *Walter Johnson: A Life:* South Bend: Diamond Communications, 1995.

_____, and Norman Macht. *Uncle Robbie.* Cleveland: Society For American Baseball Research, 1999.

Kerr, John. *Calvin: Baseball's Last Dinosaur.* Dubuque, IA: William C. Brown, 1990.

Koppett, Leonard. *Koppett's Concise History of Major League Baseball.* Philadelphia: Temple University Press, 1998.

Kowet, Don. *The Rich Who Own Sports.* New York: Random House, 1977.

Kuhn, Bowie. *Hardball: The Education of a Baseball Commissioner.* New York: New York Times Books, 1987.

Levine, Peter, ed. *A.G. Spalding and the Rise of Baseball: The Promise of American Sport.* New York: Oxford Press, 1985.

_____. *Baseball and the Great Depression.* Westport, CT: Meckler, 1989.

Lieb, Frederic G. *The Pittsburgh Pirates.* New York: G. P. Putnam's Sons, 1948.

_____. *St. Louis Cardinals: Story of a Great Baseball Club.* New York: G. P. Putnam's Sons, 1944.

_____. *The Story of the World Series: An Informal History.* New York: G. P. Putnam's Sons, 1949.

Light, Jonathan Fraser. *The Cultural Encyclopedia of Baseball.* Jefferson, NC: McFarland, 1997.

Lindberg, Richard Carl. *Stealing First in a Two-Team Town: The White Sox from Comiskey to Reinsdorf.* Champaign, IL: Sagamore, 1994.

Lowenfish, Lee, and Tony Lupien. *The Imperfect Diamond: The Story of Baseball's Reserve System and the Men Who Fought to Change It.* New York: Stein and Day, 1980.

Mansch, Larry D. *Rube Marquard: The Life and Times of a Baseball Hall of Famer.* Jefferson, NC: McFarland, 1998.

Maria, Michael Santa, and James Costello. *In the Shadows of the Diamonds: Hard Times in the National Pastime.* Carmel, IN: William C. Brown Communications, 1992.

Markusen, Bruce. *Baseball's Last Dynasty: Charlie Finley's Oakland A's.* Indianapolis: Masters Press, 1998.

Marshall, William. *Baseball's Pivotal Era: 1945–1951.* Lexington: University Press of Kentucky, 1999.

McCollister, John. *The Bucs: The Story of the Pittsburgh Pirates.* Lenexa, KS: Addax Publishing Group, 1998.

McKelvey, G. Richard. *The MacPhails: Baseball's First Family of the Front Office.* Jefferson, NC: McFarland, 2000.

Mead, William B. *Even the Browns.* Chicago: Contemporary Books, 1978.

______, and Paul Dickson. *Baseball — The President's Game.* Washington, DC: Farragut, 1993.

Miller, James Edward. *The Baseball Business: Pursuing Pennants and Profits in Baltimore.* Chapel Hill: The University of North Carolina Press, 1990.

Miller, Marvin. *A Whole Different Ball Game: The Sport and Business of Baseball.* New York: Birch Lane Press, 1991.

Moore, Joseph Thomas. *Pride Against Prejudice: The Biography of Larry Doby.* New York: Greenwood Press, 1988.

Moritz, Charles, ed. *Current Biography 1973.* New York: H.W. Wilson Company, 1973, 1974.

______. *Current Biography 1974.* New York: H.W. Wilson Company, 1974, 1975.

Murdock, Eugene C. *Ban Johnson Czar of Baseball.* Westport, CT: Greenwood Press, 1982.

Oakley, J. Ronald. *Baseball's Last Golden Age, 1946–1960: The National Pastime in a Time of Glory and Change.* Jefferson, NC: McFarland, 1994.

Okrent, Daniel, and Steve Wulf. *Baseball Anecdotes.* New York: Oxford University Press, 1989.

Peterson, Robert. *Only the Ball Was White.* Englewood Cliffs, NJ: Prentice-Hall, 1970.

Pietrusza, David. *Lights On! The Wild Century-Long Saga of Night Baseball.* Lanham, MD: Scarecrow, 1997.

Porter, David, ed. *Biographical Directory of American Sports.* Westport, CT: Greenwood Press, 2000.

Povich, Shirley. *The Washington Senators.* New York: G. P. Putnam's Sons, 1954.

Prince, Carl E. *Brooklyn's Dodgers: The Bums, the Borough, and the Best of Baseball 1947–1957.* New York: Oxford University Press, 1996.

Rader, Benjamin G. *Baseball: A History of America's Game.* Urbana: University of Illinois Press, 1992.

Rains, Rob. *The St. Louis Cardinals: The 100th Anniversary History.* New York: St. Martin's Press, 1992.

Regalado, Samuel O. *Viva Baseball: Latin Major Leaguers and Their Special Hunger.* Urbana: University of Illinois Press, 1998.

Reichler, Joseph L., ed. *The World Series: A 75th Anniversary.* New York: Simon & Schuster, 1978.

Ribowsky, Mark. *The Power and the Darkness: The Life of Josh Gibson in the Shadows of the Game*. New York: Simon & Schuster, 1996.

Riess, Steven. *Touching Base*. Westport, CT: Greenwood Press, 1980.

Rossi, John P. *The National Game: Baseball and American Culture*. Chicago: Ivan R. Dee, 2000.

Rothe, Anna, ed. *Current Biography 1948*. New York: H. W. Wilson, 1949.

______. *Current Biography 1950*. New York: H. W. Wilson, 1951.

Sands, Jack, and Peter Gammons. *Coming Apart at the Seams: How Baseball Owners, Players, and Television Executives Have Led Our National Pastime to the Brink of Disaster*. New York: Macmillan, 1993.

Scully, Gerald W. *The Business of Major League Baseball*. Chicago: University of Chicago Press, 1989.

Seymour, Harold. *Baseball: The Golden Age*. New York: Oxford University Press, 1971, 1989.

______. *Baseball: The People's Game*. New York: Oxford University Press, 1990.

Smelser, Marshall. *The Life That Ruth Built*. New York: Quadrangle/The New York Times Book Company, 1975.

Smith, Curt. *Storied Stadiums: Baseball's History Through Its Ballparks*. New York: Carroll & Graf, 2001.

Smith, Red. *Red Smith on Baseball*. Chicago: Ivan R. Dee, 2000.

Smizik, Bob. *The Pittsburgh Pirates: An Illustrated History*. New York: Walker, 1990.

Solomon, Burt. *Where They Ain't*. New York: The Free Press, 1999.

Sommers, Paul M. *Diamonds Are Forever: The Business of Baseball*. Washington, DC: The Brookings Institution, 1992.

Spinks, J. G. Taylor. *Judge Landis and Twenty-Five Years of Baseball*. New York: Thomas Y. Crowell, 1947.

Stark, Benton. *The Year They Called Off the World Series: A True Story*. Garden City Park, NY: Avery Publishing Group, 1991.

Stump, Al. *Cobb: A Biography*. Chapel Hill: Algonquin Books of Chapel Hill, 1994.

Sullivan, Dean A. *Early Innings: A Documentary History of Baseball 1825–1908*. Lincoln: University of Nebraska Press, 1995.

Sullivan, Neil J. *The Diamond Revolution: The Prospects for Baseball After the Collapse of Its Ruling Class*. New York: St. Martin's Press, 1992.

______. *The Dodgers Move West*. New York: Oxford University Press, 1987.

Thomas, Henry W. *Walter Johnson Baseball's Big Train*. Washington, DC: Phenom Press, 1995.

Tygiel, Jules. *Baseball's Greatest Experiment: Jackie Robinson and His Legacy*. New York: Oxford University Press, 1997.

______. *Past Time*. New York: Oxford University Press, 2000.

Voigt, David Quentin. *American Baseball Volume III: From Postwar Expansion to the Electronics Age*. University Park: The Pennsylvania State University Press, 1974.

______. *The League That Failed*. Lanham, MD: Scarecrow, 1998.

Vricella, Mario. *St. Louis Cardinals — First Century: A Short History of the National League's Greatest Team*. New York: Vantage Press, 1992.

White, G. Edward. *Creating the National Pastime: Baseball Transforms Itself 1903–1953*. Princeton: Princeton University Press, 1996.

Will, George. *Bunts: Curt Flood, Camden Yards, Pete Rose and Other Reflections on Baseball*. New York: Scribners, 1998.

Zimbalist, Andrew. *Baseball and Billions: A Probing Look Inside the Big Business of Our National Pastime.* New York: Harper Collins, 1992.
Zoss, Joel, and John Bowman. *Diamonds in the Rough.* New York: McMillan, 1989.

Articles

"The Baron of Beer," *Time* 65 (July 11, 1955), 82–84.
"Barney Dreyfuss." *McClures* 39 (July 1912), 247–248.
"Baseball Man." *Sports Illustrated* 3 (November 7, 1955), 12–13.
"Baseball: Trial for Life." *Newsweek* 27 (May 27, 1946), 66–67.
"Baseball's Answer to TV." *Colliers* 130 (September 27, 1952), 61–62.
"Baseball's Dynamo: Nothing That the Cleveland Indian's Prexy Does Is Surprising, for He Stands Alone." *Sportfolio* (April 1949), 5–22.
"Batter Up, Play Ball." *The Literary Digest* 121 (April 11, 1936), 37–38.
"Beer Teams Up with Baseball." *Business Week* (February 28, 1953), 32.
"Beisboleros." *Newsweek* 23 (May 29, 1944), 90.
Bennett, Biff. "Sportalk" *Sport* 16 (March 1954), 6–7.
"Big Money Is Ruining Baseball." *Sport* (February 1919), 10, 89–91.
Bingham, Walter. "Ticker Tape, Dyed Grass, Blue Cowboy Hats." *Sports Illustrated* 16 (April 23, 1962), 18–24.
Brown, Warren. "Bill Veeck." *Sportfolio* (April 1949), 4.
Cerrone, Rick. "A Conversation with Bill Veeck." *Baseball Quarterly* 2 (Fall 1978), 17–18, 67–68.
"Charlie Finley: Baseball's Barnum." *Time* 106 (August 18, 1975), 42–43, 49–51.
Cobbledick, Gordon. "Bill Veeck — Baseball's Greatest Showman." *Sport* 5 (September 1948), A61, 55–63.
Condon, David. "How Bill Veeck Got That Way." *Chicago Sunday Tribune Magazine* (May 10, 1959), 32–35.
Daniel, Daniel M. "Dreyfuss, the Last of the Baseball Squires," *Sport* (September 1931), 439.
Doherty, Lawrence E. "Baseball Braces for Promotion Binge as Veeck Returns to White Sox Helm." *Advertising Age* 46(December 23, 1975), 3, 37.
Drebinger, John. "Another Old Baseball Dynasty Passes." *Baseball Magazine* 77 (October 1946), 365–366.
Durslag, Melvin. "A Visit with Walter O'Malley." *Saturday Evening Post* 232 (May 14, 1960), 31, 104–106.
Flood, Curt, and Richard Carter. "My Rebellion." *Sports Illustrated* 34 (February 1, 1971), 24–25.
"Fun in the Basement." *Time.* 58 (September 3, 1951), 7.
Furlong, William. "Charlie Finley: Triumph and Turmoil." *Saturday Evening Post* 247 (October 1975), 30–32, 72–73.
______. "Master of the Joyful Illusion." *Sports Illustrated* 13 (July 4, 1960), 55–60.
______. "The Veeck-Yankee Feud is for Real." *Sport* 29 (April 1960), 20–21 66–69.
Gietschier, Steve. "Bill Veeck Indian Chief." *Timeline* 7 (April-May 1990), 30–39.
Greenberg, Hank. "Unforgettable Bill Veeck." *Reader's Digest* 129 (July 1986), 67–73.
Griffith, Clark C. "Building a Winning Baseball Team." *The Outing Magazine* 62 (May 1913), 131–141.
Gross, Milton. "The Artful O'Malley and the Dodgers." *True* (May 1954), 49–50, 112–115.

"Gussie Vs. the Cards." *Newsweek* 79 (June 19, 1972), 61.

Hirshberg, Al. "Bill Veeck — Ladies' Man of Baseball." *Today's Woman* (September 1952), 4, 20–26.

Hoffman, John. "Squirrel Night at the Brewers." *Esquire* 20 (September 1943), 53–54.

"Hustler's Return." *Newsweek* 86 (December 22, 1975), 50–51.

Kirshenbaum, Jerry, ed. "The Man Who Won the West." *Sports Illustrated* 51 (August 20, 1979), 5–6.

Koppett, Leonard. "Busch, Beer and Baseball." *New York Times Magazine* (April 11, 1965), 32–33 127–128.

Lane, F. C. "Will the Major Leagues Adopt Night Baseball?" *Baseball Magazine* 55 (October 1935), 487–492.

Lardner, John. "The Great Baseball Bamboozle." *Liberty* 23 (June 29, 1946), 17–19.

Leggett, William. "A Bird in Hand and a Burning Busch." *Sports Illustrated* 32 (March 23, 1970), 18–23.

Lenehan, Michael. "The Last of the Pure Baseball Men." *The Atlantic Monthly* 248 (August 1981), 35–37.

Leo, Jon. "Baseball's Happy Hustler." *Time* 127 (January 13, 1986), 61.

Linn, Ed. "Bill Veeck's Free Advice to the New Commissioner." *True* (April 1966), 59–60, 107–108.

Markusen, Bruce, and Ron Visco. "Bucky and the Big Train." *Elysian Fields Quarterly* (undated, unpaged, found on internet).

Martin, Harold H. "The Cardinals Strike It Rich." *Saturday Evening Post* 225 (June 27, 1953), 22–23, 70–75.

"One Run for Charlie O." *Sports Illustrated* 34 (January 18, 1971), 8.

"The Outsider Who Was King." *Newsweek* 107 (January 13, 1986), 62.

Palmer, Eric Harold. "What Is the Matter with Baseball?" *Harpers Weekly* 58 (August 15, 1914), 148.

Povich, Shirley. "Griff Finds Rich His Arc-Enemies" *Baseball Digest* 8 (January 1949), 47–48.

_____. "Shading Night Baseball" *Baseball Digest* (February 1945), 57–58.

Raphael, Steve, and Terry Brewster. "Bill Veeck: Send in the Clowns" *Friends* (May 1980) 13–15.

Ribowsky, Mark. "Charlie Finley Lives! Despite the A's, the Fans, Bowie Kuhn." *Black Sports* 6 (June 1977), 32, 35.

"Selling a Ball Club to the Fans." *Business Week* (October 2, 1948), 52–56.

"Shading Night Baseball." *Baseball Digest* 4 (February 1945), 57–58.

Shane, Ted. "Veeck — The Barnum of Baseball." *Baseball Magazine* 88 (April 1952), 8–9, 30.

Shrake, Edwin. "A Man and a Mule in Missouri." *Sports Illustrated* 23 (July 19, 1965), 36–38, 43–44.

"Sporting Venture." *Time* 61 (March 2, 1953), 46.

Stewart, Wayne. "Just a Regular Joe Honored with a Night to End All Nights." *Beckett Baseball Card Monthly* 8 (August 1991), 105–109.

"Time of His Life." *Time* 63. (March 22, 1954), 81.

"Unionism in Baseball." *U S News and World Report* 20 (May 10, 1946), 42–43.

Veeck, Bill. "Are Umpires Ruining Baseball?" *Sport* 28 (April 1961), 16–17.

_____. "What's Wrong with Baseball ... What Can Be Done About It? *Look* 13 (April 12, 1949), 94–99.

Veeck, Bill, and Ed Linn. "The Midget at the Bat." *Readers Digest* 81 (October 1962), 73–77.
"Walter in Wonderland." *Time* 71 (April 28, 1958), 58–62.
"What Every Team Needs." *Time* 83 (January 24, 1964), 30.
Young, A.S. (Doc). "A Blackman in the Wigwam." *Ebony* 24 (February 1969), 66–74.
_____. "A Few Hundred from the Front Office." *Ebony* 26 (January 1971), 45–50.

Newspapers

Albany (NY) Times Union
Arizona Daily Star
Boston Globe
Brooklyn Eagle
Brooklyn Spectator
Chicago Tribune
Cleveland Plain Dealer
Detroit Free Press
Kansas City Star
Leslie's Weekly
Los Angeles Examiner
Los Angeles Times
National Sports Daily
New York Daily News
New York Herald-Examiner
New York Post
New York Times
Newark Star Ledger
Newsday
Philadelphia Inquirer
Pittsburgh Post-Gazette
Pittsburgh Sun-Telegraph
Reedy's Mirror
Sporting Life
San Francisco Chronicle
St. Louis Business Journal
St. Louis Globe-Democrat
St. Louis Post-Dispatch
St. Louis Star Times
Syracuse Herald
The Press Sports
The Sporting News
The Wall Street Journal
USA Today
Vero Beach Press Journal
Washington Post

Index

9 780786 415625